W9-AXL-115

Catholicism at the Dawn of the Third Millennium

Thomas P. Rausch, S.J.

A Michael Glazier Book
THE LITURGICAL PRESS
Collegeville, Minnesota

Cover design by Greg Becker.

A Michael Glazier Book published by The Liturgical Press

Excerpts from Vatican II documents are from Walter M. Abbott, ed., *The Documents of Vatican II,* New York: The America Press, 1966.

Excerpts are taken from the New American Bible, © 1991, 1986, 1970 by the Confraternity of Christian Doctrine, 3211 Fourth Street N.E., Washington, DC 20017-1194, and are used by permission of the copyright holder. All rights reserved.

4	5	6	7	8

Library of Congress Cataloging-in-Publication Data

Rausch, Thomas P.
    Catholicism at the dawn of the third millennium / Thomas P.
Rausch.
        p. c.m.
    "A Michael Glazier book."
    Includes bibliographical references and indexes.
    ISBN 0-8146-5770-2
    1. Catholic Church–Doctrines.   2. Catholic Church–History–20th
century.   3. Spiritual life–Catholic Church. I. Title.
BX1751.2.R36   1996
282–dc20   96-14518
                                           CIP

For Michael Glazier

Contents

Abbreviations

DOCUMENTS OF VATICAN II

DH   *Dignitatis humanae:* Declaration on Religious Freedom

DV   *Dei Verbum:* Dogmatic Constitution on Divine Revelation

GS   *Gaudium et spes:* Pastoral Constitution on the Church in the Modern World

LG   *Lumen gentium:* Dogmatic Constitution on the Church

NA   *Nostra aetate:* Declaration on the Relationship of the Church to Non-Christian Religions

OE   *Orientalium ecclesiarum:* Decree on Eastern Catholic Churches

PC   *Perfectae caritatis:* Decree on the Appropriate Renewal of the Religious Life

PO   *Presbyterorum ordinis:* Decree on the Ministry and Life of Priests

SC   *Sacrosanctum concilium:* Constitution on the Sacred Liturgy

UR   *Unitatis redintegratio:* Decree on Ecumenism

OTHER

BEM   *Baptism, Eucharist and Ministry.* Geneva: World Council of Churches, 1982

CDF   Congregation for the Doctrine of the Faith

DS   Denzinger-Schönmetzer. *Enchiridion Symbolorum.* 33rd ed. Freiburg: Herder, 1965

PL   J. Migne. *Patrilogia latina*

RCIA   Rite of Christian Initiation of Adults

USCC   United States Catholic Conference

WCC   World Council of Churches

Introduction

I have often been asked to recommend a manageable book that gives an adult account of Catholic faith and life and at the same time says something about what is happening in the contemporary Catholic Church—in other words, something between a sophisticated adult catechism and a theological text. I've never been sure quite what to suggest.

Perhaps the best book on Catholicism is Richard McBrien's volume by the same name.[1] Methodologically sound and comprehensive, faithful to the sources yet critical, it is an excellent reference, the closest thing to a contemporary *summa* of Catholic faith. It should be in every Catholic home, but its very size can make it intimidating. Another excellent reference is Anthony Wilhelm's *Christ Among Us,* probably the most widely used introduction to Catholicism.[2] Now in its fifth revised edition, it is a classic in the category of adult catechisms.

The new and official *Catechism of the Catholic Church,* mandated by the 1985 Extraordinary Synod of Bishops and published in its English version in 1994, was designed primarily as an aid for the bishops with the hope that it would lead their episcopal conferences to produce local catechisms adapted for their own churches. As a compendium of Catholic doctrine it is comprehensive, orderly, and authoritative; but it is not particularly reflective of either modern scholarship or contemporary concerns. Still, surprising its critics, it has turned out to be a bestseller. It is a valuable resource; Pope John Paul II refers to it in his introduction as a "reference text."[3]

There are a number of good theological works on contemporary Catholicism. Timothy G. McCarthy's *Catholic Tradition: Before and After Vatican II* is a fine study, done in terms of events, themes, and personalities, particularly

---

[1] *Catholicism,* rev. ed. (San Francisco: Harper, 1994).

[2] *Christ Among Us: A Modern Presentation of the Catholic Faith for Adults* (San Francisco: Harper, 1990).

[3] *Catechism of the Catholic Church* (Vatican City: Libreria Editrice Vaticana, 1994) 3.

the last nine popes.[4] It is an excellent introduction to contemporary issues as shaped by the Church's recent history, particularly the council. T. Howland Sanks' study of the Church, *Salt, Leaven, and Light,* another fine book, combines theological analysis with a sociological and historical approach.[5] Both are scholarly works, but neither treats the broader issues of Catholic faith and practice. Joseph Eagan's *Restoration and Renewal? The Church in the Third Millennium* moves in this direction.[6] His book is a study of the contemporary Church and its challenges with an ecumenical emphasis.

I would like this present volume to fall somewhere between the adult catechism and the theological text. It is structured around two questions: what is Catholicism and where is the Catholic Church headed as it approaches the third millennium? These are not the same questions, but they are closely related.

An Overview of Catholicism

"Catholicism" is used most generally for a particular experience of Christianity shared by Christians living in communion with the Church of Rome. In this popular sense "Catholicism" refers to a particular community of believers, a visible, historical Church, and a living tradition, all with roots reaching back to the Church of the apostles. In a broader sense, "Catholicism" is sometimes understood as including other Churches such as the Orthodox and those of the Anglican communion, which share to a significant degree in the Catholic tradition. Without denying that these and other Churches share in the Catholic tradition, we are concerned here with Catholicism in the popular sense, which associates it with the Church called simply "Catholic."

The adjective "catholic," from the Greek *kath' holou,* "referring to the whole," was first applied to the Church in the sense of "whole" or "universal" by Ignatius of Antioch around the year 115. The First Council of Constantinople (381) added it to the creed in its description of the Church as "one, holy, catholic and apostolic." After the division between Eastern and Western Christianity in 1054, the Eastern Churches began to speak of themselves as "Orthodox," while the Western Church continued to be known as the "Catholic Church." From the time of the Reformation in the sixteenth century it became increasingly common to add "Roman" to the word "Catholic," but that Church continues to refer to itself simply as the "Catholic Church" in its official documents.

---

[4] *The Catholic Tradition: Before and After Vatican II: 1878–1993* (Chicago: Loyola Univ. Press, 1994).

[5] *Salt, Leaven, and Light: The Community Called Church* (New York: Crossroad, 1992).

[6] *Restoration and Renewal? The Church in the Third Millennium* (Kansas City: Sheed & Ward, 1995).

What, then, does "Catholicism" mean for those who are members of the Catholic Church? It means first of all an inherently ecclesial way of experiencing Christian faith. The Church for Catholics is much more than a visible, religious institution. It has a deeply mystical, sacramental dimension, mediating for and through its members the mysterious divine life. From at least the second century onward this nurturing character has been recognized, often in maternal imagery, as bringing men and women to new birth through baptism, instructing them through the Word, drawing them to a deeper life in Christ through the sacraments.

"Catholicism" also means having a sense for the universality, or catholicity, of the Church. When a Catholic says "Church," he or she generally thinks of the whole Church. The Church is much more than the local congregation or the sum of all the particular Churches. The *ecclesia catholica* means both the fullness of the Church and the communion of Churches, for the one Church exists in many Churches. The pope as bishop of Rome and chief pastor presides over the communion of the Church, symbolizing its universality and catholicity.

The catholicity of the Church is not just spatial or geographical; "catholicity" implies an inclusiveness toward Church membership. As James Joyce said in *Finnegan's Wake,* "Catholic means here comes everybody." Because of its mission of proclaiming the universality of salvation in Jesus, the Church must embrace all peoples, classes, races, and cultures. "Catholicity" means that the Church includes within itself all humanity–saints and sinners, rich and poor, adults and children, even infants. The Catholic Church exalts in this rich diversity; it includes in its fellowship warriors and pacifists, liberation theologians and the members of Opus Dei, anarchist Catholic Workers and Catholics United for the Faith, charismatics, feminists, traditionalists, singles, married and divorced, gays and straights, monks and nuns, hermits, married priests in Eastern Rite Catholic Churches, celibate clergy in the West, faith healers and philosophers, mystics and activists. The doctrine of the communion of saints extends this fellowship to all those who have died in the Lord, the saints–canonized or not–the holy ones of the Hebrew Scriptures, and the souls who have died but not yet entered the fullness of eternal life.

A list of those things that Catholics would take for granted as characteristic of Catholicism, though not always unique to it, would have to include the following: Catholics have a sense for the historical uniqueness of their Church, its hierarchical ministry and teaching authority, and a reverence for its tradition. Catholic faith is characterized by an incarnational theology, sacramentality, a strong liturgical tradition centered on the Eucharist, a reverence for Mary and the veneration of the saints, and a rich tradition of spirituality, mysticism, and contemplative prayer. Catholicism includes the monastic life, religious orders, an appreciation of the religious value of the arts, a deep sense for the complementarity of faith and reason, a communal understanding of both sin and redemption and thus of the importance of community, a vast educational and health-care system, a social doctrine based on the dignity of the human person, a commitment to missionary activity, and of course, the papacy. We will consider most of these aspects of Catholicism in this volume.

Approach

Any study of Catholicism must first offer an overview of Catholic faith and doctrine. That is our properly theological task, to show how the faith of the Church emerges out of Scripture and Christian history—that is, out of the life of God's holy people—and takes on expression in symbol and story, in ritual and sacrament, and finally, in theological language and doctrinal statements. Good theology helps make this process of development clear. It also has a critical role to play in probing the tradition, clarifying its religious language, reinterpreting doctrines that have lost their power to communicate, and testing their truth claims in light of other areas of knowledge and the entirety of the Christian tradition.

Second, to understand contemporary Catholicism we need to know something of those forces and movements that have defined it in the twentieth century. Catholicism is not just a historical tradition; it is a living tradition as well, one that continues to develop and grow, even to change. In particular we need to consider the great impact the Second Vatican Council has had in reshaping Catholicism. According to Church historian John O'Malley, "never before in the history of Catholicism had so many and such sudden changes been legislated and implemented which immediately touched the lives of the faithful, and never before had such a radical adjustment of viewpoint been required of them."[7]

O'Malley compares Vatican II to two other great reforming movements in the history of the Church, the Gregorian Reform in the eleventh century and the Lutheran Reformation in the sixteenth. The Gregorian Reform, in its struggle against the abuses of the selling of Church offices and the lay investiture of bishops, represented a rejection of the feudal system; it gave the Church considerable independence in the temporal order and led to the development of the powerful papacy that has characterized the Catholic Church in the second millennium. The Lutheran Reformation effected a theological paradigm shift that has resulted in divisions in the Western Church down to our own day.

Hopefully, the Second Vatican Council, through the self-examination and renewal it initiated, will someday be seen as a step toward reconciliation and a preparation of the Church for the third millennium, which is to dawn shortly. But as the community of faith seeks to read "the signs of the times"

[7] *Tradition and Transition: Historical Perspectives on Vatican II* (Wilmington: Glazier, 1989) 17.

(GS 4) and to discern God's mysterious presence in the light of new challenges and changed circumstances, there are serious problems confronting it. In many ways the Church is divided, and there are issues that, if not dealt with wisely, could do it immeasurable harm. Therefore, we must also consider some of the issues the contemporary Church is facing and some of the questions contemporary Catholics are asking. To do this we will begin with the Second Vatican Council and end with what might be considered the council's unfinished agenda.

Finally, our study must try to communicate something of the culture of Catholicism. Like any culture, the culture of Catholicism is a socially constructed environment, a world of symbolic forms that embody and transmit meaning and value. Culture transforms the natural world and enables us to relate to one another in a human way. The culture of Catholicism transforms our human cultures, relating us to God and to God's presence in the world and especially in our human community. As a sacramental faith, Catholicism is mediated as much by the culture it has created—its richly textured world of liturgical seasons, sacred spaces, sacramental symbols, vocational choices, and diverse communities—as it is by the theologies through which it is expressed. So we need to give some idea of the culture of Catholicism, its worldview, the ways it experiences the holy, its different visions of the Christian life, its sense for ritual, its ways of prayer and different spiritualities.

Perhaps communicating this culture is the real challenge today. Theology can always be found in books, libraries, and graduate schools. But the culture of Catholicism is the embodiment of its way of life. At its best it speaks not just to the head but to the heart. Today that culture is in danger of being lost. In the years after the council most Catholics were assimilated into the dominant culture with its secular ethos, which left little room for the sacred. Many devotional traditions disappeared and, with them, a popular Catholicism that has survived in the United States only in some more-recently arrived ethnic communities. Catholic colleges and universities reduced significantly the number of required theology courses at the same time they broadened their offerings; most students in Catholic institutions today take only two courses, often outside their own religious tradition. The majority of Catholic undergraduates attend secular institutions and don't take any theology at all.

For most Catholics continuing education in the faith is limited to the Sunday liturgy. When I ask my students to name the Catholic journals or periodicals their families subscribe to, few can name any, with perhaps the exception of the diocesan newspaper. Many no longer practice their faith, as most Catholic campus ministers could attest, discovering in their campus RCIA programs an increasing number of Catholic students who have been baptized but have never made their First Communion. Many religious communities have discovered that they have to provide courses in basic Catholic doctrine for their novices, even though their candidates have often been active in a parish, campus community, or social ministry.

At the same time, many Catholics want to learn more about their faith. They are embarrassed by their inability to answer the questions other Christians often ask of them and want to have something to pass on to their children. Parishes with good programs in adult religious education find many who want to participate. At secular or non-Catholic private campuses the weekly Catholic liturgy draws more students than any other religious service. Some Catholics admit they are confused about what to believe; they find themselves in the middle of battles between conservatives and liberals or between the official Church and popular opinion, particularly as it is refracted by the media, and they are not at ease with either side. Others want to find some way of connecting what they were once taught with what the Church seems to be saying today.

Hopefully, this volume can supply those connections. It is designed for those who are familiar with Catholicism but want to investigate it on a more mature level. Some of these might be young Catholics who have not had the opportunity to study theology. Others might be Catholics who have become reconnected with the Church as adults and are asking themselves how they might better understand their faith and make sense of it to others. Or they might be those who are simply interested in what Catholics believe and why they do what they do. I hope they will find this a nontechnical book, one that combines a faithful presentation of the tradition as well as a critical theological reflection and interpretation of where the Church is today and where it might be moving.

As an aid to readers who might want to compare particular passages of this volume with the new *Catechism of the Catholic Church,* an outline is provided in an appendix, with references to the appropriate sections of the catechism. However, it is important to note that this present volume is not based on the catechism and makes no claims to being as comprehensive. The structure and purpose of the two works are different. One is a compendium of official Catholic doctrine. It is not concerned with historical development or contemporary issues. The other, as a presentation of Catholic faith in a contemporary North American context, is more historically conscious and thus interpretative. It deals with many subjects not covered in the catechism. Hence not every point treated in the text will have a corresponding section in the catechism or may not be presented in the same way. For these reasons the references to the catechism are not always adequate. Another appendix lists a number of basic works for further investigation of Catholic faith and life.

I have tried to keep footnotes to a minimum, though the nature of some chapters has demanded more extensive documentation. I have also made an effort to use inclusive language throughout, but that has not always been possible in quoting historical texts. I ask the reader's indulgence.

Acknowledgments

I am grateful to Michael Glazier, who suggested that I might do this book when he invited me to contribute an article on Catholicism for his *Modern Catholic Encyclopedia.* His contribution to Catholic scholarship in the United States has been enormous. Bill Cain, a Jesuit colleague and friend here at Loyola Marymount, has several times suggested to me the need for such a book. Much of the work on it was done at the Institute for Ecumenical and Intercultural Research at Collegeville in the fall of 1994. The interest and support of all at the institute, both colleagues and staff, made those months there most enjoyable. Finally, I want to thank Elizabeth Montgomery for her work in preparing the manuscript for publication.

1. The Church and the Council

When Pope Pius XII died in 1958, the Catholic Church was, to all casual observers, in excellent shape. In the first half of the twentieth century the Church had been led by a number of strong popes, particularly Pius XII himself, who had guided the Church through the Second World War and focused its energies against the postwar threat of Communism. The Church was continuing to grow in both numbers and influence. Seminaries, convents, and monasteries were filled to the bursting point. New religious houses were being built throughout the United States and in many other countries. Catholic theology, if not very creative, was very orthodox; there was almost no dissent, no public disagreement. Catholics knew who they were; they were proud of their Church and had a clear sense of their own identity.

PRE-VATICAN II CATHOLICISM

But there was a shadow side to this picture. The Catholic Church in the middle of the twentieth century considered itself very much a Church under siege. Deeply suspicious of the modern world, the Church was on the defensive. Catholic scholarship had been crippled by the atmosphere of suspicion and distrust that followed the Modernist crisis at the beginning of the twentieth century. Books by Catholic authors were rarely published without a review by ecclesiastical authorities; they had to obtain an *imprimatur* from the bishop or a *nihil obstat* from an official censor of books. The only really acceptable model for theology was that of the dogmatic manuals of the Roman schools, a textbook theology that relied on an abstract and ahistorical neoscholasticism. Rather than asking new questions and investigating biblical and historical sources, this textbook theology demonstrated traditional positions by citing biblical proof texts and numbers from Denzinger's *Enchiridion Symbolorum,* a compendium of papal and conciliar teachings.

When Pius XII died at the end of the 1950s, a number of progressive Catholic scholars like Karl Rahner, Yves Congar, Henri de Lubac, Marie-Dominique Chenu, Teilhard de Chardin, and the American Jesuit John Courtney Murray had been either silenced, forbidden to write on certain topics, or disciplined. The threat of having their books placed on the Index of Forbidden Books hung over them. Seminary professors were required to take an oath against Modernism each year. In the United States, where Catholic scholarship was particularly undistinguished, Msgr. John Tracy Ellis and Thomas O'Dea had just asked in two important books why the American Church and its universities had contributed so little to the intellectual life of the country.[1]

The Catholic Church officially was not interested in ecumenism, the movement aimed at restoring unity to the divided Christian Churches. What became the modern ecumenical movement resulted from a gathering of Protestant Christians at the World Missionary Conference at Edinburgh, Scotland, in 1910. From that came the Faith and Order Conference, which met for the first time at Lausanne, Switzerland, in 1928. Shortly afterward Pope Pius XI issued his encyclical *Mortalium animos,* forbidding Catholics to participate in ecumenical meetings of non-Catholics. The Catholic approach to Christian unity was quite clear: "There is only one way in which the unity of Christians may be fostered, and that is by promoting the return to the one true Church of Christ of those who are separated from it."[2] This "one true Church" approach was characteristic of Catholic thinking for the first half of the twentieth century. Catholics looked upon Christians in other Churches as good but misguided people. Though the Holy Office published a letter in 1949 allowing Catholic participation in the ecumenical movement under certain very strict conditions, in the years immediately before Vatican II most Catholics were warned not to attend a Protestant service or even to send a child to a Protestant summer camp.

A genuine theology of the laity was only beginning to emerge. The lay movement known as "Catholic Action" began in Italy in 1930. Particularly through its Belgian and French expressions, it was to give a new energy to the Church in Latin America, laying the ground for what would be known in the late sixties as the theology of liberation. But the official Church seemed unable to recognize that lay men and women had a real share in the mission of the Church. In Church documents the "lay apostolate" was defined as "the collaboration of the laity in the apostolate of the hierarchy."[3] Ministry was the prerogative of the clergy.

[1]John Tracy Ellis, *American Catholics and the Intellectual Life* (Chicago: Heritage Foundation, 1956); Thomas O'Dea, *American Catholic Dilemma: An Inquiry into the Intellectual Life* (New York: Sheed & Ward, 1958).

[2]*Acta apostolicae sedis* 20 (1928) 14.

[3]"Allocution to Italian Catholic Action," *Acta apostolicae sedis* 32 (1940) 362.

Liturgically, although a liturgical movement had been growing in the Church since late in the nineteenth century, at the time of Pius XII's death Rome was trying to discourage the "Dialogue Mass," which had people praying and responding to a leader in English while the priest at the altar prayed quietly in Latin. In many Catholic colleges and universities Catholic college students were required to read a popular book called *The Thirteenth: Greatest of Centuries.*[4] The sense that the Catholic Church had its attention fixed firmly on the past rather than on the future could not have been more clearly illustrated.

How had the Catholic Church become so stuck? In a very real sense the Church had never completely recovered from the shock of the Reformation in the sixteenth century. As a result of the Reformation, within a period of some forty years half of Europe had become Protestant. But there were other causes for the Church's distrust of the modern world as well. The scientific revolution and the rationalism of the Enlightenment, or Age of Reason, in the seventeenth and eighteenth centuries with the accompanying assaults on Church doctrine, authority, and ritual left the Church on the defensive; both movements presupposed an autonomous human reason that left no room for revelation or the transcendent. Then came the revolutions of the late eighteenth and nineteenth centuries, including the French Revolution. The latter sought to change the nature of Church government by forcing the clergy to obey a civil constitution that stripped the pope of any juridical authority over the Church in France. Finally, it attempted to restrict the practice of the faith itself.

In 1863 Pope Pius IX, considered quite liberal in the early days of his pontificate, published his *Syllabus of Errors,* a list of eighty concepts and movements that he considered typical of modern civilization. Among the errors condemned was the proposition that "the Roman Pontiff can and should reconcile himself and reach agreement with 'progress,' Liberalism and recent departures in civil society" (DS 2980). Even the territory the Church considered its own was under attack. In 1870 Garibaldi seized the Papal States for what was to be the newly united Italian state. The loss of this vast area of central Italy ruled by the popes for more than a thousand years was traumatic.

Modernism

The Modernist crisis at the beginning of the twentieth century left the official Church even more fearful of the new scholarship.[5] The movement

---

[4]James J. Walsh, *The Thirteenth: Greatest of Centuries* (1907; reprint, New York: Fordham Univ. Press, 1952).

[5]See Gabriel Daly, *Transcendence and Immanence: A Study of Catholic Modernism and Integralism* (Oxford: Clarendon, 1980).

designated by the term "Modernism" was never really a coherent theological system; what it represented was an attempt by some Catholic scholars to enter into a dialogue with modernity by using modern methods of biblical and historical investigation. These "critical" methods, developed largely by Protestant scholars in Germany, opened up a rich new world of biblical scholarship that gave new insight not just into the texts themselves but also into the way that God's revelation emerged out of the history of God's people.

Unfortunately, many who used those methods, both Protestant and Catholic, inherited to a considerable degree the rationalistic presuppositions stemming from the Enlightenment. In too many cases they relativized doctrines, rationalized whatever could not be explained scientifically, and reduced the content of revelation to subjective human experience. Doctrines became symbols without any propositional truth, miracles were explained away, and Christian revelation was reinterpreted as something devoid of any supernatural influence, a particular expression of a general religious experience available to all. Thus, in a number of ways, "Modernism" can be seen as a Catholic version of Liberal Protestantism.

Characteristic of all of these thinkers was a concern to bring history and subjectivity into the work of theology. Alfred Loisy (1857–1940) was a French biblical scholar whose book, *The Gospel and the Church,* published in 1902, attempted to show how the Church resulted from a necessary institutionalization of Jesus' preaching of the kingdom of God. George Tyrell (1861–1909), an English Jesuit and convert to Catholicism, was a philosopher of religion. His main interest was in revelation as an inner religious experience, something that could be expressed symbolically but could never be understood simply as a group of propositions. Friedrich von Hügel (1852–1925), a theologian and spiritual teacher, interpreted Christianity in terms of its institutional, intellectual, and mystical elements. Though not considered a Modernist himself, he was in frequent contact with Modernist thinkers and is often associated with them.

The Catholic Church reacted strongly to what it perceived as a threat to its faith. In 1907 two documents were published condemning Modernism, Pius X's encyclical *Pascendi* and a decree of the Holy Office, *Lamentabili.* The encyclical pointed out some real errors in what it understood as Modernism, though scholars today are not in agreement about the extent to which those errors were actually present in the thought of the scholars against whom the encyclical was directed. Loisy and Tyrell were excommunicated; von Hügel escaped condemnation.

Over the next fifty years Catholic scholarship was to pay a heavy price for the measures enacted to excise the Modernist threat from the Church. *Pascendi* had encouraged strict censorship, the setting up of diocesan vigilance committees to watch over Catholic teaching, and the turning in the names of those suspected of Modernist ideas to the Holy Office. With the pope's approval a secret society known as the *Sodalitium Pianum* was set up to keep under surveillance even members of the hierarchy suspected of Modernist tendencies.[6]

What followed was a long period of suspicion and repression. Bishops and seminary professors were required to take annually the oath against Modernism, mentioned earlier. Any teaching that did not conform to the theology of the Roman manuals was suspect; scholars were not infrequently dismissed from their positions, and others had their books placed on the Index. The congregations of the Roman Curia, the Vatican bureaucracy that was to assist the pope in his leadership of the Church, became even more powerful. The members of these curial congregations and commissions, for the most part Italian clerics, watched over doctrine and morals, decided what positions were to be held and taught by Catholic professors, disciplined dissenters, kept a close eye on seminaries, appointed bishops, and set up new dioceses. They dispatched apostolic nuncios and delegates to represent Rome in national Churches, supervised religious orders and congregations, particularly those of women, and regulated the sacramental and liturgical life of the Church.

CURRENTS OF RENEWAL

The picture was not completely a bleak one. The brightest side of the period from 1920 to 1960 has been described by the French word *ressourcement*, "return," understood as a return to the sources of Catholicism in Scripture, the Fathers of the Church, the liturgy, and philosophy.[7] This return to the sources gave rise to or supported a number of currents of renewal that were ultimately to play a major role in reshaping the face of Catholicism at the Second Vatican Council. Furthermore, in the period after the Second World War the world itself was changing. After the horrors of Nazism the Christian Churches experienced a resurgence of faith. There was a new optimism and a new sense of freedom. We need to consider briefly those currents of renewal.

The Modern Biblical Movement

The modern biblical movement was made possible by the development in the largely secular German universities of various critical, historical, and

[6]Carlo Falconi, *The Popes in the Twentieth Century* (London: Weidenfeld & Nicolson, 1967) 54–55.

[7]See Stephen Happel and David Tracy, *A Catholic Vision* (Philadelphia: Fortress, 1984) 134–36.

literary methods of investigating biblical texts (historical criticism, form criticism, redaction criticism, source criticism, textual criticism). Fearing that it was tainted by the Modernist spirit, the new biblical criticism was for a long time resisted by the Church. The Pontifical Biblical Commission issued a number of decisions between 1905 and 1915 that required Catholic biblical scholars to hold positions critical scholarship was beginning to call into question, among them the substantial Mosaic authorship of the Pentateuch, the historical nature of the first chapters of Genesis, the view that the Book of Isaiah was the work of a single author, that Matthew was the first Gospel to be written, and so on.[8]

The turning point came with the 1943 encyclical of Pope Pius XII, *Divino afflante Spiritu,* a document that has often been referred to as the Magna Carta of Catholic biblical scholarship. In it the pope gave Catholic scholars the freedom to use the methods of historical-critical scholarship that had previously been denied them. Catholic biblical scholarship, which had previously lagged behind that of Protestants, began to flourish as Catholic scholars instructed in the new methods began teaching in seminaries and universities. Subsequent decrees from the Pontifical Biblical Commission confirmed this new direction, even reversing previous directives when in 1955 the secretary of the commission gave Catholic scholars complete freedom in regard to those earlier restrictive decisions of 1905–1915 except where faith or morals were involved.

The Liturgical Movement

The liturgical movement represents a second current of renewal, which began long before the Second Vatican Council. If today some people at times associate the liturgical movement with guitars and folk songs, with liturgical drama, dance, and banners in church, it actually describes an attempt to recover the symbolic and communal riches of traditional Christian worship, thus giving new life to the official prayer and worship of the Church. Its roots are to be found in the Benedictine monasteries of Germany, Switzerland, and France, which in the nineteenth century began to popularize the use of Gregorian chant and to encourage a more active participation in the liturgy on the part of the laity. Dom Prosper Guéranger (1805–1875) of Solesmes in France, with his writings on the liturgical year, is often considered the founder of the movement. In Belgium Dom Lambert Beauduin (1873–1960) stressed that the liturgy was a profound way to deepen the life of faith, that it was an action not just of the priest but of the gathered faithful.

---

[8]See Raymond E. Brown, *Biblical Reflections on Crises Facing the Church* (New York: Paulist, 1975) 6–10.

The liturgical movement in the United States is most often associated with St. John's Abbey in Collegeville, Minnesota, and with the name of Virgil Michel (1890–1938), a monk of the abbey. Father Michel became familiar with the liturgical movement during his studies in Europe. When he returned to the United States in 1925, he dedicated himself to promoting liturgical renewal as well as to addressing the social ills that were the product of an increasingly industrialized society. He began publishing a monthly liturgical review, *Orate Fratres,* and founded The Liturgical Press. Through these publishing efforts several generations of North Americans were to become familiar with the liturgical movement. After Michel's death in 1938 one of his former students, Fr. Godfrey Diekmann, took over the review. He was to edit it for twenty-five years, changing its name in 1951 to *Worship.* Collegeville, with its abbey, university, and press, has remained a center of the liturgical movement in the United States.

For many years prior to the council those interested in liturgy would withdraw to various progressive monasteries to make retreats, to take part in the monastic liturgy, and to learn Gregorian chant. In 1940 the Benedictines in the United States began sponsoring The Liturgical Week, a series of seminars, or congresses, on the liturgy. The first of a number of international congresses of liturgical scholars convened in 1951 at Maria Laach in Germany. The great body of scholarship produced by the liturgical movement was to bear fruit in the council's Constitution on the Sacred Liturgy.

The New Theology

For too long the Catholic theology favored in Rome had been confined to the categories of the Scholastic philosophy and theology inherited from the great universities of the Middle Ages. Particularly influential was the work of the Dominican Thomas Aquinas. Indeed, Leo XIII in his encyclical *Aeterni Patris* (1879) had attempted to impose Thomism on the entire Church, while Pius X made Thomas' *Summa theologiae* the textbook to be used in all pontifical institutions.[9] The Modernist "crisis" at the turn of the century was occasioned by one attempt to break out of this narrow approach and to enter into dialogue with contemporary thought. The so-called *nouvelle théologie* ("new theology"), a term used to describe the work of some scholars in France and Germany in the two decades before the council, represented another.

The term *nouvelle théologie* was apparently used for the first time by the Holy Office's Msgr. Pietro Parente in February 1942 in *Osservatore Romano,* the official Vatican newspaper, and it was used pejoratively. But, like Modernism,

[9]See Avery Dulles, *The Craft of Theology: From Symbol to System* (New York: Crossroad, 1992) 120.

the new theology was not really a system. It was an attempt by a wide range of scholars—Yves Congar, Henri de Lubac, Jean Daniélou, and Marie-Dominique Chenu in France; Karl Rahner and Otto Semmelroth in Germany; Hans Urs von Balthasar in Switzerland—to return to the biblical, patristic, and liturgical sources that had so enriched the self-understanding of the Church of the first millennium. Ecclesiology was a key issue for these theologians. Other topics included the development of doctrine, creation, evolution, original sin, grace, and the Eucharist.

Because the approach of these scholars was biblical and historical rather than neo-Thomist, they were attacked by the Scholastic representatives of the Roman orthodoxy, who saw their work as a new kind of Modernism. This seems to have been the concern of Pius XII in his 1950 encyclical *Humani generis*. The encyclical called for a return to a Thomistic approach in both philosophy and theology; it also argued that the proper task of theologians was to show how those things taught by the magisterium of the Church are found in Scripture and tradition (DS 3886). A number of those associated with the new theology were disciplined; they "were removed from their professorial chairs, prevented from upholding their views in lectures or writings, condemned to silence and inactivity."[10]

In 1954 in what has been described as a "raid on the Dominicans," three French Dominican provincials were removed from office, and a number of Dominican scholars, among them Chenu and Congar, were disciplined at the insistence of the Holy Office, fearful of what were considered to be dangerous innovations in their teaching. Chenu, a distinguished medieval theologian, had been comparing changes in thirteenth-century society and Church to those in the twentieth. Congar's writings took up issues such as the organic nature of tradition, Church reform, the theology of the laity, and ecumenism. Both were dismissed from their teaching positions. Nevertheless, both attended the Second Vatican Council, where their work was to help shape a number of the council's documents.[11]

Pius XII

Humani generis was not a progressive encyclical. It has frequently been used as evidence that Pius XII was not a reformer. But contemporary scholars are coming to a new appreciation of the extent to which this austere, patrician pope prepared the way for Vatican II. His encyclical *Divino afflante Spiritu* (1943) brought modern biblical criticism into the Church, even if the officials in the Roman Curia continued to snipe at those who used it. As late

---

[10]Falconi, *The Popes in the Twentieth Century,* 283.

[11]Thomas O'Meara, "'Raid on the Dominicans': The Repression of 1954," *America* 170 (1994) 8–16.

as 1962 these officials launched several attacks on the Jesuit-run Biblical Institute in Rome and sought to have two of its professors removed from the faculty.

Another important encyclical of Pope Pius XII was *Mystici Corporis* (1943), with its sacramental vision of the Church as the body of Christ. It was followed in 1947 by *Mediator Dei,* the pope's great encyclical on the liturgy. Though the latter warned against the excesses of some liturgical reformers, it encouraged the liturgical movement and commended the Dialogue Mass.

John XXIII

Then, in 1958, Pius XII died. His death marked the end of an era. Few suspected that a new one in the life of the Church was about to begin. When the cardinals gathered in the Sistine Chapel to elect a successor, the expectation was that nothing would change. Most of those assembled wanted someone who would continue Pius XII's strong, conservative leadership. But the conclave deadlocked; none of the front runners was able to receive sufficient votes to be elected. Finally a compromise was reached. The cardinals turned to a seventy-six-year-old by the name of Angelo Roncalli (1881–1963). He was to be a transitional pope. The general sense was that he was too old to do any damage.

Roncalli, or John XXIII, as he is known to history, was a round, thickset Italian with a face like something out of a Michelangelo painting. He came of solid peasant stock, farmers from northern Italy. But in spite of his appearance, Roncalli was a shrewd and sophisticated churchman. Ordained in 1904, he served in his early years as a seminary professor at Bergamo, as a chaplain during the First World War, and as a counselor to university students. Most of his career had been spent outside of Rome in the papal diplomatic service. He had represented the Vatican in Bulgaria and Turkey, gaining in the process a deep appreciation for Orthodox Christianity as well as a familiarity with the languages and problems of eastern Europe. In 1944 he was appointed apostolic nuncio to France, where he was exposed to the theological and pastoral renewal taking place there. During this time he befriended an ecumenical group of Protestants trying to live a monastic life in a little village in Burgundy called Taizé. But in spite of all his accomplishments, his heart was first of all the heart of a pastor. Finally, in 1953 he was made patriarch of Venice, where he could give full expression to his pastoral concerns.

Shortly after his election to the papacy the new pope, talking to his secretary of state about the problems facing the world and the Church, told him that he was going to call a council. Pope John's council was to radically change his Church.

THE SECOND VATICAN COUNCIL: 1962–1965

On January 25, 1959, Pope John and seventeen cardinals, many of them from the Roman Curia, met at the Basilica of Saint Paul-Outside-the-Walls for a pontifical vesper service to conclude the octave of prayer for Christian unity. In a brief address the pope announced that he intended to summon an ecumenical council, adding at the end a prayer for "a renewed invitation to the faithful of the separated communities that they also may follow us amiably in the search for unity and grace, to which so many souls aspire in all parts of the earth."[12] The cardinals greeted his announcement with a stunned silence. Why couldn't the new pope leave well enough alone? The last thing the leaders of the Roman Curia wanted was to bring together all the bishops of the Church, particularly some of the more progressive bishops of France, Germany, Austria, Belgium, and Holland.

The Preparatory Phase

In convening a council, to be called the Second Vatican Council, or Vatican II, the pope made clear that it was to be an ecumenical council for the whole Church. In the months that followed he clarified his goals for the council. First, he wanted it to be an *aggiornamento,* a renewal or, more accurately, a "bringing up to date" of the Catholic Church. The story is often told that the pope once described what he wanted the council to accomplish by going to the nearest window and opening it up to let in some fresh air.

Second, Christian unity was to be a primary aim of the council; indeed it had been his purpose from the beginning. To promote his ecumenical intentions Pope John took a number of concrete steps, each of them highly symbolic. First, he asked that official observers be delegated by the Orthodox and Protestant Churches. Second, he arranged to have them seated in a place of honor in the front of the Basilica of St. Peter close to the section reserved for the cardinals. Finally, he established a new Vatican congregation, the Secretariat for Promoting Christian Unity, charged with bringing the Catholic Church into the ecumenical movement, and placed its resources at the service of the observers.

When it became clear that the pope was not to be dissuaded from having a council, the Curia leaders adopted the strategy of stage managing it so that it would remain firmly under their control. The ten commissions and two secretariats set up to prepare the council were stacked with officials from the corresponding curial congregations. These bodies prepared seventy schemata, or drafts, on various dogmatic and disciplinary issues to be con-

---

[12]"Pope John's Announcement of Ecumenical Council," *Council Daybook,* Sessions 1–2 (Washington: National Catholic Welfare Conference, 1965) 2.

sidered by the bishops when they gathered in Rome. The plan, obviously, was to overload the council, making the work of the Curia indispensable.

But in two important addresses the pope made clear to the bishops assembling for the council that its work was to be their own. In a radio address on September 11, 1962, he spoke of the need for the Church to address issues of peace, the equality and rights of all peoples, the problems of underdeveloped countries, and the miseries faced by so many, and he suggested that the Church be presented as "the Church of all, and *especially of the poor*.[13] None of these topics had been raised by the preparatory commissions.

Then, on October 11, in his address officially opening the council, he called on the twenty-five hundred bishops gathered from all over the world at a solemn liturgy in the Basilica of St. Peter to look not to the past but to the future. Disassociating himself from "those prophets of gloom who are always forecasting disaster," meaning his critics in the Curia, he said that the council was not to be a discussion of this or that fundamental doctrine, but rather "a step forward toward a doctrinal penetration and a formation of consciousness" faithful to the Church's authentic doctrine, but one that "should be studied and expounded through the methods of research and through the literary forms of modern thought." Most often quoted was his affirmation of the renewal of the Church's theological language: "The substance of the ancient doctrine of the deposit of faith is one thing, and the way in which it is presented is another."[14]

The Work of the Council

At the first working session of the council on October 13 the agenda called for the election of members for the council's ten commissions, which were to present the schemata to the council fathers and consider whatever amendments they might propose. The Curia hoped that those members who had served on the preparatory commissions would simply be reelected; to help the fathers, a list of their names was handed out. But in an important intervention Cardinal Liénart, Archbishop of Lille, suggested a delay so that before so important a step was taken, the bishops could consult in their national or regional conferences about those they wanted to elect. His proposal was endorsed by Cardinal Frings of Cologne, and both interventions were greeted with loud applause from the council fathers. With such a strong show of support, the motion to delay the election was approved. The bishops had begun to assume control of the council.

[13]Cited by Peter Hebblethwaite, "John XXIII," in Adrian Hastings, ed., *Modern Catholicism: Vatican II and After* (New York: Oxford Univ. Press, 1991) 30.

[14]The text of his address is in Walter M. Abbott, ed., *The Documents of Vatican II* (New York: Herder & Herder, 1966) 710–19; see 712, 715.

The council met in four sessions. The debating and voting on the various documents took place on the floor of the Basilica of St. Peter, where the council fathers, the twenty-five hundred bishops and heads of the religious orders of men, were seated. But much of the real business of the council took place less formally in the conference rooms, restaurants, and coffee bars of Rome, where innumerable conversations took place among the different groups gathered for the council—bishops meeting with one another, with their *periti* or theological advisors, with scholars and journalists, and with the observers from the Protestant, Anglican, and Orthodox Churches.

Inviting official observers from the other Christian Churches gave an ecumenical flavor to the council from the beginning. There were some forty observers present when the council opened on October 11, 1962; by the time it closed, their number had risen to eighty. In spite of the secrecy that the Curia tried to preserve in regard to the deliberations of the council, the observers received advance copies of the drafts of the council's documents. Treated as honored guests, they were able to be present for all the daily sessions in the basilica and to attend some of the meetings of the commissions. A translation service was also set up for them.

After Cardinal Suenens observed that no women were present for the council's deliberations, some were added as "auditors." By the end of the council there were twenty-two women present, among them Sr. Luke Tobin, superior of the Sisters of Loretto in the United States.

The council generated an enormous amount of interest. In occasionally reversing previously held positions, even positions taught by popes, the council illustrated the dynamic character of Catholicism. Two of the documents drafted by the conservative Theological Commission, the schema on the Church and the one on divine revelation, were sent by the council fathers back to the commission to be rewritten. The sixteen documents that emerged from its deliberations established the guidelines for Church renewal, still unfinished, in a number of areas.[15]

The Church

The Dogmatic Constitution on the Church *(Lumen gentium)* represents an attempt to articulate a contemporary self-understanding of the Church that stands in marked contrast to the clerical and monarchical ecclesiology of nineteenth- and early twentieth-century Catholicism, often symbolized by a pyramid in which all authority descends from the top down. Particularly significant is its stress on the Church as the people of God, its doctrine of episcopal collegiality, and its theology of the laity.

---

[15]Two of the documents, those on the Church and on divine revelation, were dogmatic constitutions; the document on the liturgy was a constitution, the one on the Church in the modern world a pastoral constitution, and the rest were decrees or declarations.

Chapter 1 introduces the Church as a "sacrament of intimate union with God, and of the unity of all mankind" (LG 1). Treating the nature and mission of the Church, it touches on the relation between the Catholic Church and other Churches. In speaking of "the unique Church of Christ," the constitution states: "This Church, constituted and organized in the world as a society, *subsists in* the Catholic Church" (LG 8). The earlier 1963 draft had read "This Church . . . *is* the Catholic Church."[16] This small change of "is" to "subsists in," made by the Theological Commission after the second session, was immensely significant ecumenically; it meant that the Catholic Church was no longer proclaiming an exclusive identity or strict equation between the Church of Christ and itself. Even though the council understands the Catholic Church as a realization of the Church of Christ in its essential completeness or fullness (LG 14), it implies that the Church of Christ is also present in various ways in other Churches and ecclesial communities (LG 8).

Rather than beginning with the hierarchy, chapter 2 describes the whole Church as the people of God, the ruling image in the council's ecclesiology. Reference to the diverse "charismatic gifts" (LG 12), elsewhere described as "both hierarchical and charismatic" (LG 4), is evidence of a recovery of the rich theology of the charismata that play such an important role in 1 Corinthians 11–14. The distinction between the "ministerial" or "hierarchical priesthood" and the "common priesthood" (priesthood of all believers) underlines the share of all the faithful in the priesthood of Christ (LG 10).

Chapter 3 developed a collegial understanding of the episcopal office. The battle over collegiality was one of the most important of the council; it implied a return to the ancient understanding of the Church and its government. Together with the pope, the bishops have supreme authority over the universal Church (LG 22) and share in its infallible teaching office (LG 25). Bishops are thus not to be understood as vicars of the pope but as heads of local Churches (LG 27). The Church itself becomes a communion of Churches, as it understood itself in the first millennium, rather than a single, monolithic institution. By making clear that the bishops share in the Church's charism of infallibility, the council provided a new context for the interpretation of the teaching of the First Vatican Council (1870) on papal infallibility.

Chapter 4 turned to a theology of the laity, stressing that through their baptism and confirmation lay men and women share in the mission of the Church (LG 33) and in the threefold office of Christ as prophet, priest, and king (LG 31). From this emphasis was to come the multiplicity of lay ministries in the postconciliar Church, a recognition of the obligation of competent lay people to express their opinion for the good of the Church (LG 37), and a new involvement of lay men and women in the Church's task of theological reflection (cf. GS 62). The constitution envisions lay men and women as living out

[16]Italics added.

their vocation precisely "by engaging in temporal affairs," working "for the sanctification of the world from within, in the manner of leaven" (LG 31).

Chapter 5 is on the call of the whole Church to holiness, chapter 6 on religious, and chapter VII on the union of the Church on earth with the heavenly Church, the saints in heaven, and the souls in purgatory. Its description of the Church as a "pilgrim Church" moves away from the notion of the Church as a "perfect society," dominant in Catholic ecclesiology since the time of Robert Bellarmine. The final chapter is on the role of the Blessed Virgin Mary in the mystery of Christ and the Church.

Revelation

The council's Dogmatic Constitution on Divine Revelation *(Dei Verbum)* takes a personalist rather than a propositional approach. Revelation is not something "contained" in sources, even though the first chapter of the Theological Commission's rejected original draft was entitled the "Two Sources of Revelation." The council defined revelation as God's self-communication in history, which reaches its fullness in the person of Jesus, and through life in the Spirit offers men and women a share in God's own divine nature (DV 2). In the council's understanding, then, revelation is personal rather than propositional, it is Trinitarian in form, Christological in realization, and historical in its mediation.

Chapter 2 discusses the transmission of God's revelation in Scripture and tradition. Chapter 3 reflects the influence of the modern biblical movement in its discussion of the interpretation of Scripture. Echoing Pius XII's *Divino afflante Spiritu,* it stresses the importance of searching out the biblical author's intention and identifying the text's literary form. The final chapter outlines measures to restore the Word of God to its central place in the life of the Church and particularly in its liturgy (DV 21); it calls for new translations from the original texts, encourages biblical scholars in their work, and points to the central place of Scripture in theology. Priests, deacons, and catechists are exhorted to share the Word of God with those entrusted to them and the faithful urged to read the Bible frequently and to use it for their prayer. Thus the Constitution on Divine Revelation ended the benign neglect of the Bible, which had characterized the Catholic Church since the Reformation, and emphasized the central role of the Word of God in the liturgy.

The Liturgy

The Constitution on the Sacred Liturgy *(Sacrosanctum concilium)* initiated a thorough renewal of the Church's official prayer and worship. It encouraged greater participation in the liturgy on the part of the laity (SC 14) and mandated the revision of liturgical texts and rites to make the liturgy more fruitful in the life of the Church (SC 21). Its most obvious reform, reflecting its emphasis on the importance of the Word, was its provision for the celebration of the liturgy in the language of the people (SC 36). Many of its suggestions and tentative steps toward renewal have in the years since the council become commonplace: the liturgical homily, the prayers of the faithful or universal prayers of the Church, the kiss of peace, Communion under both species, concelebration, congregational singing, and a multiplicity of new liturgical ministries for lay men and women.

Ecumenism

Moving beyond the Church's earlier suspicion of the ecumenical movement, Vatican II firmly committed the Catholic Church to the search for Christian unity. The Decree on Ecumenism *(Unitatis redintegratio)* recognizes that Christians from different Churches and ecclesial communities are already in an imperfect communion with one another through baptism (UR 3). They are already sharing to some degree in the life of grace. It stresses that all ecumenism begins with conversion of heart and in the name of the Catholic Church officially begs pardon of God and of other Christians for its own sins against unity (UR 7). Then it outlines the principles for Roman Catholic ecumenical involvement. It recommends joint prayer services, though it is more cautious about common worship (UR 8). Ecumenical dialogue is encouraged, and those engaged in dialogue are reminded that "there exists an order or 'hierarchy' of truths." In other words, not all doctrines are of equal importance, since "they vary in their relationship to the foundation of Christian faith" (UR 11).

Religious Freedom

The greatest battle at the council took place over the Declaration on Religious Freedom. The schema was bitterly contested by those who followed the traditional argument that "error has no rights" and who therefore wanted the Church to continue maintaining that in predominantly Catholic countries it should in principle be able to prohibit the practice or spread of religions that it considered false. Other faiths, including other Christian faiths, might be tolerated for political reasons, but they had no intrinsic right to equality of treatment. According to John Courtney Murray, the principle author of the decree, the council was clearing up a long-standing ambiguity: "The Church does not deal with the secular order in terms of a double standard—freedom for the Church when Catholics are a minority, privilege for the Church and intolerance for others when Catholics are a majority."[17]

[17]John Courtney Murray, introduction to "Religious Freedom," *The Documents of Vatican II,* ed. Walter M. Abbott, 673.

In the heated debates over religious freedom, the experience of the bishops from the United States played an important role. On Wednesday, September 23, 1964, three American cardinals spoke in favor of the document. It was finally approved, though by the narrowest margin of any vote of the council (1,114–1,074). Reversing the teaching of Pius IX and Leo XIII, *Dignitatis humanae* proclaimed that human beings have a right to religious freedom, to worship freely according to the dictates of their consciences, rooted in their dignity as human persons (DH 2).

Non-Christian Religions

Moving beyond the traditional axiom "no salvation outside of the Church," the council acknowledged that those who sincerely seek God and open themselves to God's grace can be saved even if they have no explicit knowledge of Christ (LG 16). According to the Declaration on the Relationship of the Church to Non-Christian Religions *(Nostra aetate),* the Catholic Church looks upon the great world religions with respect, recognizing that their teachings often reflect a ray of divine truth (NA 2).

The Church and the Modern World

Perhaps the most significant shift represented by the council was the turn toward the world and especially toward the poor. From its opening sentence, the Pastoral Constitution on the Church in the Modern World *(Gaudium et spes),* the longest of the council documents, calls attention to the plight of the poor and the afflicted: "The joys and the hopes, the griefs and the anxieties of the men of this age, especially those who are poor or in any way afflicted, these too are the joys and hopes, the griefs and anxieties of the followers of Christ. Indeed, nothing genuinely human fails to raise an echo in their hearts" (GS 1). In addition to stressing that great efforts must be made to satisfy the demands of justice and equity (GS 66) and to its calling Christians to a new level of concern for the poor (GS 69), the constitution devotes chapters to the subjects of marriage and the family, including the concept of responsible parenthood, the development of culture, socioeconomic principles, the right of all to participate in political life, and the question of war and the arms race. *Gaudium et spes* was to help inspire a host of contemporary socially conscious religious movements, among them, Latin American liberation theology, indigenous theologies in Africa and Asia, the pastoral letters of the American bishops on peace and economic justice, and feminist theology.

CONCLUSION

The documents of the Second Vatican Council reflect the divided nature of the council itself. Some of them seem schizophrenic, juxtaposing side by side traditional and progressive views. For example, the Dogmatic Constitution on the Church balances almost every statement on episcopal collegiality with a reaffirmation of traditional papal prerogatives.

But the council was enormously successful in unleashing the currents of renewal in the Church. Within relatively few years Catholicism experienced sweeping changes in its liturgy and worship, its theology, its understanding of authority and ministry, its religious communities, its parish life, even its popular culture. Not all the changes have been beneficial for the Church, and for many Catholics there has been and remains considerable confusion.

The situation of the Church at the end of the twentieth century cannot be attributed only to the council. The second half of this century has seen a number of movements—among them an increasing secularization, a widespread crisis of authority and of social institutions, the so-called sexual revolution, national liberation movements, feminism, and a growing concern for social justice—that would have brought about massive changes in the Church and in Catholic life even without the council, just as they have in society at large. But the council brought to the Church a new vitality, and by calling the Church to the renewal of its structures, theology, and life, has enabled it to play a conscious role in its own change and transformation.

One of the most useful concepts to appear at the time of the council was that of "non-historical orthodoxy," developed by Michael Novak in his book *The Open Church.*[18] "Non-historical orthodoxy" describes a belief that, over time, has mistakenly assumed the certainty of a doctrine held to be orthodox, a matter of faith, even though it represented at best a theological position that had no real biblical or historical foundation. Catholics in the period prior to Vatican II grew up and took for granted a host of "Catholic" positions—on papal infallibility, the nature of the Church, the source or sources of revelation, the sacral nature of the priesthood, the existence of limbo, and so on—all of which could be considered examples of non-historical orthodoxy.

It is also true that positions taught by the ordinary magisterium and held—in some cases for centuries—as Catholic doctrine have ultimately been changed as a result of theological critique and a lack of reception by the faithful. Examples from Church history include teachings on the temporal power of the popes; the denial of salvation outside the Church; the conciliarist teaching of the Council of Constance; the Church's acquiescence in the practice of slavery, sanctioned by four ecumenical councils; and the justification and

[18] *The Open Church: Vatican II, Act II* (New York: Macmillan, 1964); see especially ch. 5, "The School of Fear."

authorization of the use of torture for obtaining an admission of guilt.[19] Examples of more recent papal teachings modified or rejected by Vatican II include Pius IX's inability to find any truth or goodness in non-Christian religions, his condemnation of the proposition that Church and state should be separated, his denial of religious freedom as an objective right, and Pius XII's exclusive identification of the Catholic Church with the mystical body of Christ.[20]

The council not only began a renewal of Catholic life; it also changed the way Catholics understood themselves and their Church. In the chapters that follow we will attempt to present a contemporary understanding of Catholic life and faith, building on the work of the Second Vatican Council.

[19]See Luis M. Bermejo, *Infallibility on Trial: Church, Conciliarity, and Communion* (Westminster: Christian Classics, 1992).

[20]J. Robert Dionne, *The Papacy and the Church: A Study of Praxis and Reception in Ecumenical Perspective* (New York: Philosophical Library, 1987).

2. Faith and the Believing Community

Faith, according to the author of the Letter to the Hebrews "is the assurance of things hoped for, the conviction of things not seen" (Heb 11:1, RSV). There is much that all of us take on faith, for our experience gives us confidence in the truth or reality of many things we cannot prove to ourselves or have not had the opportunity to demonstrate. Even the most critical scientist takes for granted that the world is ordered and intelligible; he or she has faith that it is governed by certain discoverable natural laws.

Religious faith is concerned with ultimate reality, with the ultimate questions we ask in our more reflective moments. Are we alone in this world, or is there a presence beyond it, a mystery transcending our comprehension, that reaches out to offer us compassion, companionship, and love?

THE NATURE OF FAITH

We have all experienced revelatory moments—gazing across a grassy prairie moving gently in the breeze, or perhaps on a beach watching the ocean break against the shore, or under the night sky with the Milky Way arching across the dark heavens like a brilliant road of stars—when we have felt our hearts expand and sensed that the universe is so much more than clouds of burning gas, swirling matter, transient life forms, and dying stars. In moments like these the universe appears benevolent; it seems personal, and we sense a mysterious presence at its heart. Parents have sensed it, rejoicing in a newborn child. Husbands and wives who have grown old together often glimpse it in their shared life. Poet Kathleen Norris finds it in the words of one of her students, a little girl who writes of the Dakota sky: "The sky is full of blue / and full of the mind of God."[1] In such moments of

---

[1] *Dakota: A Spiritual Geography* (New York: Houghton Mifflin, 1993) 21.

solitude, or joy, or communion, we know more than we are able to put into words; we sense the presence of the ultimate.

But how can we fathom the mystery? How can we draw closer to the presence that draws us unless that mysterious other in some way reaches out to encounter us? What is that other like? These are the questions that Christianity attempts to answer. And what Christian faith tells us is that the mystery at the heart of reality that we call God has taken the initiative and is disclosed to us in the person of Jesus of Nazareth. This encounter in faith with the mystery of God impacts on our experience in a number of ways. In speaking of it, the Catholic tradition has long distinguished between the act of faith and the content of faith. We will consider both these aspects of faith as well as its source in the Holy Spirit.

The Act of Faith

The act of faith describes the acceptance of God and God's love, which is made known to us in the person of Jesus. It implies a personal encounter with God that leads to trust, confidence, surrender, and love. The act of faith can be compared to the moment in the Gospels when individuals like the woman with the hemorrhages (Mark 5:28), the centurion with the sick servant (Matt 19:8), and the father with the possessed son (Mark 9:24) open themselves to Jesus and come to experience the power of God's reign present within him. In the Synoptic Gospels especially, faith in Jesus always involves a deep personal trust. Thus the act of faith is the moment when God becomes real for an individual and he or she enters into personal relationship with God and with Jesus. It is the beginning of one's personal "journey of faith," which Avery Dulles, taking St. Francis of Assisi as an example, describes as "a progressive assent to God, which may reach the point of mystical ecstasy as its culmination in the present life."[2]

The act of faith involves the total response of the person. The gospel word for this response is *metanoia* (Mark 1:15), usually translated as "repentance" or "conversion." But *metanoia* means not just repentance or sorrow for sins but a complete change of heart. It is a creative act that reorders a person's priorities and gives him or her a new sense of self as one loved and cherished by God, cherished even in spite of one's sins. The act of faith is essentially a free act, for God always respects our human freedom; God does not coerce us. It is a response to God's invitation, to grace, to God's presence, but as a personal response it can sometimes coexist with doubt, for the object of faith is not seen directly (cf. Heb 11:1). In this life, as Paul says, "we see indistinctly, as in a mirror" (1 Cor 13:12).

---

[2] *The Assurance of Things Hoped For: A Theology of Christian Faith* (New York: Oxford Univ. Press, 1994) 32.

If the act of faith is genuine, it will express itself in deeds; it cannot be reduced to mere acceptance and trust. The Catholic tradition takes seriously the words of James 2:17: "Faith . . . if it does not have works, is dead."

Evangelical Christians describe this moment of coming to a personal faith in Jesus as being "born again" or as "letting Jesus into one's life" or as "accepting Jesus as one's personal Lord and Savior." Catholics, particularly those from some European backgrounds, are often uncomfortable with this very personal language. Their own religious language is more formal; they are uncomfortable with anything that seems overly emotional, or too personal, or that reveals too much of their own feelings; they prefer to say "the Lord" or "Christ" rather than "my Lord" or "Jesus."

There is much Catholics can learn from this evangelical language. Too many Catholics unconsciously reduce faith to its theological content, that is, to believing all the "teachings" or "doctrines" of the Church. They overlook the important dimension of the act of faith, the personal encounter with Jesus that comes so strongly to expression in evangelical language. After all, this language describes a very real experience, a moment of conversion or of decision when one makes a very personal commitment to the Lord in faith.

Yet many Catholics have had such moments when their faith has been tested, and they have affirmed it and made it their own in a very personal way. Others experience their faith as something that has always been part of their lives, as an awareness and knowledge of God that grows over time and deepens within them. Still others find their faith very real in spite of their own lapses and sins. A certain hesitancy or formality in expression does not mean someone has not made an act of faith, even if that act has not been expressed in explicitly evangelical language.

But there are some deeper reasons as well for the Catholic suspicion of a religious language that is overly personal and emotional. For Catholics, knowledge of God is always a mediated knowledge; God is not experienced directly in some kind of spiritual inwardness or personal revelation. Faith is more than the subjective "born again" experience, and it cannot be reduced to some interior feeling or illumination. Though Catholicism has a strong mystical tradition and recognizes the possibility of visions, it tends to be suspicious of an overly privatized faith experience; it has always emphasized the social and communal dimensions of faith, which is the faith not just of individuals but of a community. God's revelation comes to us precisely as a community of God's holy people and is mediated by the community that is the Church.

Reflect for a moment on your own faith journey. How did you come to a personal faith? Who is God for you? How do you image God? Have you ever felt God's presence in a special way? Who is Jesus? Do you feel that Jesus is a person for you, and that you have a personal relationship with Jesus? In what ways has Jesus helped you to know who God is? Or put another way, is the God you know the God of Jesus in the Gospels? Is your experience of God Trinitarian; do you think of God as Father, Son, and Spirit?

Who or what has informed and influenced your faith? Did your parents play an important role? Grandparents, siblings? Can you remember moments, perhaps family rituals, prayers before meals, a moment of silent reflection before the crib at Christmas in the midst of gifts and packages, or giving thanks for a new brother or sister, experiences that made you aware of God's presence in the life of your family? Were there teachers, priests or sisters, spiritual guides or friends, who might have helped you come to a deeper sense of faith? Have you ever had a serious discussion about your struggles to believe, to know God, with a close friend?

Usually when we ask ourselves questions like these, reflecting on where our own faith has come from, we become aware of the people who have helped us to know and to believe, men and women who have shared their own faith with us, who have helped us to understand the Scriptures, who have celebrated their faith with us in ritual and song and narrative, who have been for us the community called "the Church." We will return to this notion of faith mediated by the Christian community, but first we must ask how the Word becomes life for us, how we are enabled to recognize Jesus as Lord, how we are helped to accept the God of Jesus as our God.

The Revealing Spirit

If the act of faith is to be understood as our personal response to God, that response is brought about by the person of the Spirit, who enables us to know God and Jesus Christ, whom God has sent (cf. John 17:3). The Spirit is thus the source of our faith. Often last in the order of theological formulation, at least in Western theology, the Spirit is first in the order of our experience. The Spirit is God's life and breath in and to the world, the continuation of the mystery of the incarnation after the historical life of Jesus.

But the Spirit is difficult to talk about. We don't experience the Spirit directly. The Spirit is "discerned"; we sense the Spirit's movements. The very word "Spirit" suggests something more felt than understood, a quickening and warming, a drawing that gives life and communion. The Hebrew word for "spirit," *rûach*, is difficult to translate. It means in various contexts "breath," "wind," "the principle of life." The Greek *pneuma* is similar. Breath is the sign of life. Wind can be gentle, cool, or warm. The *Veni Sancte Spiritus,* the sequence prayer in the liturgy for the feast of Pentecost, invokes the Spirit's transforming presence:

> Heal our wounds, our strength renew;
> On our dryness pour thy dew;
> Wash the stains of guilt away;

Bend the stubborn heart and will;
Melt the frozen, warm the chill.

In the Hebrew Scriptures, particularly after the Exile, "spirit" is often a personification of God's presence and activity. The spirit of God is creative and life giving (Ps 104:29-30). In the beginning it hovers over the primordial waters as God brings order and life out of chaos (Gen 1:2). The spirit of God enables the prophets to speak God's word and thus to recognize God's presence in the life of the community (Num 11:17ff.; 2 Sam 23:2; Ezek 3:8). It is also associated with God's judgment and concern for justice (Mic 3:8; Isa 11:2-4; 42:1; 61:1-2).

The Spirit of God is present and active throughout the life of Jesus; he is conceived through the Spirit (Matt 1:20; Luke 1:35), receives the Spirit at his baptism (Mark 1:10), undertakes his ministry of bringing good news to the poor (Luke 4:18-19) and his miracles and exorcisms in the Spirit (Matt 12:28), and pours out the Spirit on his disciples, the Church (Luke 24:49). For Paul the Spirit is the principle of life of the Church. The Spirit gives new life to the believers (Rom 8:11) and in baptism unites them into the one body of Christ (1 Cor 12:13). It is the source of the Church's charismatic structure and its ministry (1 Cor 12). In the Acts of the Apostles, the Spirit guides the growth of the primitive Church. The Trinitarian baptismal formula at the end of Matthew's Gospel (28:19) and the Johannine reference to the Paraclete (John 14:16, 25) are perhaps the closest the New Testament comes to personifying the Spirit in relation to the Father and the Son.

What is the experience that lies behind this "Spirit" language in the New Testament? Perhaps a clue can be found in St. Paul's letters. Paul sees the Spirit as the gift of the risen Jesus; to be "in Christ" is to have new life "in the Spirit," which enables us to know God's love (cf. Rom 5:5), to call on God as *Abba,* "Father" (Rom 8:15), and to pray from the heart (cf. Rom 8:26-27).[3] In 1 Corinthians Paul writes, "No one can say, 'Jesus is Lord,' except by the holy Spirit" (1 Cor 12:3). We might paraphrase Paul's view by saying that it is the Spirit that helps us to recognize and accept Jesus as Lord, that enables us to know God's love and to call out to God in prayer. In turn, "the fruit of the Spirit" in our lives "is love, joy, peace, patience, kindness, generosity, faithfulness, gentleness, self-control" (Gal 5:22-23). These habits of the heart, or "virtues," are experienced signs of the Spirit's presence.

Paul identifies love as the greatest of the gifts of the Spirit (1 Cor 13:13); it is the trace of the Spirit's presence in our life. Later theology would develop this insight. For Augustine the Spirit is the mutual love of the Father

[3]According to Kilian McDonnell, "'Being in the Spirit' and 'being in Christ' mutually interpret each other"; see "A Trinitarian Theology of the Holy Spirit?" *Theological Studies* 46 (1985) 204.

and the Son into which we are drawn, so that we truly share in the divine life. In the Church's Trinitarian theology, the self-communication of God takes place in the Son (incarnation) and transforms our own lives in the Spirit (grace). The Spirit in turn draws us to a deeper life in Christ and so back to the Father.

From the earliest days of the Church the liturgy of baptism has celebrated this awakening to faith in God through Christ in the Spirit. The one being baptized is not so much receiving the Spirit as acknowledging the Spirit's activity, leading him or her to God in Christ. As sacramental incorporation into Christ and the Church, baptism is precisely a response to grace, to the Spirit's presence in one's life. This becomes clear in the liturgy when the one to be baptized renounces the works and allurements of evil and makes the Trinitarian profession of faith.

We have all had moments when we have experienced the Spirit's presence drawing us to believe, moments when our faith came alive in a special way. This action of the Spirit in drawing us to a deeper life in God is reflected in the traditional language of the seven "gifts of the Holy Spirit," wisdom, understanding, counsel, fortitude, knowledge, piety, and fear of the Lord. Notice how each "gift" in some way relates us to God.

For Catholics this experience of the Spirit is always a mediated experience. It may originate in an experience of a gracious and healing love that accepts us for the person we are, mediated by the love of a friend, a spouse, a parent, as we saw earlier. Such an experience expands our hearts and fills them with wonder; it often moves us to seek the ultimate source of this love. We might also experience the Spirit's drawing us to Christ in the prayer and worship of the Christian community. It could come from the preaching of the Word, encouraging us to trust, to open ourselves to God. Or it might happen in a sacramental moment, when we become aware of Christ's presence in the bread broken and the wine poured out, or in the community, or in receiving forgiveness. These are moments in which we sense the Spirit's presence within us.

In these last two sections we have seen that Catholic faith is a communal, ecclesial faith. Though each individual must ultimately respond to the Spirit, to God's grace, by making a personal act of faith, Catholics find God's presence mediated by the Church, with its community, its history, its symbols of the sacred, its sacraments, even its institutional structures. Catholic faith is rooted in the history of Israel, is revealed in its fullness in the life, death, and resurrection of Jesus, and has been carried down the centuries from the communities of primitive Christianity by a living tradition. This brings us to the content of faith.

The Content of Faith

If the Synoptic Gospels emphasize faith as trust in Jesus, John's Gospel is equally insistent that faith involves not just trust in Jesus but also acceptance of his teachings; to believe in Jesus means that we accept who Jesus is (John 6:69), where he comes from (John 16:30), and the words he has spoken (John 2:22; 5:47; 8:45). In other words, faith involves also a content, the story of God and God's holy people, which finds its expression in Sacred Scripture, in the creeds, and in the teachings of the Church.

How can we briefly summarize the content of Christian faith? To do so we must review the story of the people of God as it emerges from the pages of the Hebrew Scriptures, that collection of Jewish sacred writings that Christians generally call the Old Testament. Then we will consider the story of Jesus, his teachings, his life, death, and resurrection, and the way that what happened to Jesus was interpreted and understood by his disciples, the first Christians. Finally, we need to consider how the early Church formulated its faith in Jesus in the language of its official creeds.

THE PEOPLE OF GOD

The Hebrew Scriptures open with the Book of Genesis. The first eleven chapters serve to introduce the biblical narration of God's saving work. They tell the story of the creation of the world, the origin of humankind, the fall, the spread of sin and its disastrous effects, and the promise of salvation, using a collection of myths and stories, some of them borrowed from the Israelites' pagan neighbors.

Creation and Fall

Though the story of creation comes at the very beginning of the Bible, creation theology developed relatively late within the Old Testament tradition. The Israelites did not initially think of their God as a cosmic creator. Their original understanding of God was dynamic and personal; the God of the patriarchs, variously known as "the God of Abraham," "the Mighty One of Jacob," or "God Most High," was a tribal deity who traveled with the clan, or people. This was the Israelites' basic experience of God. Later, through the influence of Moses, they began to speak of their God as "Yahweh," a God who ruled over the Israelite people as king. Later still in what represents a considerable theological development, they extended Yahweh's reign over the other nations as well (Pss 22:29; 47; 99). And as they encountered the creation stories of their neighbors, they began to see their God also as creator. The psalms describe God as exercising his royal power as king over all creation in virtue of his work as creator (Pss 74:12; 93; 95–99).

If we understand a myth as a prescientific way of trying to explain a mystery, we can say that the two creation stories in Genesis are mythical, that is, they present a religious truth in a highly imaginative, poetic way. The first creation story (Gen 1–2:4a) presents a magnificent picture of the God of Israel fashioning a world of order, light, and life out of the primeval waters of chaos by the sheer power of the divine word. From a literary perspective it represents the sacred author's careful reworking of the ancient Near Eastern creation myth known to us as the *Enuma Elish* in its Babylonian form.[4] The Israelites borrowed it from their neighbors, preserving its basic structure but "demythologizing" it by eliminating its original story of the creation of the earth through a violent struggle between rival gods and goddesses and recasting it to show their God creating effortlessly and alone.

The second story (Gen 2:4b-25) focuses more on God's creation of humankind from the clay of the earth. It is followed by the story of the fall, which reintroduces into the world the very destructive forces of chaos that God overcame and confined in the work of creation. Once the man and woman succumb to the temptation of the serpent to "be like gods" themselves (Gen 3:5)—that is, placing themselves first by refusing to acknowledge the one who alone is God, thus assuming the place of the creator—the world God has given them begins to come apart. They lose their innocence and must leave the garden; their children begin killing each other; and as the lawlessness spreads, it is not long before the human race itself is nearly destroyed by the return of the primordial waters in the Great Flood.

What does this mythical "prehistory" have to teach? There are a number of important themes that emerge from a careful reading of the texts. Note that they are concerned with religious truths, not scientific ones. First of all, the Genesis prehistory teaches that creation itself is good, for it comes from the hand of God. The first creation story repeats over and over the refrain that accompanies the divine work like a liturgical antiphon: "God saw how good it was."

Second, Genesis affirms the immense dignity of humankind. The Catholic reverence for all human life, from the life of the unborn to that of the elderly, the terminally ill, the convicted criminal, is rooted here in the affirmation that man and woman are created "in the image of God." In some mysterious way each person mirrors the divine glory. Furthermore, the man and woman are partners, created in mutuality as equals, male and female (cf. Gen 1:27). Recent criticism has pointed out that the creature *ha adam,* translated as "man" (Gen 2:7) does not become sexually differentiated until God creates woman. In other words, there is no subordination of one to the other; humankind only exists as man and woman. Before the fall they are equal partners and enjoy a relationship of intimacy with God, who comes to

[4]See Alexander Heidel, *The Babylonian Genesis* (Chicago: Univ. of Chicago Press, 1942).

talk with them in the garden in the cool of the evening. In a lovely symbol of the innocence in which they live, created for each other, they are untroubled by their nakedness in each other's presence.

Third, the intimate relationship between humankind and God is destroyed by sin. Because of the sin of our first parents a threefold alienation comes about (Gen 3:16-19). First, they no longer enjoy friendship with God. Second, their relationship with the natural world is altered. The woman must bear her children in pain and labor. The man must toil for his food against the very earth, which now resists him. Finally, their relation to each other is changed. Their sexuality now introduces an alienation into the mutuality of their relationship; they are no longer comfortable with their nakedness and the woman loses the equality with her husband that God intended.

Yet there is a final point. In spite of the chaos and alienation man and woman have brought into the goodness of creation, it is clear that God's will is to save, to deliver humankind from the results of their sin. God's graciousness is revealed in multiple interventions. When Adam and Eve are embarrassed by their nakedness, God makes clothes to cover them. God places a mark on Cain to protect him from those who would try to avenge Abel's murder, delivers Noah and his family—and thus humankind—from the ravages of the flood, and finally, in Abraham, promises a blessing in which all the nations of the earth will one day share (Gen 12:3).

Exodus and Covenant

With God's saving work grounded in creation itself, the actual story of the people of God begins with Abraham, the father of the Jewish people and biblical model of the person of faith. God calls Abraham to leave his father's house and tribe and to set out for the unknown land of Canaan. His descendants settle there, but generations later a famine causes them to migrate down into Egypt, where in time they became an exploited minority, migrant workers reduced to virtual slavery within an oppressive empire. The Book of Exodus tells the story of God's deliverance of this people from bondage and oppression under the leadership of Moses.

They were not an important people. Historically, those who left Egypt with Moses to become Israel included "a crowd of mixed ancestry" (Exod 12:38), Hebrews from various tribes, other fugitive slaves, even some Egyptians. But the story of the Exodus is at the center of what was to become the identity of the Jewish people (just as the Holocaust experience is inseparable from what it means to be a Jew today). To be a Jew is to be a member of that disadvantaged group that God chose, delivered, and fashioned into a people. It is to belong to the people that God chose from among the nations, led through the desert with powerful deeds, guided through Spirit-filled figures like Moses and Miriam, delivered from the pursuing Egyptians at the

Red Sea, and established a covenant with on Mount Sinai. The Decalogue, the Ten Commandments given to Moses on the holy mountain, represents the earliest expression of the covenant, a relationship between Yahweh and Israel that was to make Israel God's holy people: "I, the LORD, am your God, who brought you out of the land of Egypt, that place of slavery. You shall not have other gods besides me" (Exod 20:2-3).

Sin and Salvation

For the Israelites, the Exodus event *was* God's salvation. It was an act of God in Israel's past; an act in their history by which God delivered these enslaved migrants from oppression and made them a people. The Israelite tradition continued to look back on that great foundational event and celebrate it (Ps 103:23-45; Isa 63:11-14). The miraculous crossing of the Red Sea, the cloud by day and the pillar of fire by night, the appearance of God at Mount Sinai, the two tablets with the Ten Commandments inscribed on them; all these are symbols of God's presence with the people during their migration from Egypt to the land of Canaan. Passover was the ritual meal that symbolically reenacted their deliverance. But the subsequent history of Israel was to effect a shift in the religious imagination of the people, and salvation began to be seen as something God would do in the future rather than as an event in the past. Among the factors lying behind this shift is the experience of failure and guilt, or in theological terms, of sin.

While sin and grace are always co-present in the life of a people, Israel as a community went through a number of crises in the period between the ninth and the sixth centuries. The unity that David had forged between the northern and southern tribes collapsed in 922 B.C. as the one kingdom became two, Israel in the north and Judah in the south. Both kingdoms were weakened by a series of weak kings and the greed of their upper classes. In addition, the people of Judah, falsely confident in God's choice of the house of David, particularly as expressed in the Oracle of Nathan (2 Sam 7:16), turned their religious tradition into a political ideology. A long series of prophets tried to call the people to conversion, condemning them for their worship of false gods, for their trust in armaments and foreign alliances rather than in Yahweh, and particularly for their injustice and oppression of the poor. Prophets like Amos, Isaiah, Micah, Jeremiah, Habakkuk, Ezekiel, and Malachi denounced the leaders of the people and the upper classes for their greed, dishonesty, lack of compassion, for their substituting a religion of external observance for the justice and mercy demanded by the Law (Amos 5:7-12, 21-24; 8:4-6; Isa 1:1-17; 10:1-4; 58:3-7; Jer 7:3-7).

It is difficult to overemphasize this biblical, prophetic view of religion: religious ritual without justice and compassion for the poor is an abomination to the Lord (Isa 1:13-15). We need to hear this message today just as much as Israel of old. But Israel's prophets were without success; both kingdoms fell, Israel in 721 to Assyria, Judah in 587 to the Babylonians. The prophets saw this as God's judgment on the people for their infidelity, their sinfulness.

But the prophetic preaching had not been without a promise of future deliverance; always the prophets held out the hope that God would again intervene in the life of the people, showing the divine loving kindness, destroying the evil oppressing them, and manifesting the salvation that only God could bring. So salvation becomes something yet to come, a future intervention, God's promise not to leave the people chosen and loved to the fate brought on by their sins.

The prophets could not paint a concrete picture of that future; their hope is general, not specific. But one finds in the prophetic writings a variety of messianic images and figures to express their confidence in God's coming salvation. They speak of a future Davidic king or "messiah" who will restore the religious life of the people and govern wisely (Isa 9:16; Mic 5:1-5; Jer 23:5; Ezek 37:24; Zech 9:9). Some speak of a "Day of Yahweh," when God's judgment will be revealed, bringing justice for the poor, comfort for the sorrowing, and condemnation for the evildoer (Isa 2:11; Joel 4:14; Zeph 1:14-18; 2:4-15). Isaiah (10:20-22; 11:11), Jeremiah (31:7), Micah (1:12; 5:6), Zephaniah (2:7, 9; 3:13), and Zechariah (8:10-12) speak of a "remnant" of the survivors of Israel who will once again know Yahweh's blessing.

Ezekiel speaks of a renewal of the covenant (Ezek 27:26; 34:27); Jeremiah, more pessimistic, sees God establishing a new covenant (31:31-34). In his beautiful Servant Songs (Isa 42:1-4; 49:1-6; 50:4-9; 52:13–53:12) Second Isaiah uses the enigmatic figure of the Servant of Yahweh, who will himself bring God's salvation. The apocalyptic tradition in postexilic Judaism, developed in a time of extreme crisis when observant Jews were dying for the right to practice their faith, looks to the end of history and a new order that includes the resurrection of the dead (Dan 12:1-3; 2 Macc 12:44); for the first time the idea of a life beyond the grave enters the Jewish tradition.

The preaching of the prophets and the hope for a general resurrection of the dead in the apocalyptic tradition led to an expectation in first-century Palestinian Judaism, variously expressed, that God was about to do something new. In the preaching of John the Baptist, that expectation takes the form of a warning about a coming judgment: "You brood of vipers! Who warned you to flee from the coming wrath?" (Luke 3:7). The preaching of Jesus of Nazareth, in contrast, was from the beginning a message of good news, which is the literal meaning of the word "gospel."

JESUS AND GOD'S REIGN

It is very possible that Jesus had been for a while a member of John the Baptist's movement.[5] Certainly his own baptism at John's hands was a turning point in his life. The Gospels tell of a theophany following his baptism; Jesus is anointed with the Spirit and proclaimed as God's Son. Though it is not possible to discern Jesus' inner experience behind the texts, Luke notes that the theophany took place while Jesus "was praying" (Luke 3:21), and the Synoptics agree that he withdrew afterward into the desert to spend a considerable period of time in prayer and solitude. When he returned he began to preach, gathering around him a group of disciples of his own. From them he chose twelve, a number symbolic of a renewed Israel.

The Preaching of Jesus

In the few brief years of his ministry Jesus did not talk much about himself, nor was his message primarily about a future life. According to Luke, Jesus "was a prophet mighty in deed and word" (Luke 24:19) who "went about doing good and healing all those oppressed by the devil, for God was with him" (Acts 10:38). Even today we can sense the power of his parables. We often find them difficult to accept, for they challenge our ordinary way of thinking. As Eamonn Bredin points out, they present us with a new vision that is shocking, even subversive: "It is the *Samaritan* who is neighbor, it is the *last* who are first, it is the *lost* who are rejoiced over, the *stranger* who is at table, the *wastrel* son who is embraced and feted."[6]

The image that dominates Jesus' preaching is that of the kingdom of God, for he proclaimed that God's kingdom, or reign, was at hand (Mark 1:15). Though the term "kingdom of God" has roots in the Old Testament, particularly in the concept of the kingship of Yahweh, it is for the most part a New Testament expression. In Jesus' preaching it functions more as a symbol than a clearly defined concept; he does not explain it but illustrates its meaning by his parables and its coming through his ministry. The term "kingdom" *(basileia)* is often and more accurately translated as "reign," for it refers to a dynamic event, not a place. In Jesus' preaching the reign of God is both present and future.

The future dimension of God's reign is clearly evident in Jesus' preaching. In the Our Father he taught his disciples to pray for the coming of God's kingdom (Matt 6:10). The Beatitudes promise comfort and joy to the poor, the sorrowing, and the hungry in the kingdom (Matt 5:3-12; Luke

---

[5] John P. Meier judges this "the more probable hypothesis"; see *A Marginal Jew: Rethinking the Historical Jesus* (New York: Doubleday, 1994) 2:123.

[6] *Rediscovering Jesus: Challenge of Discipleship* (Mystic, Conn.: Twenty-Third, 1986) 40.

6:20-23). The gospel sayings about the Son of Man coming in judgment bring out the future dimension of God's reign (Luke 12:8-9). As John P. Meier says in his study of the historical Jesus, "The eschatological kingdom Jesus proclaimed . . . would mean the reversal of all unjust oppression and suffering, the bestowal of the reward promised to faithful Israelites (the beatitudes), and the joyful participation of believers (and even of some Gentiles!) in the heavenly banquet with Israel's patriarchs (Matt 8:11-12 par. and the bread-petition of the Lord's Prayer)."[7]

But the kingdom is in some way already present in Jesus' ministry, becoming real in the lives of others through his preaching and parables, his miracles and exorcisms, his proclamation of the forgiveness of sins, and his practice of table fellowship. After driving out a demon from a person unable to speak, Jesus replies to his critics, "But if it is by the finger of God that [I] drive out demons, then the kingdom of God has come upon you" (Luke 11:20). Certainly the core of the gospel miracle-tradition is historical, those miracles that concerned healing the injured and the sick, though some of the more extravagant "nature" miracles, for example, changing water into wine at the wedding feast at Cana, may be creations of the evangelists.

The table fellowship tradition, the meals that Jesus shared with his friends and with sinners and others considered by the religious authorities as being outside the Law (Mark 2:16-19), shows that God's reign is inclusive; no one is excluded. Jesus was constantly criticized for associating with "tax collectors and sinners." The Church's Eucharist has its roots in this tradition of table fellowship. The parables of the kingdom—the farmer and the seed, the weeds and the wheat, the mustard seed, the yeast kneaded in the flour, the net cast into the sea (Matt 13:1-53)—bring out both present and future dimensions of God's reign.

Thus the kingdom of God "is Jesus' comprehensive term for the blessings of salvation insofar as it denotes the divine activity at the center of all human life."[8] It means that God is to be found in our midst, that God's saving power is to be discovered among us when we open ourselves to God by faith and reach out compassionately to others as Jesus did. Yet we still must wait for the fullness of our salvation.

Though all are called to share in God's reign, Jesus makes a connection between entering the kingdom and one's personal response. One must become like a little child to enter the kingdom (Mark 10:15; Luke 18:17). He called those who would listen to a personal conversion (Mark 1:15) to discipleship in the service of God's reign, taught them to love others with an all-inclusive and self-sacrificial love (Matt 5:38-48), to be faithful to their marriage partners (Matt 5:31-32), and warned against the dangers of wealth

[7]Meier, *A Marginal Jew,* 2:349.
[8]Michael L. Cook, *The Jesus of Faith* (New York: Paulist, 1981) 56–57.

(Mark 10:24-25; Luke 12:16-21). The Beatitudes are at the center of his preaching; they describe those who will find fulfillment in the kingdom. Entrance into the kingdom is dependent on one's conduct toward others, especially the poor and unfortunate (Matt 25:34-46).

Who is the God that Jesus preached? Jesus was a wandering preacher, a storyteller, not a theologian. He did not give abstract lectures on the nature of God. His pictures of God are personal and concrete. In his preaching God appears as the loving father who watches for his erring son to return and rushes out to embrace him when he finally appears on the road (Luke 15:20). God is the shepherd who leaves the ninety-nine sheep to go out in search of the one who has strayed (Matt 18:13). God's activity at the heart of the world is hidden but inexorable; God is the woman who mixes yeast into the flour until it gradually makes the whole loaf rise (Matt 13:33). God is the incredibly generous landowner who in his concern for the disadvantaged pays the unemployed laborers hired at the end of the day the same amount as those taken on at dawn (Matt 20:1). God is the one who shows a special care for the poor, the hungry, and the sorrowing (Luke 6:20-21), who reverses the normal order of things, making the first last and the last first (Mark 10:31; Luke 1:52-53). God is the owner of the vineyard who makes himself vulnerable by risking his only beloved son after his tenants have abused and murdered those he had previously sent to collect his share of the produce (Mark 12:6). God is the one whom Jesus sought continually in prayer, the one he called "Abba," an intimate term used by a son or daughter of a father.

Death and Resurrection

In preaching God's compassionate love, a love that embraced even the "tax collectors and sinners," Jesus was implicitly challenging the Jewish community's religious leaders. Their sense that their own authority was being threatened led them increasingly to oppose Jesus. Ultimately they conspired with the Roman government officials to have him put to death. In a very real sense the evil present in the world, the evil that is the result of human sinfulness, took on concrete expression in these political and religious leaders who refused to recognize the presence of God in the ministry of Jesus. Having poured himself out for others in his life, he continued to pour himself out even to his death on the cross. Thus his death, freely accepted, was the completion of his life of giving himself for others, a self-offering that was part of his service on behalf of God's reign. The early Christians saw it at once as a sacrifice. Sacrificial language is already present in the words spoken by Jesus over the bread and the cup at the Last Supper: "my body . . . given for you . . . the new covenant in my blood, which will be shed for you" (Luke 22:19-20).

Jesus went to his death alone, deserted by his friends and perhaps feeling abandoned even by his God (cf. Mark 15:34). But he did not despair; to the end he continued to trust that the one he called "Abba" would vindicate him.[9] And God raised him up to everlasting life.

The resurrection of Jesus stands at the very heart of the New Testament tradition. Without it the story of the early Christians does not make sense; it does not hold together. Though we sometimes say Jesus "rose" from the dead, that language is less than correct. In the New Testament, the resurrection was something that happened to Jesus. God raised him up. Even if the resurrection is not something that can be proved by ordinary methods of historical investigation, it is no less real. It cannot be reduced to a subjective experience on the part of the disciples. Yet there remains something mysterious about the disciples' encounter with the risen Jesus. They do not immediately recognize him (Luke 24:31); they are terrified and think they are seeing a ghost (Luke 24:37); some continue to doubt even when Jesus manifests himself to them (Matt 28:17); even Mary of Magdala, who was so close to Jesus, does not recognize him (John 20:14). The appearance stories in the Gospels suggest there is something about the Easter experience of the disciples that cannot be objectified.[10] Jesus does not appear to his enemies but only to his friends, to those who had a relation with him (Paul is the exception here, but Paul too was one who was genuinely if mistakenly seeking God). It is as though Jesus has to lead them to belief in him. Perhaps their experience of coming to faith in the risen Jesus, while unique, is still not so different from our own.

The resurrection of Jesus is an event that lies on the other side of history; it is an eschatological event, very different from the resuscitation of a corpse. It means that God has vindicated Jesus, has raised him to everlasting life "at the right hand of God" (Acts 2:33), that Jesus now lives in God's eternal present. The resurrection also means that God's power is stronger than death, that just as Jesus has been raised to life, so too we can look forward to life everlasting. The resurrection of Jesus is the promise of our own ultimate triumph over sin and death. The poor especially see it as God's power overcoming injustice and evil.

Christology and Soteriology

The death and resurrection of Jesus transformed the disciples' understanding of Jesus. Jesus proclaimed the reign of God. The early Christians,

[9]Edward Schillebeeckx speaks of the "Abba experience" of Jesus in his *Jesus: An Experiment in Christology* (New York: Seabury, 1979) 256–71.

[10]Dermot Lane states that "the reality of the risen Jesus is a transcendent reality and . . . cannot be confined to ordinary everyday categories" in *The Reality of Jesus* (New York: Paulist, 1975) 60; the term "Easter experience" is from Schillebeeckx, *Jesus,* 380.

grasping intuitively what God had done in the death and resurrection of Jesus, proclaimed Jesus. They saw the intrinsic connection between the man and his message, and so the preacher became the preached.

In writing to the Church at Corinth, St. Paul cited an early Christian formula that says that "Christ died for our sins in accordance with the scriptures" (1 Cor 15:3). In his letters he used various terms drawn from his Jewish tradition to express the salvific meaning of what God had accomplished in Christ Jesus. In Christ God has "justified" us, made us righteous (Rom 4:25; 5:16-18), "reconciling the world to himself," not counting our sins against us (2 Cor 5:19). Jesus has thus brought about our reconciliation with God (Rom 5:10). He has accomplished our "redemption," the paying of a price for someone or something held under a penalty, to express the idea that Jesus paid the price for our sins with his blood (Rom 3:23-25; 1 Cor 1:30). Most importantly, Paul sees that Jesus' victory over sin means that the power of death has been destroyed (Rom 8) and that those who believe in Jesus will also share in his resurrection. Jesus himself is the "firstfruits" of the resurrection from the dead (1 Cor 15:23).

The resurrection also raised for the early Christians the fundamental Christological question: Who is this Jesus? And as they were Jews, they drew upon their own religious tradition, using salvific images and titles from their Scriptures in their efforts to give expression to their experience of Jesus.[11] Jesus was the "Messiah," or Christ, the anointed son of David promised by the prophets who would bring God's salvation, even though the historical Jesus did not speak of himself as the Messiah and seemed reluctant to accept the title from others (cf. Mark 8:30). Jesus was also identified with the "Son of Man," the figure who in the apocalyptic tradition would come in the last days as ruler and judge. Jesus himself spoke of the Son of Man as one who would exercise God's judgment (Luke 12:8-9).

Jesus was called "Lord," a title of respect like "Sir," but also in its Aramaic usage addressed to God as "Lord" or "the Lord." This ambiguous usage is preserved today in the German *Herr* and the Spanish *Señor*. "Lord" was used of the risen Jesus as one who represented God's lordship, or reign in the world. But the title "Lord" was a powerful one. The Greek word for "Lord," *kyrios,* had been used in the Septuagint, the Greek translation of the Hebrew Scriptures, to translate the sacred name of Yahweh. When applied to Jesus, the term implied that Jesus shared God's authority and that those passages in the Jewish Scriptures referring to Yahweh could also refer to Jesus.

Jesus was also called "Son of God," a title that in the Gospels has several meanings. Mark, whose Gospel has no Christmas story, sees Jesus as God's Son by adoption, declared or adopted as God's Son at his baptism (Mark 1:11). Behind this lies the Old Testament image of the promised descendant

[11]See Bredin, *Rediscovering Jesus,* 247–59.

in the Davidic line, who according to the Oracle of Nathan would be adopted as God's Son (2 Sam 7:14). Recent scholarship has stressed the importance of the Wisdom tradition in late Judaism for the earliest Christians; they saw Jesus as the truly righteous man, called a Son of God and able to call God his Father (Wis 2:13, 16-18). Jesus was seen as having a unique relationship with the Father (Luke 10:22).[12]

In the later New Testament the term "son of God" is used in a much more metaphysical sense: Jesus is the natural son of God, as in Matthew and Luke, who proclaim that Jesus is conceived not by human generation but by the Holy Spirit (Matt 1:20; Luke 1:35); or in John, where Jesus is preexistent Word and eternal Son of God. From John's Gospel comes the foundational dogma of the incarnation, the belief so basic to Catholicism that the divine Word, or *Logos,* has become flesh and lived among us (John 1:14), in other words, that God has entered into human space and time and history in the person of Jesus.

It is clear that by the end of the New Testament period the divinity of Jesus was clearly grasped, and there is considerable evidence that Paul was aware of the mystery of the divine sonship of Jesus much earlier (cf. Phil 2:6-11). One senses in Mark's Gospel an awareness of the mystery of Jesus' relation to God that far exceeds what he is able to express in the traditional language available to him. What is fascinating to reflect on today is not that it took the early Christians so long to recognize the divinity of Jesus but, just the reverse, that these early Christians, so many of them Jews, with their unshakable Jewish faith in the oneness of God, were within a relatively short period of time confessing that Jesus was himself divine (cf. John 20:28). But this was what their experience of Jesus, their faith in him, led them to do. It is as though their faith in Jesus constantly overflowed the confines of the religious imagination they had inherited, and the biblical images and figures they used took on new meanings as they struggled to find an expression adequate to their faith in Jesus.

From the New Testament to Chalcedon

As Christianity moved out of its cradle in the Jewish Christian world and into the Roman Empire, the Church faced the new challenge of finding a language that would make sense of its faith in the very different culture in which it was now living. The early Christian writings that would soon be known as the New Testament had used the mytho-poetic language of the Jewish Scriptures; for the most part, Jesus was described functionally, in terms of his relation to us. Jesus was the Messiah bringing God's salvation;

---

[12]Marinus de Jonge, *Christology in Context: The Earliest Christian Response to Jesus* (Philadelphia: Westminster, 1988) 79–82.

he was the Son of Man exercising divine judgment, the Son of God, the Word of God, as we have seen.

Now, in the Greco-Roman world, the ontological or metaphysical question of what Jesus was in himself was increasingly raised, and new ways of expressing this were formulated using the more abstract language of Hellenistic Greek philosophy. Hellenistic thought did not have much trouble accepting the divinity of Jesus as the Word *(Logos)* of God, for Neoplatonic philosophy was full of divine emanations and cosmic principles, but the idea that the divine Word could take on flesh was a different matter. It was repugnant to the prejudice against matter so typical of Greek philosophy. Early heresies such as Docetism and Gnosticism were unable to accept Jesus' humanity. The difficult issue was that of preserving the biblical unity of Jesus while acknowledging both his humanity and his divinity.

Not all attempts to give expression to the unity of Jesus were successful. One of the greatest crises faced by the early Church was the heresy of Arianism in the third century. Arius was a priest of Alexandria in Egypt, born in Libya in the year 256. In an effort to defend the true humanity of Jesus, which he felt was being threatened by the teaching of his bishop, Arius ended up denying his divinity. He taught that the *Logos,* or Son, is a creature, one who received existence "before time and before the ages" but nonetheless a creature who had a beginning, or, as his famous theological slogan expressed it, "there was a time when he was not."

The teaching of Arius spread rapidly, dividing Christians from one another and threatening the unity of the empire. Finally, in an effort to restore peace, the emperor Constantine in 325 summoned all the Church's bishops to a council at Nicaea in Asia Minor, really the first universal or ecumenical council. The assembled bishops rejected the Arian proposition "there was a time when he was not" and hammered out a profession of faith, or "creed," to express what the Church believed about Jesus:

> We believe in one God, the Father almighty, maker of all things visible and invisible. And in one Lord Jesus Christ, the Son of God, only-begotten, born of the Father, that is, of the substance of the Father, God of God, light of light, true God of true God, born, not made, of one substance *(homoousios)* with the Father, through whom were made all things in heaven and on earth. . . .

The language of Nicaea is much more philosophical than that of Scripture. It speaks of Jesus and his relation to God in ontological terms, using the Greek *homoousios,* "of the same substance." Jesus is one substance with, one in being with the Father. This creed of Nicaea was slightly revised and expanded by another council a few years later at Constantinople (381), which affirmed the divinity of the Holy Spirit, "who together with the Father and the Son is adored and glorified." Though some Churches at first resisted the creed, it was gradually accepted or "received" by most of the ancient

Churches as an expression of their faith. Known today simply as the Nicene Creed, it is still recited as part of the Sunday worship of the Catholic, Orthodox, and mainline Protestant Churches.

With Constantinople the Church had progressed from its experience of God's self-disclosure in history as Father, Son, and Spirit to a formulated dogma of the Trinity, still present in its essential form. The Council of Chalcedon in 451 resolved the problem of the unity of Jesus by adopting the terminology of one person in two natures. Subsequent councils would further develop and refine the Church's Trinitarian language. God is a unity that transcends but does not negate difference. The one God exists as one being or substance in three distinct but equal persons. In more contemporary language, the inner life of God is constituted by relationships of mutual love and communion, a communion in which we are called to share.

CONCLUSION

It is not easy to be a person of faith today. Contemporary American culture—like much of Western culture today—no longer presupposes the value of religious faith and provides little support for those who seek to live out their faith in their everyday lives. In such a pluralistic, secular culture there is a tendency to regard any religious value or sentiment as a private matter, not as something that might have a contribution to make to the public community.[13] Our culture approaches religious belief as it does any other belief or value; it presupposes that each person has the right to believe whatever he or she chooses, for there are no absolutes save one: in the area of belief questions of truth are to be decided on the basis of personal taste. Such an individualistic perspective completely privatizes faith.

Catholicism's approach to faith is personal rather than propositional, communal rather than individualistic. The act of faith is a personal encounter with the God made known in Jesus, but that encounter is the work of the Spirit through the mediation of the believing community. We come to know God as a member of the people that God had first chosen and entered into relationship with. From the time of Abraham and Sarah, of Moses and Miriam, this people is God's people, and through their history with its struggles and tragedies as well as its achievements of the human spirit, through its prophetic men and women who speak in God's name, naming sin and assuring the people of God's faithfulness, God's self-disclosure takes place. That self-disclosure or revelation reaches its full realization in the life, death, and resurrection of Jesus.

---

[13]See Stephen L. Carter, *The Culture of Disbelief: How American Law and Politics Trivialize Religious Devotion* (New York: Basic Books, 1993).

Therefore, faith is much more than a private, subjective experience; it has a content, a content rooted in human experience while at the same time transcending it. Faith is historically transmitted, disclosed through symbols, and expressed in the stories and language of the believing community. That community through which we come to know God as Father, Son, and Spirit is the community of the disciples of Jesus that we call Church. We must consider now more carefully the nature of that Church.

3. A Visible Church

Over the desk in my office I have a picture by a California artist, John August Swanson, called "The Procession." In the foreground a crowd of worshipers is emerging from a great church led by servers with candles and incense; they are accompanying the Eucharist, carried by a priest under a canopy. In the center the church is open to view, its towers rising to embrace Jesus and the disciples in a boat hauling in a great net full of fish.

The whole picture is filled with people—in the procession, on banners carried by those in the congregation, and in niches or compartments, little icons, like those in a great stained glass window, which merge with and extend the walls of the church. Some figures are biblical—Adam and Eve leaving the garden, Noah's ark, the sacrifice of Isaac, Jacob's dream of a ladder to heaven, Moses being discovered by Pharaoh's daughter on the Nile, David and Goliath, Judith slaying Holofernes, Jonah being swallowed by the great fish, the three young men in the fiery furnace, Mary at the annunciation, the child Jesus in the stable at Bethlehem, the Magi, Jesus being baptized by John, the woman in the Gospel washing his feet with her tears, his Palm Sunday procession, crucifixion, his appearances to the disciples. Some are holy men and women from Christian history—St. Jerome in his cave translating the Scriptures, St. Francis and the wolf of Gubbio, St. Clare, St. Patrick, St. Elizabeth of Hungary. Some are apocryphal—Veronica wiping the face of Jesus, St. Christopher carrying the child Jesus across the river, St. George and the dragon.

The figures look Indian or Hispanic; the colors are rich Central American tones; the picture is packed, full of people—diverse, colorful, playing music, celebrating, meeting the Lord. This procession of life is the Church—in its history, its diversity, its sacramental life.

THE CHURCH AND THE COUNCIL

When the fathers of the Second Vatican Council set out to develop a document on the Church, really a contemporary Roman Catholic ecclesial self-understanding, they had to wrestle with a number of schemas, or drafts. The first draft (1962) was prepared by a subcommittee of the conservative Roman Theological Commission, chaired by Cardinal Alfredo Ottaviani, head of the Holy Office. The cardinal's episcopal coat of arms bore the legend *Semper Idem,* "always the same." The draft produced by his commission was rejected by the fathers; they found that it was not sufficiently biblical in its development, that it defined the Church almost exclusively in terms of the hierarchy, and that it did not meet the ecumenical concerns of Pope John XXIII, who had made Christian unity one of the primary aims of the council. In the words of Bishop de Smedt of Bruges it was too triumphal, too clerical, and too juridical.[1]

The second draft, presented to the bishops in the autumn of 1963, was a considerable improvement. After some further revisions it was approved by the bishops on November 21, 1964, with 2,151 voting for and only 5 against it. The document, called the Dogmatic Constitution on the Church *(Lumen gentium),* opens with a chapter entitled "The Mystery of the Church." The second chapter treats the whole Church as "The People of God." Chapter 3, "The Hierarchical Structure of the Church, with Special Reference to the Episcopate," is focused on the Church's official ministry, particularly its episcopal office.

The Church is the community of the disciples of Jesus. It should still be such today. But what is the relation between the Church as community and the Church as institution? And how do Catholic Christians understand the Church? In this chapter we will investigate the dialectic between the Church as community and its visible, institutional expression. We will consider the Church as a community of disciples, its official ministry, and its one, holy, catholic, and apostolic nature.

A COMMUNITY OF DISCIPLES

The Church has existed from the moment that the friends and disciples of Jesus, scattered by his arrest and crucifixion, were gathered together again by his new, risen presence among them. In its essential nature the Church is the community of the disciples of Jesus.

In what sense can we say that Jesus "instituted" the Church? On the one hand, the historical Jesus did not design and plan the Church as an organization, with an order of ministers, seven sacraments, and a constitution. On the other hand, Jesus did gather the men and women who were his disciples into a community, gave them a share in his own ministry of proclaiming the good news of God's reign, appointed twelve of them as apostles, told them

---

[1]For a fascinating review of the debates on the council's floor, see Xavier Rynne, *Vatican Council II* (New York: Farrar, Straus and Giroux, 1968).

to carry on his tradition of table fellowship by breaking the bread and sharing the cup in his memory, and empowered them with the Spirit. One can trace "continuities of belief, personnel, and practice between the group gathered around Jesus in his earthly ministry (the disciples) and the group gathered around the risen Lord (the church)."[2] As this community expanded and grew, it gradually developed the institutional and ministerial structures that would ensure its fidelity to its origins and to its mission. All this happened under the guidance of the Spirit, poured out by the risen Jesus. Thus the Catholic Church can claim divine institution for its historical structures.

Church

The New Testament word for "Church," *ekklesia,* from the Greek words *ex* (out) and *kaleo* (to call), means literally "those who have been called out," that is, "assembly" or "congregation." It is a Pentecost word, not a gospel word, appearing only three times in the Gospels, specifically in Matthew 16:18 and 18:17.

Paul uses the word *ekklesia* three different ways in his letters. He sometimes uses the expression "church at their house," or house church, for a local gathering of Christians in a private home (1 Cor 16:19; Rom 16:5; Col 4:15). These domestic assemblies were the earliest expression of Church; here Christians gathered for teaching *(didache),* fellowship *(koinonia),* and worship *(leitourgia),* and from these assemblies came much of the early Church's leadership. Theologically, the house-church setting indicates that the place of God's presence for the primitive Christian community was not a sanctuary, temple, or holy place but the community itself; the reality of Church is in the assembly of the faithful.[3]

Most often Paul uses *ekklesia* to refer to the local Christian community, as in "the church of God that is in Corinth" (1 Cor 1:2) or in reference to all the Churches (1 Cor 11:16). Occasionally he uses "church" generally, in the sense of the whole Church (Gal 1:13; 1 Cor 12:28; Col 1:18), a usage that became much more common in the later New Testament (cf. Col 1:24; Eph 5:29). Today we speak of the "whole," "universal," or "catholic" Church as well as the "local" or "particular" Church presided over by the bishop.[4]

Body of Christ

Paul's other term for Church is "body of Christ." As a community of different members with different gifts and ministries (1 Cor 12:4-7) made one

[2]Daniel J. Harrington, *God's People in Christ* (Philadelphia: Fortress, 1980) 29.

[3]See Thomas F. O'Meara, *Theology of Ministry* (New York: Paulist, 1983) 102–4.

[4]See Joseph A. Komonchak, "The Local Church and the Church Catholic: The Contemporary Theological Problematic," *The Jurist* 52 (1992) 416–47.

body in the Spirit by baptism (1 Cor 12:13) and the Eucharist (1 Cor 10:17), the assembly, or Church, constitutes the body of Christ (1 Cor 12:27).

Basic to Paul's understanding of Church as the body of Christ is the reconciliation of peoples that comes with baptism and Eucharist. He tells the Christians at Corinth that they are sinning against the body and blood of the Lord because their community is divided in its Eucharistic assembly (1 Cor 11:17-34). He reminds them that "in one Spirit we were all baptized into one body, whether Jews or Greeks, slaves or free persons" (1 Cor 12:13). He uses similar language to the Galatians: "For all of you who were baptized into Christ have clothed yourselves with Christ. There is neither Jew nor Greek, there is neither slave nor free person, there is not male and female; for you are all one in Christ Jesus" (3:27-28). In other words, all artificial divisions based on race, social status, or sex are done away with for those incorporated into Christ through baptism. There is necessarily an inclusive quality to being Church.

Life in the Spirit

Paul generally speaks of Christian life as life in the Spirit. He sees the Christian community as rich in a variety of Spirit-given charisms and ministries. These include service gifts *(charismata)* such as wisdom, faith, healing, discernment, administration, giving alms, and works of mercy as well as more permanent roles or ministries *(diakoniai)* like that of the apostle, prophet, teacher, and presider, all given for the building up of the Church (1 Cor 12:4-7; Rom 12:4-8). He also names both marriage and celibacy for the sake of the kingdom as charisms (1 Cor 7:7). The Church in Paul's view is a Spirit-filled community in which everyone has something to contribute: "To each individual the manifestation of the Spirit is given for some benefit" (1 Cor 12:7).

The Second Vatican Council stressed in a number of different ways that lay people share in the mission and ministry of the Church. If it did not go so far as to speak specifically of lay ministries, it is clear that it was moving the Church in that direction. The Dogmatic Constitution on the Church reclaims for Catholics the Pauline vision of the Church as equipped with a multiplicity of charismatic gifts. Several times it speaks of the diversity of gifts (LG 12) "both hierarchical and charismatic" (LG 4). It also stresses that both the hierarchical priesthood and the common priesthood of all the baptized share in the one priesthood of Christ (LG 10), and that the laity share both in the priestly, prophetic, and kingly functions of Christ (LG 31) and in the mission of the Church itself (LG 33).

It has never been easy for the Church to be what it must be, a community of disciples. Perhaps the greatest challenge faced by the New Testament Church was the working out of this new unity between Jews and Gentiles brought about by God's reconciliation in Christ. It was not immediately apparent to the first Christians, who of course were Jews, just what this would mean. For many of them it was inconceivable that one could be a disciple of Jesus and member of the Christian community without first becoming a Jew, which meant observing the Jewish Law with all its dietary restrictions and for males, circumcision (cf. Acts 15; Galatians). Paul himself saw clearly that being Jew or Gentile made no difference; the great message of his Letter to the Romans was that all were justified by faith in Jesus Christ. It took the Church much longer to challenge slavery as an institution. While Paul taught that relations between slaves and masters were to be different in virtue of their new partnership in Christ Jesus (Phlm; Eph 6:5-9), he did not challenge the institution of slavery, taken for granted in the ancient world. The Church accepted slavery for centuries. A number of popes began to speak out against the slave trade in the sixteenth century, though it was not until the pontificate of Leo XIII (1878–1903) that the Church officially began to correct its teaching in regard to slavery.[5] And it can be argued, as many do today, that the Church has yet to recognize the full equality of women and men, not just in principle but in the Church itself.

How did the Church develop from the community of the disciples of Jesus to a Church with a structured, hierarchical ministry of bishops, priests, and deacons, presided over by the bishop of Rome, the pope?

AN OFFICIAL MINISTRY

From the earliest days the community of the disciples of Jesus had a leadership group in the Twelve, that core group chosen by Jesus during his historical ministry. The New Testament recognizes a wider circle of apostles from the beginning as well as the unique place of the Twelve. The apostles were the original witnesses to the resurrection of Jesus, those who had an "Easter experience" of the risen Jesus. Though the risen Jesus manifested himself to both men and women, women were not given the title of "apostle" by the New Testament writers,[6] most probably for the cultural reason that in Jewish society a woman's word was not considered as legally binding testimony. Most of the apostles worked as roving evangelists rather than resident pastors; they were constantly on the move founding communities, or Churches, like Paul himself.

---

[5]See John Francis Maxwell, *Slavery and the Catholic Church* (London: Barry Rose, 1975) 115–20. On the unwillingness of the Catholic Church in the United States to support the abolitionist movement, see Patrick Granfield, *Ecclesial Cybernetics: A Study of Democracy in the Church* (New York: Macmillan, 1973) 61–67.

[6]Paul refers to Andronicus and Junia as "prominent among the apostles" (Rom 16:7). Junia is a woman's name, though it has often been interpreted by editors as a man's name. The text does not explicitly call them apostles.

From the beginning the Twelve chose to share their own apostolic ministry with others (Acts 6:1-6). Furthermore, the apostles were not the only ministers or evangelists in the primitive Church. All of the disciples were called to a share in the mission of Jesus. Paul speaks of a wide variety of spiritual gifts and ministries (1 Cor 12:4), and the list of the names of his "co-workers" at the end of many of his letters is evidence of his dependence on others, a number of them husband and wife teams (cf. Rom 16). In the early days the language is quite fluid, though even here there is a certain order. In 1 Corinthians Paul speaks of "first, apostles; second, prophets; third, teachers; then, mighty deeds; then gifts of healing, assistance, administration, and varieties of tongues" (12:28). In Romans 12:6-8 he refers to the gifts of prophecy, the teachers, the exhorter, the almsgiver, the presider or leader, and the one who does works of mercy.

Ministry and Leadership

It might be good to reflect on the nature of the language used by the early communities for their ministers and leaders.[7] First, the language is functional. Ministers and leaders are usually identified in terms of the roles they play; teaching, presiding, overseeing, shepherding. The New Testament does not use the word "priest" *(hiereus)* for Christian ministers. Second, the language used suggests something about the style of leadership and the way authority is to be exercised in the Christian community. Power words are avoided. Jesus' teaching on leadership as service in the community of disciples is remembered and passed on: "You know that those who are recognized as rulers over the Gentiles lord it over them, and their great ones make their authority over them felt. But it shall not be so among you. Rather, whoever wishes to be great among you will be your servant; whoever wishes to be first among you will be the slave of all" (Mark 10:42-44; cf. Luke 22:25-26). Very early the word "shepherd" (Latin, *pastor*) was associated with teachers (Eph 4:11) and the presbyter-bishops (Acts 20:28; 1 Pet 5:2-4). Peter is made shepherd in a special sense (John 21:15-17). Think for a moment about how a shepherd functions in regard to a flock. Generally the shepherd follows rather than leads, as the sheep know where they are going. The shepherd only intervenes when a sheep strays away or when danger threatens. The role is one of guidance and protection, not domination. We still speak of "pastoral" leadership or ministry and object when it is exercised in an authoritarian way.

The basic New Testament word for "ministry" is the Greek *diakonia,* from *diakonos,* "servant." *Diakonia* was translated into Latin as *ministerium,*

[7]See Kenan Osborne, *Priesthood: A History of the Ordained Ministry in the Roman Catholic Church* (New York: Paulist, 1988) 40–85; Paul Bernier, *Ministry in the Church: A Historical and Pastoral Approach* (Mystic, Conn.: Twenty-Third, 1992) 15–49.

from which we get our English word "ministry." Ministry is service on behalf of the Christian community; like any spiritual gift or charism, its purpose is for building up the Church (1 Cor 14). Paul describes himself as a minister to the Gentiles (Rom 15:16), and he refers to Phoebe "our sister" as a "minister" (not "deaconess," as *diakonos* here is frequently translated) of the Church at Cenchreae (Rom 16:1).

Local Church leaders were described by various terms, among them, "leaders" or "presiders" (cf. 1 Thess 5:12; Rom 12:8); "prophets" and "teachers" (1 Cor 12:28; cf. Acts 13:1); "pastors and teachers" (Eph 4:11); "leaders" (Heb 13:7, 17, 24); "presbyters" (Acts 14:23; 20:17; 1 Tim 5:17-22; Titus 1:5); or "presbyter-bishops," since the two terms were not always clearly distinguished (cf. Acts 20:17-35; 1 Pet 5:1-4).

Increasingly the presbyter-bishops took over the roles exercised earlier by the prophets, teachers, and leaders. Their responsibilities included both community leadership and, increasingly, the teaching and liturgical functions exercised by the prophets and teachers (Acts 13:2). From this single ministry, variously identified, were to emerge two distinct offices, that of the presbyter, or "priest," as he would later more popularly be known, and that of the bishop. The later New Testament also knows a group identified as "deacons."

Ordination

By the end of the New Testament period presbyters were being installed in office, probably with the laying on of hands (1 Tim 4:14; 5:22). This appointment to office with ritual and prayer became known as "ordination," a term derived from the Latin *ordo*, meaning "an established body." By ordination a person was incorporated into the *ordo episcoporum*, the *ordo presbyterorum*, or the *ordo diaconorum*, thus into the Church's official pastoral office. There were also unordained "orders" of virgins, widows, catechumens, and penitents in the early Church. In the tradition the appointment to the pastoral office through prayer and the laying on of hands became known as the sacrament of "holy orders."

Bishops

The word "bishop," from the Greek *episkopos*, means "overseer." The role of the *episkopos* was to watch over the community, exercising a shepherd's care for its well-being. In *1 Clement*, a letter written from the Church at Rome around the year 96, the terms "presbyter" and "bishop" are still being used interchangeably. But in 1 Timothy the twofold office of presbyter-bishop and deacon seems to be in the process of evolving into the traditional threefold office of a bishop assisted by presbyters and deacons. The letter describes some presbyters as adding to their roles of community supervision the duties of preaching and teaching (1 Tim 5:17). In other words, the group of presbyter-bishops seems to be in the process of further differentiating itself into presbyters and some presbyters with additional leadership responsibilities, who may well have received the title *episkopos* at Ephesus (cf. 1 Tim 3:1-7). At Antioch the threefold ministry is already in place by the year 115. By the year 150 it has spread through most of the Church and is well on the way to becoming universal.

From the time of Ignatius of Antioch (ca. 115) the role of bishop has been to preside over a local Church and to maintain the communion *(koinonia)* between that Church and the other Churches through communion with their bishops. Thus there is an important symbolic dimension to the episcopal office; bishops symbolize and maintain the communion between their local Churches and the apostolic Church as well as with the worldwide communion of the Church. Catholic teaching maintains that bishops succeed to the function of leadership once exercised by the apostles (LG 20). They constitute a college, which together with its head, the bishop of Rome, possesses supreme and full authority over the universal Church (LG 22). United with the pope, they share in the Church's charism of infallibility (LG 25).

Presbyters

The Greek *presbyteros,* from which our English word "priest" is derived etymologically, originally meant "elder." Presbyters first appeared in Jewish Christian Churches, borrowed from the synagogue where the responsibility of the elders was to advise and guide the community. Most presbyters, or "priests," assist the bishop by presiding over local communities of the faithful, preaching the word, celebrating the sacraments, and exercising a ministry of pastoral leadership and care (LG 28). Because they belong to the local Church or diocese they are known as diocesan or "secular" priests. Priests belonging to religious orders or congregations often exercise a more kerygmatic or prophetic priesthood, combining liturgical and sacramental ministry with a broader ministry of the word that includes preaching, teaching and scholarship, spiritual direction, and the various ministries of social justice.

Deacons

Within much of the New Testament *diakonos* seems to have been used for those in ministries of leadership. It was only in the later New Testament period that *diakonos* began to be used for a specific office, the office of deacon (1 Tim 3:8-13). In the post-New Testament Church deacons functioned as assistants to the bishop, often managing the temporal concerns of the Church, a role that made some deacons quite powerful. They were entrusted with various charitable and liturgical duties, foremost among them the dispensation of gifts to the needy of the community and assisting in the rites of Christian initiation.[8] They were often in charge of instructing those preparing for baptism. Deacons were appointed to office by ordination with the laying on of hands or were sometimes merely installed and had their own roles in the liturgy.

Women served as deaconesses in both the Eastern and the Western Churches; their function seems to have been that of anointing the women among those being baptized and visiting the sick. Some deaconesses were ordained, but their ministry was generally subordinated to that of the deacon and did not last much longer than the period in which adult baptism was the norm. By the tenth or eleventh centuries deaconesses had disappeared even from the Eastern Churches.[9]

In the Western Church the ministry of the deacon was gradually reduced to a step on the way to ordination to the priesthood. The permanent diaconate as an expression of the Church's traditional threefold ministry was not restored until the Second Vatican Council. Deacons are authorized to preach the gospel and to preside at baptisms, weddings, and funerals (cf. LG 29). Because they are ordained, permanent deacons are technically "clerics" and take on the obligation of celibacy, though the Church also ordains married men as deacons.

While the roles of bishops, presbyters, and deacons have been shaped and conditioned by different periods in the history of the Church, there are some constants. They are first of all ministers; like all ministries, their offices exist for the sake of serving and building up the Church.

Priesthood

Though the New Testament speaks of the whole community as a "royal priesthood" (1 Pet 2:9), it was only in the early third century that the cultic terms "high priest" and "priest" began to be used of Christian ministers, first in reference to the bishop, and later, by extension, to the bishop's assistants, the presbyters. Our English word "priest" carries the connotations of both cultic minister *(hiereus)* and community leader *(presbyteros)*. The sixteenth-century Protestant Reformers, following a strict principle of "Scripture alone," referred to ordained ministers as "ministers" or "pastors." Lutherans spoke of God as having established a "preaching office" for the Church. But the language of priesthood for bishops and priests should not be dismissed as something novel or contrary to the nature of the ordained ministry; it

[8]See James M. Barnett, *The Diaconate: A Full and Equal Order* (New York: Seabury, 1981) 57–93.

[9]See Aimé Georges Martimort, *Deaconesses: An Historical Study* (San Francisco: Ignatius, 1986) 182–83.

emerged early in the Church's tradition as the sacrificial dimension of the Eucharist became more clearly recognized. The Second Vatican Council returned to the ancient understanding of the episcopal office, which saw the bishops possessing the fullness of the priesthood. It also taught that both the ministerial or hierarchical priesthood and the common or baptismal priesthood of all the faithful share in the one priesthood of Christ (LG 10).

The Papal Ministry

A sense for the universality and catholicity of the Church, centered on the bishop of Rome, the pope, is basic to a Roman Catholic understanding of the Church. The papacy is Catholicism's most obvious symbol. At its foundation lie two separate but related traditions, that of Peter's leadership among the first disciples of Jesus and that of the primacy of the Roman Church.

Simon, son of John, whose name Jesus changed to Cephas, or Peter ("rock"), was the most prominent of the disciples of Jesus. His name always appears first in the lists of the apostles and is mentioned more than any other in each of the four Gospels. Peter predominates in the early Church, partly because of his prominence among the Twelve and partly because he was the first to whom the risen Jesus manifested himself (although another tradition, equally ancient, reports that Jesus appeared first to Mary Magdalene and some other women).

The Church of Rome enjoyed a preeminence from the beginning. Besides being the capital city of the Roman Empire, the city claimed a unique apostolic heritage in that both Peter and Paul had worked and died there. Already within the New Testament period, the Church of Rome was instructing other Christian communities. The First Letter of Peter was most likely written from Rome in Peter's name to a group of Christians in Asia Minor in the mid 80s. And the letter known as *1 Clement* was written from Rome around the year 96 to admonish the Christians in Corinth. As Raymond Brown has observed, it is quite possible that the reason the Roman Church did not hesitate to instruct other Churches was because it considered itself to have inherited the pastoral responsibilities of Peter and Paul for the Churches they had founded.[10]

A few years after *Clement,* Ignatius of Antioch referred to Rome's "presidency of love," saying that Rome had "taught others." Irenaeus spoke of Rome's "more powerful origin" on the basis of its two founding apostles. Cyprian (d. 258) called it the "principal church." As the Roman Church continued to make suggestions to other Churches and those Churches appealed to Rome as a kind of court of appeal, its authority grew.

---

[10]Raymond E. Brown and John P. Meier, *Antioch and Rome: New Testament Cradles of Catholic Christianity* (New York: Paulist, 1983) 165–66.

By the fourth century a series of bishops at Rome were appealing to the authority given to Peter in Matthew 16:18 as the source of their own authority. Pope Leo the Great (440–461) spoke of himself as "the vicar of Peter," a title used as late as the eleventh and twelfth centuries. Gregory the Great (590–604) rejected the title "universal pope" because it took away from the honor due his brother bishops, choosing instead the title *servus servorum Dei,* "servant of the servants of God." The title "vicar of Christ" was made popular by Innocent III (d. 1216). One familiar papal title, *Pontifex maximus,* or "sovereign Pontiff," has an interesting history. Originally a pagan title used for the head of the ancient Roman college of priests, it was used as an appellation for the pope only after the fifteenth century. To us today "sovereign Pontiff" sounds particularly sacerdotal and hierarchical. But a popular etymology has long translated the phrase as "chief bridge builder," certainly an appropriate title for a pope.

The First Vatican Council (1869–1870) solemnly declared that the Roman pontiff has full and supreme power over the universal Church not only in regard to faith and morals but also in matters that pertain to the discipline and government of the Church throughout the whole world. In regard to teaching authority, it said that when the pope speaks *ex cathedra,* he "is possessed of that infallibility with which the Divine Redeemer willed that his Church should be endowed for defining doctrine regarding faith and morals" (DS 3074). It is important to note that the council viewed the charism of infallibility as belonging primarily to the Church, not to the pope alone. The key question is, how does the Church's infallibility come to expression?

The Second Vatican Council, with its collegial theology of the episcopal office, put Vatican I's teaching on papal primacy and infallibility in a new context. As head of the college of bishops, the bishop of Rome presides over the communion of the Church and safeguards its unity. The bishops in communion with the pope have authority over the universal Church and share in its infallibility (LG 25). At the same time, the pope's authority cannot be just symbolic, for as universal pastor and head of the episcopal college the pope must have the power to act.

The Magisterium

The teaching office of the pope and bishops is called the "magisterium," from the Latin word *magister,* meaning "master" or "teacher." The fathers of the Second Vatican Council were careful to distinguish between the infallible exercise of the magisterium and what are generally referred to as the teachings of the ordinary (or noninfallible) magisterium. Both are authoritative. But the kind of assent owed to each is different. The faithful owe a "submission of faith" to those teachings that have been proclaimed infallibly (LG 25). These infallible teachings, proclaimed with the Church's highest authority,

are called "dogmas"; they include the articles of the Creed, the solemn teachings of the ecumenical councils, and the *ex cathedra* teachings of the papal
magisterium. Dogmas constitute the Church's rule of faith. To reject a dogma
would be to place oneself outside the believing community. Dogmas are ir-
reformable in the sense that the judgment contained in a dogma cannot be
changed, though like any expression of faith that emerges historically, they
are historically conditioned and thus subject to reinterpretation.

Doctrines are authoritative but noninfallibly proclaimed teachings of the
Church. Whether of Scripture, councils, or the ordinary papal magisterium,
doctrines are owed a "religious submission" *(obsequium religiosum)* of will and
mind (LG 25). The presumption of the believer is always in favor of the teaching because it comes with the authority of the Church. But since doctrines are
not proclaimed infallibly, the possibility of error cannot be excluded.
Therefore, unlike dogmas, doctrines can be not just reinterpreted but occasionally changed, as a close study of the history of the Church's doctrinal tradition would indicate. Theology serves the Church by probing the tradition
and seeking more adequate ways to bring the Church's faith to expression.

Some Catholics misunderstand the magisterium as a teaching authority
placed over the Church and equipped with the special assistance of the Holy
Spirit to define faith and doctrine rather than an office through which the faith
entrusted to the entire Church comes to expression. From this perspective the
magisterium was described as the *ecclesia docens,* the "teaching Church," placed
over and separate from the *ecclesia discens,* the "learning Church."

Similarly, some Catholics continue to imagine the pope as the source, after
God, from which all power and authority flow and as the chief decision maker
for contemporary questions. Such people still perceive the Church monarchi-
cally. Disputed questions are answered simply by citing what the pope has said.
Thus complicated questions are decided simply on the basis of an appeal to authority, and the whole complex process of doctrinal development is ignored.
This approach represents the Catholic version of the fundamentalist attitude,
though it is a papal or magisterial fundamentalism rather than a biblical one.

In the real order, the magisterium functions quite differently. The
Church is not fundamentally an institution, exercising teaching authority
from the top down. The Holy Spirit is active in the whole Church, not just
in the hierarchy. The doctrine of the *sensus fidelium* ("sense of the faithful")
shows that the Church's doctrines and dogmas emerge out of the faith of
the entire Church. The formulation of doctrine is not based on a majority
opinion, but emerges out of a consensus, which under the guidance of the
Holy Spirit embraces both pastors and laity (LG 12).

The ecclesial practice of the "reception" of doctrine is further evidence
of a mutuality or interdependence between hierarchical authority and the
body of the faithful in the formulation of doctrine, leading occasionally to
the modification or revision of the teachings of the ordinary papal magis-

terium. For example, Pius XII's exclusive identification of the Catholic Church with the mystical body of Christ in his encyclical *Mystici corporis* was changed by the Second Vatican Council; the council said that the Church of Christ "subsists in" rather than "is" the Roman Catholic Church, as the original draft had stated (LG 8).[11] The development and formulation of doctrine is always a complex process involving the work of theologians, the sense of the faithful, the process of reception, and the authoritative teaching of the Church's bishops. To believe that Christian truth is discerned simply by magisterial pronouncement without taking this complex process into account is a variety of the papal fundamentalism mentioned above.

Even in the occasional exercise of the extraordinary or infallible magisterium, the pope is defining what the Church believes. This was evident in the only two cases of infallible definitions of the extraordinary papal magisterium, the immaculate conception of Mary (1854) and her assumption (1950), both of which were made only after a process of consulting the Church through a polling of the bishops. Thus the Church functions as a communion in which all members, faithful and hierarchy, are mutually interdependent. Neither functions independently of the other. A clearer acknowledgment of this interdependence would do an enormous amount of good toward reassuring Christians of other Churches who remain suspicious of the papal magisterium.

ONE, HOLY, CATHOLIC, AND APOSTOLIC

From the time of the Council of Constantinople in 381 Christians have professed that they believe in "one, holy, catholic, and apostolic Church." These four "notes" or "marks" characterize the Church of Christ. In the ancient Church they served to distinguish the true Church from heretical assemblies or false churches. Since the Reformation they have often been used polemically, to justify the claim of one Church against another. And there is the problem. To many today, the marks seem much more a description of what the Church should be rather than what it actually is. It is obvious that the Church today is not one but many. For a considerable number of people the holiness of the Church is not immediately apparent; it seems more clearly a sinful Church. If some Churches still identify themselves as Catholic, they must also further specify themselves as Anglo Catholic or Old Catholic or Roman Catholic. And most Churches claim to be apostolic, in the sense of being in succession to the Church of the apostles. How should these marks of the Church be understood?

[11]See Francis A. Sullivan, *The Church We Believe In: One Holy, Catholic, and Apostolic* (New York: Paulist, 1988) 23–33.

It would be a mistake to reduce the marks of the Church to purely eschatological predicates, qualities that the Church receives from the Lord only in the fullness of time. The marks are attributes of the Church of Christ as it exists in time and space. To take refuge in eschatology is to say there is no way to recognize the visible, historical Church. It leads to a kind of ecclesial relativism—similar to the modern tendency to overlook questions of historical claims, fidelity to the apostolic tradition, a concern for right preaching and proper administration of sacraments—and to emphasizing instead a congenial community, good music, a personal fit. This is one extreme, which by making one Church as good as another takes away from all the Churches any incentive of striving to become more fully the Church of Christ.

At the other extreme is the "one true Church" approach, which makes a claim of exclusive identity between a particular community and the Church of Christ. Such an approach today is more common of sectarians. It overlooks the complexity of the Church. The Church is both visible and invisible, one and many, mystical body and visible assembly, united by the Spirit and expressed in structures of sacraments, ecclesiastical government, and communion (cf. LG 8).

The Church Is One

From the beginning the Church was one, for the Church of the New Testament was a communion of Churches. The word *koinonia,* generally translated as "communion" or "fellowship," was first used by Paul. It refers to a relationship of communion between believers based on sharing certain things in common *(koinon).* The basis of this communion is primarily spiritual; it comes from sharing a common life in the Spirit given in baptism (1 Cor 12:13) and particularly from sharing in the Eucharist. The members of the Church are "one body" because they have a participation or communion *(koinonia)* in the body and blood of Christ (1 Cor 10:16-17).

Koinonia was expressed through visible signs. Paul tells us that after going to Jerusalem to present before the leaders of the Church the gospel as he preached it to the Gentiles, he received the handclasp of fellowship *(koinonia)* from James, Cephas, and John (cf. Gal 2:9). Paul's effort to have his Churches contribute financially to assist the poor in the mother Church of Jerusalem (Rom 15:25-26; 1 Cor 16:1-4; 2 Cor 8:1-5) was another sign of his desire to maintain *koinonia.* Throughout the first millennium the authentic character of the respective Churches was exhibited through the visible signs of the *communio,* which linked them together into the *ecclesia catholica,* Eucharistic hospitality, letters of communion, communion between the bishops themselves, and as early as the third century, communion with Rome.

But the Church was not able to maintain unity and communion with all those who professed Christian faith. Some ancient Churches lost their communion with the universal Church because of their inability to accept the Church's developing Christological doctrine: the Nestorian or East Syrian Churches after the Council of Ephesus (431), the Copts in Egypt and Armenians after Chalcedon (451). The first great division came in 1054 because of tensions and misunderstandings between Rome and Constantinople. After the legates of Pope Leo IX excommunicated the patriarch, Michael Cerularius, and were in turn excommunicated by a local synod, communion between the Eastern Churches and the Latin West was broken. The Churches of the East became known as "Orthodox," a word that had been used particularly in the East to describe those Churches that remained faithful to the teachings of the Councils of Ephesus and Chalcedon.

The Western Churches living in communion with and increasingly under the bishop of Rome continued to be known as the Catholic Church, though its unity suffered a further loss through the sixteenth-century Reformation. In western Europe three new Church traditions emerged, the Lutheran in Germany and Scandinavia, the Reformed or Calvinist in Switzerland and France, and the Anglican in England. In addition, the so-called radical or left-wing Reformation led to a number of communities referred to collectively as the Anabaptists: the Swiss Brethren, the Hutterites in Moravia, and the Dutch Mennonites. These communities sought not just to reform the Church but to restore Christian life on the model of the Church of the New Testament.

Part of the tragedy of the Reformation was its inability to preserve unity within itself; new Churches continued to appear. As Calvin's thought spread, Churches in the Reformed tradition were established in eastern Europe, the Netherlands, Scotland, England, Ireland, and ultimately the United States. In the seventeenth century the Baptists developed out of the Puritan movement in England; Roger Williams established the first Baptist Church in Rhode Island in 1639. The Methodists began as a renewal movement within the Church of England in the eighteenth century, led by John and Charles Wesley, and came to the United States with circuit-riding preachers such as Francis Asbury, Thomas Coke, and Philip Embury. American Protestant denominationalism includes mainline Churches, Evangelicals, Fundamentalists, Pentecostals, and various sects.

Today there are over 1.8 billion Christians in the world, constituting 33.5 percent of the world's population. They are divided into a multiplicity of Churches. Roman Catholics number over 1 billion, Orthodox Christians 173 million, Protestants 382 million, and Anglicans 75 million.[12] There are well over three hundred Churches in the membership of the World Council of Churches, an association of Protestant and Orthodox Churches established in 1948.

---

[12]Based on statistics in the 1994 *Britannica Book of the Year,* 271.

How can we best understand the relationship between the one Church and the many Churches and, at the same time, make sense of the claim of the Second Vatican Council that to be "fully incorporated" into the Church one must be in full visible communion with the Catholic Church (LG 14)?

The Church cannot be reduced simply to the local congregation, or to the sum of all the particular Churches, as many Protestants tend to do. Such an atomistic concept of the Church is contrary to the way the Church of the first millennium held both unity and diversity together in a delicate balance. If the Church is a communion of Churches, then each local or particular Church, to be fully Church, must be part of the communion. At the same time, the Church cannot be understood as a single, worldwide, monolithic institution. Too many Catholics continue to think of the Church in this way. According to Vatican II, the particular Churches are "fashioned after the model of the universal Church," while "in and from such individual churches there comes into being the one and only Catholic Church" (LG 23).

As a worldwide communion of Churches, the Catholic Church is at once one and many Churches. The local or particular Churches are linked to one another and to the bishop of Rome through the bonds of communion between their bishops. Included in this communion are the Eastern Catholic Churches, sometimes referred to incorrectly as "Uniate" Churches. These are communities that were formerly Orthodox but that have at various moments in history reestablished communion with the bishop of Rome; they maintain their own distinct theological, liturgical, and canonical traditions, including a married clergy. The council's Decree on Eastern Catholic Churches recognizes their rites as of equal dignity with the Latin Rite (OE 3). The communion linking the Churches is not just theological but institutional as well, which means that the communion of Churches can act as one, as it did at the Second Vatican Council. According to the council, the unity or oneness Christ bestowed on his Church already exists in the Catholic Church as something it can never lose; yet this unity is not yet perfect, for the council expresses the hope that "it will continue to increase until the end of time" (UR 4).

The Catholic Church has always recognized the Orthodox Churches as Churches, and the council spoke of the separated "Churches and ecclesial Communities" (UR 19) to refer to the divisions in the West. The expression "Churches and ecclesial Communities" is used to distinguish between those that are recognized as having valid orders and those that do not, and so "have not preserved the genuine and total reality of the Eucharistic mystery" (UR 22); the latter are not recognized as Churches in the full theological sense. At the same time, they are called *ecclesial* communities because the Church of Christ is in some way present in them, even if imperfectly. They are analogous to particular Churches of the Catholic Church.[13]

[13]Sullivan, *The Church We Believe In*, 54.

The Church Is Holy

One of the most fascinating aspects of the experience of God that emerges from the Hebrew Scriptures is the idea that God is "holy" and that God's people are to be holy also. "Be holy, for I, the LORD, your God, am holy" (Lev 19:2). The idea of "holiness" (from the Hebrew root *qds,* meaning "separate") describes the essential character of God—otherness, difference, or apartness from all that is created, limited, and imperfect. God's holiness implies both divine power and moral righteousness; it is shown in God's deliverance of the chosen people, justice, and abhorrence of sin.

In a secondary sense persons, places, and things are called holy by their association with God. The ground around the burning bush is holy because God is there (Exod 3:4-5). Israel is holy because of the covenant relationship—spelled out in the Ten Commandments—between the people and Yahweh (Exod 19:5-6). The objects associated with the cult or liturgy are seen as holy, the tent of meeting, the temple, the altar, the sacred vestments, the priests, the Sabbath, the sacrifice. All these are holy not in some magical sense but because of their closeness or association with the divine.

The Church is called "holy" in this derivative sense. The Church is holy because it is the locus of God's abiding presence. In Christ God has sanctified the disciples; they have become united as "Christ's body" (1 Cor 12:27); the community is "God's building" (1 Cor 3:9), and through Christ the community becomes "a temple sacred in the Lord" and "a dwelling place of God in the Spirit" (Eph 2:21-22). The community is "a royal priesthood, a holy nation, a people of his own" (1 Pet 2:9). The earliest New Testament documents frequently refer to the members of the Church as "holy ones" *(hagioi)* or "saints" (Rom 1:7; 12:13; 15:25; 1 Cor 14:33; 16:1; Phil 4:22; Acts 9:13, 32), "sanctified" in Christ Jesus (1 Cor 1:2) or by the Holy Spirit (Rom 15:16).

The Second Vatican Council echoes this theology, grounding it in baptism: "The baptized, by regeneration and the anointing of the holy Spirit, are consecrated into a spiritual house and a holy priesthood" (LG 10). But if God has made the Church holy as a sanctified people, a "holy People of God" (LG 12), it is equally clear that as individuals they must cooperate with grace; they must become holy (1 Cor 1:27; Rom 1:7); they must respond in obedience (1 Pet 1:14-16).

The Church is also holy because God has given it holy gifts: the Word of God (Jas 1:21; 1 Pet 1:23), the Church's ministry (2 Cor 5:18; Eph 4:11-12), the sacraments (John 3:5; 20:23; 1 Cor 6:11; 11:27; Jas 5:14-15), to sustain and sanctify the people. These endowments or structures of the Church are holy in themselves because they are divine gifts; they enable the Church to be an effective, sacramental sign of holiness in the world in spite of the unworthiness of the Church's people or ministers. In the liturgy of the Eastern Churches these two dimensions of the Church's holiness are joined when the deacon invites the assembly to come forward and receive the Eucharist with the words "holy things for the holy."

Can the Church be at once holy and sinful? The official tradition has been reluctant to speak of the Church as sinful, but the council acknowledges that the Church's holiness is an imperfect one: the Church remains "in need of being purified" (LG 8); its radiance "shines less brightly" because of the sins of its members (UR 4); and as a pilgrim Church has need of "continual reformation" (UR 6), echoing the Protestant emphasis on the Church always needing reform *(ecclesia semper reformanda)*.

Others are less hesitant to acknowledge that the holy Church, because it is made up of both saints and sinners, is also sinful. Sullivan calls attention to the council's owning the responsibility it shares for the sins against unity in the sixteenth century (UR 7) and adds other examples of "historical sins for which the Church in some way shares a collective responsibility: . . . ill-treatment of the Jewish people, racial discrimination, the exploitation of colonized nations, and the tolerance of slavery."[14] Thus, just as the Church can become more fully one, so can it also become more perfectly holy.

The Church Is Catholic

The Greek adjective *katholikos,* meaning "general," "total," or "universal," was first applied to the Church in the sense of the whole or universal Church by Ignatius of Antioch around the year 115. Ignatius wrote, "Wherever the bishop is, there his people should be, just as, where Jesus Christ is, there is the catholic church" *(Smyrn.* 8.2). Ignatius was arguing that just as Christ is the head and center of the whole Church, so the bishop is the head and center of the local congregation.

But as early as the third and fourth centuries the word "catholic" was being used more polemically to distinguish the great or true Church from heretical groups or movements separate from it. Augustine (d. 430), listing the true Church's characteristics—universal consent, authority, a succession in the priesthood from the seat of Peter—refers finally to "the name 'catholic' itself, which not without reason amid so many heresies, only this one Church has retained, so that, although all the heretics would like to be called 'catholics,' not one of them would dare answer a stranger's questions as to where the Catholic Church meets by pointing to his own basilica or house."[15]

Augustine also contributed to the emergence of a third meaning of the word "catholic": in the controversy with the Donatists the *ecclesia catholica* was understood geographically as referring to the Church spread throughout the whole world.

---

[14]Sullivan, *The Church We Believe In,* 82–83.
[15]*Contra ep. Manichaei* 4.5; *PL* 42, 175.

Thus the word "catholic" has meant the Church in its fullness or totality; it has been used polemically for the true Church, and it has had a geographical or universal sense for the Church present everywhere. Cyril of Jerusalem (d. 387) brought together several senses of the word when he described the Church as catholic because it extends to the ends of the earth, teaches all the doctrines necessary for salvation, instructs all peoples, heals every kind of sin, and possesses every virtue (*Catechesis* 18).

The catholicity of the Church implies an inclusiveness toward Church membership. As a sign of reconciliation in Christ and communion in the Spirit, the Church must embrace all peoples, reconciling differences of race, class, and culture, as its birth on the feast of Pentecost suggests (Acts 2:5-11). The Church's mission of embodying Christ's redemption demands its catholicity; it is to be a sign of the unity of all humankind (cf. LG 1). A Church that excluded others on the basis of race, ethnicity, or social status would not be catholic.

Both the unity and the catholicity of the *ecclesia catholica* were diminished by the division between the Eastern and Western Churches in 1054 as well as by new divisions that resulted from the Reformation. With Christianity in fact divided, catholicity cannot belong only to the Catholic Church, which since the sixteenth century has usually been called the "Roman Catholic Church," though it continues to refer to itself in its official documents simply as the "Catholic Church." In its total membership, the Catholic Church constitutes little more than half of all Christians.

A local Church is catholic if it is in communion with the communion of Churches that constitutes the universal Church. Vatican II teaches that there is a fullness of catholicity that belongs to the Catholic Church, though it also acknowledges that because of the historic divisions the Church "finds it more difficult to express in actual life her full catholicity in all respects" (UR 4). Certainly there are elements of catholicity in other traditions. The rich theological, liturgical, and spiritual traditions of the separated Eastern Churches belong to the catholicity of the undivided Church. A number of traditions show a catholicity through their membership in world confessional families such as the Anglican Communion, the Lutheran World Federation, and the World Alliance of Reformed Churches, though each member Church generally remains juridically independent. The World Council of Churches represents a desire for catholicity on the part of its member Churches, though it is not itself a church but a council of independent Churches that remain free to disassociate themselves from any position or statement of the council. If the Catholic Church is to claim a fullness of catholicity, it has perhaps a special responsibility to find ways to include other Churches in that fullness.

The Church Is Apostolic

In Luke's summary sketch of the primitive Christian Church in Jerusalem, he says that all "devoted themselves to the teaching of the apostles" (Acts 2:42). Today all Christians agree on the unique and irreplaceable role of the apostles in the foundation of the Church. All agree that the contemporary Church needs to be apostolic in the sense of being in succession to the Church of the apostles. But since the Reformation in the sixteenth century, apostolic succession has been differently understood.

The Anglican, Catholic, and Orthodox Churches have traditionally emphasized succession through the historic episcopal office. The Catholic Church holds that "by divine institution bishops have succeeded to the place of the apostles as shepherds of the Church" (LG 20). The Protestant Churches broke with the episcopally ordered Church in the sixteenth century. In the case of the Lutherans, the bishops were unwilling to ordain their pastors. John Calvin argued that apostolicity was to be found in conformity with the teaching of the apostles (*Institute* 4.2.6); this became the traditional position of the Protestant Churches. Apostolic succession was understood in terms of succession in apostolic faith.

The principle of apostolic succession was established as early as A.D. 96 by the author of *1 Clement*. In admonishing the Christians of Corinth for expelling their *episkopoi* from office, Clement states that the apostles themselves, in order to prevent intrigues over the episcopate, had "appointed their first converts . . . to be the bishops and deacons of the future believers" (42.4) and provided that when these died "other approved men should succeed to their ministry" (44.2).

Most scholars today consider Clement's principle as more theological than historical, but the idea of succession to the ministry of the apostles is already present in the New Testament. Local Church leaders are frequently portrayed as succeeding to the pastoral responsibilities of the apostles, both in terms of guarding the apostolic tradition (Acts 20:29-31; 2 Tim 1:14; 2:2) and by various efforts to link their ministry with that of the apostles themselves (1 Pet 5:1; Acts 14:23; 1 Tim 5:22; Titus 1:5). On the one hand, there is enough evidence to suggest that the picture of the apostles appointing leaders who would later be known as presbyter-bishops may have some historical foundation. On the other, it probably was not the only practice. For example, the communities addressed by the *Didache* were instructed to "appoint for yourselves bishops and deacons worthy of the Lord" (15.1).

In the post-New Testament Church, troubled by the heretical communities and Gnostic claims of secret, unwritten traditions going back to Jesus, writers such as Hegesippus (ca. 180), Irenaeus (d. ca. 200), and Tertullian (ca. 200) appealed to the true apostolic tradition handed on through the Churches with apostolic foundation, using lists of the bishops of these

Churches to demonstrate their visible continuity with the apostolic Church. Tertullian challenged Marcion to produce one Marcionite Church that could trace its descent from an apostle (*Marc* 1.21.5). Thus bishops were recognized as successors to the apostles and guardians of the apostolic tradition from at least the second century.

There is liturgical evidence for the collegial nature of the episcopal office in the *Apostolic Tradition* of Hippolytus, dating from late second or early third century; in the ritual for the ordination of a bishop, the new bishop receives the laying on of hands only from the other bishops present (2.3). Their participation is a sign that the new bishop and his Church are in communion with the other Churches and in succession to the Church of the apostles.

Today it is common to distinguish between the succession of the Church in apostolic faith and life and succession in the historical episcopal office; succession in faith is the basic requirement, while episcopal succession is the *sign* of that succession. The World Council of Churches text, *Baptism, Eucharist and Ministry (BEM)*, accepted at the 1982 meeting of the Faith and Order Commission at Lima, Peru, takes this approach.[16] It sees the episcopal succession "as a sign, though not a guarantee, of the continuity and unity of the Church" (M no. 38), and suggests that those Churches that lack it may need to recover the sign (M no. 53b). Thus it offers a nuanced argument for the recovery of an episcopal office in the historic succession. The only thing that *BEM* cannot accept is that idea that a ministry of a particular Church is invalid until it enters the line of the episcopal succession (M no. 38).

The Catholic Church has yet to officially receive the WCC *Baptism, Eucharist and Ministry* text, nor has it been able to acknowledge ordained ministries in the Protestant Churches as valid. But a broad theological consensus along the lines suggested above is emerging in ecumenical documents like *BEM*, which is challenging for all the Churches.[17] The Catholic Church is called to recognize the apostolic faith and authentic nature of ordained ministry in the Protestant Churches, even if they lack the sign of apostolic succession. Protestant Churches are being called to share more fully in the Church's episcopal ministry and to ordain their presiding ministers or bishops in a way that can invite their recognition by Churches in the Catholic tradition. With such theological consensus developing, it will become more important to look at the other reasons, not all of which may be theological, that may prevent the Churches from moving toward reconciliation and communion.

[16]World Council of Churches, *Baptism, Eucharist and Ministry* (Geneva: WCC, 1982).
[17]For a fuller analysis of some of these documents see Sullivan, *The Church We Believe In*, 185–209; also Thomas P. Rausch, *Priesthood Today* (New York: Paulist, 1992) 116–28.

CONCLUSION

The Church as the community of the disciples of Jesus is a visible, historical reality. Catholicism understands that community as mediated and preserved by sacramental symbols and institutional structures, the expressions of a living tradition reaching back to the time of the apostles, as we have seen. There is a ministerial office in the Church, linked to the ministry of the apostles, but it is not the only source of authority. The Church's authority is to be found in Scripture, tradition, the witness and lives of the saints, the *sensus fidelium,* as well as in the decisions of the magisterium.

Protestant Christians, nurtured in a tradition that stresses the sovereign freedom and transcendence of God, the one mediatorship of Christ, and the primacy of the Word, are often suspicious of this Catholic emphasis on tradition, symbols, and structures. For many Protestants, following Calvin, the true Church is an invisible gathering of the elect. What is important is the community of the faithful gathered in response to the preached word, not the denomination or the institution. Faith and life are more important than historical credentials. For Protestants, then, the Church of Christ exists in many different Churches.

Catholics also understand the Church of Christ as existing in many different Churches, but they approach the question differently. From the beginning, the word "church" meant both the local Church and the whole Church, referred to as "catholic" at the beginning of the second century. The papacy belongs to the fullness of the Church. Catholics see the Church of Christ as subsisting in the Catholic Church in its essential fullness because of that Church's historic structures and its unique claims to unity, holiness, catholicity, and apostolicity. They do not deny that the Church of Christ can also be present in different ways in other Churches and ecclesial communities.

The Catholic Church is a world Church; it exists in every land. The majority of Catholics is shifting from the Northern to the Southern Hemisphere. At the Extraordinary Synod of Bishops, which met in Rome in 1985, 74 percent of the bishops came from countries other than Europe and North America, and it is estimated that by the year 2000, 70 percent of the Church's members will live in Third World countries.[18]

Vatican II recognized that there already exists real but imperfect communion between other Christians and the Catholic Church in virtue of baptism (UR 3; LG 15). The Roman Catholic *Ecumenical Directory,* revised in 1993, goes further; it speaks much more clearly of a real though not yet perfect communion that exists not just between Christians but between the Catholic Church and other Churches and ecclesial communities (no. 18).[19]

[18]See Walter Bühlmann, *The Church of the Future* (Maryknoll, N.Y.: Orbis, 1988) 3–11.
[19]See "Directory for the Application of Principles and Norms on Ecumenism," *Origins* 23 (1993).

If the one Church is a communion of Churches, the ecumenical task is to find a way to reestablish full communion between the different Churches and ecclesial communities. In this way the unity already present in the Catholic Church might embrace all the Churches and so become that perfect unity for which Jesus prayed (John 17:22).

4. A Living Tradition

Some people are put off by the notion of tradition. The very word suggests to them something frozen, authoritarian, locking one into the past. They see it as a challenge to personal autonomy. Elizabeth Bennett Johns, an art historian recently received into full communion with the Catholic Church, once saw tradition in this way. In a memoir on her journey to Catholicism she describes her struggle with her own individualist heritage and how she learned, particularly through a number of directed retreats, to see tradition in terms of community: "To assent to the authority of tradition one has to assent to the authority of a community that has existed before oneself, that exists outside of oneself now, and that will continue into the future."[1] This sense of becoming part of a greater community nicely captures what tradition means for Catholics.

The word "tradition" (Greek, *paradosis;* Latin, *traditio*) means literally that which has been "handed over" or "passed on." Too often the term is identified with its secondary meaning of "traditions," all those customs, practices, beliefs, and teachings that are popular but unofficial expressions of the community's faith. Catholics once had a multitude of such traditions—fasting during Lent or from midnight before receiving Holy Communion, abstaining from meat on Fridays, men tipping their hats when passing the front of a Catholic church (because of the presence of the Blessed Sacrament within), women covering their heads in church, even if with a piece of tissue clipped to the hair. These traditions were once part of popular Catholic culture and helped reinforce a Catholic identity, but they were time-conditioned and ultimately unimportant.

In its most basic sense "the tradition" is the shared faith experience of the Christian community, its life in Christ, and its communion in the Spirit. For the Fathers of the Church, that tradition as something handed on from the Apostolic Age was characterized by the three marks of "antiquity, uni-

[1] "A Journey into Spiritual Community," *America* 171 (October 22, 1994) 26.

versality, and consensus." A sense for this principle of tradition enabled the early Church to gather those sacred writings recognized as apostolic by all the Churches into a biblical canon, to identify false teachers and heterodox teachings as such, and to develop normative creeds and confessions of faith. In this way God's revelation is preserved and comes to expression in the life of the community.

But tradition is much more than a respect for what is ancient; it is a living reality that bears the faith experience of the community—received, proclaimed, celebrated, and passed on to subsequent generations. Vatican II spoke of this active role of tradition in its Constitution on Divine Revelation: "And so the Church, in her teaching, life, and worship, perpetuates and hands on to all generations all that she herself is, all that she believes." The tradition "develops . . . with the help of the Holy Spirit," there is a "growth in the understanding of the realities and the words which have been handed down," and "the Church constantly moves forward toward the fullness of divine truth" (DV 8). In this sense tradition has an orientation toward the future, a "forward thrust."[2] Jaroslav Pelikan captures this nicely: "Tradition is the living faith of the dead; traditionalism is the dead faith of the living."[3]

In this chapter we will consider first the relationship between the life or tradition of the community and revelation, the dialogue or self-disclosure that God has initiated with humankind. Next we will consider various official expressions of the tradition of the Church. Finally, we will consider some specific characteristics of the Catholic tradition.

REVELATION AND TRADITION

Many Christians, familiar with God's apparently direct way of dealing with humankind in the Scriptures, long for the clarity of the biblical period with a certain nostalgia. Everything was so simple. God spoke through the burning bush to Moses, and to the people from the smoke and fire of Mount Sinai. God gave them ten tablets with the Law clearly inscribed on them. The people were led through the desert with a cloud by day and a pillar of fire by night. There were great miracles, like the plagues in Egypt, the parting of the Red Sea during the Exodus, the sun standing still in the heavens at Gibeon, and the explicit oracles of the prophets.

There seems to be an equal clarity in the New Testament. Jesus has a clear sense of his own identity, telling the Jews in John's Gospel that he and

[2] Avery Dulles, *The Craft of Theology: From Symbol to System* (New York: Crossroad, 1992) 95; see also ch. 6, "Tradition as a Theological Source."
[3] *The Emergence of the Catholic Tradition (100–600)* (Chicago: Univ. of Chicago Press, 1971) 9.

the Father are one (John 10:30), that he existed even before Abraham (John 8:58). In Matthew's Gospel he gives explicit instructions to the apostles after the resurrection; they are sent to make disciples of all nations (Matt 28:19). Their preaching after Pentecost is accompanied with wondrous miracles, including the raising of the dead (Acts 9:40), and when there is a question to be decided, Peter or Paul is blessed with a revelatory dream or vision, so that God's will is easily discerned (Acts 10:10-16; 23:11).

How do we account for this marvelous divine help in biblical times and explain the apparent silence or hiddenness of God in our own? Why did God so favor our ancestors and leave us so much to our own resources? Perhaps the situation in biblical times was not as simple as it might appear at first glance. Indeed, a careful reading of the Acts of the Apostles shows that the situation of the early Church was not so different from that of our own today. New circumstances raised new questions, the answers to which were not immediately known.

The first great crisis faced by the infant Church was the question of what to do about the Gentiles, those non-Jewish men and women who also came to believe in Jesus and wanted to be baptized into the Christian community. This presented the Church with a great question: Did these prospective Christians first have to become Jews, to take on the obligations of the Jewish Law, which for men included circumcision? The question was not an easy one for the early Church, and in spite of the apparent clarity of gospel texts such as Matthew 28:19, instructing the apostles to baptize all nations, it took the Church considerable time to resolve the dilemma it faced.

Models of Revelation

So how does God communicate with us? Various answers have been proposed.[4] Some understand revelation as God's communication of certain "truths," which are then formulated in explicit propositions. This makes God seem like a theologian who speaks in clear concepts, or Jesus like a teacher who hands over a specific body of doctrines to his apostles. Catholics have often spoken of the "deposit of faith" in this sense; it has been understood statically, as though Jesus entrusted the faith to the apostles as a complete collection of truths.

The Council of Trent (1546–1563) came close to such a propositional understanding of revelation when it spoke of the Gospel as the "truths and rules . . . contained in the written book and unwritten traditions which have come down to us, having been received by the apostles from the mouth of Christ himself" (DS 1501). The Oath against Modernism described faith as "a genuinely intellectual assent to truth received from outside by hearing" (DS 2145).

[4]See Avery Dulles' fine work, *Models of Revelation* (Garden City, N.Y.: Doubleday, 1983).

For many Protestants the doctrine of the verbal inspiration of Scripture reflects a similar propositional understanding of revelation. The words of Scripture are to be understood as true in their literal sense, dictated to the sacred author by the Holy Spirit. For example, there are many fundamentalists who are ready to see in the Book of Revelation, an early Christian work that barely made it into the New Testament canon, a divinely revealed code for all those historical events that will herald the end of the world and the second coming of Christ.

A propositional approach to revelation rightly grasps that there is an element to God's self-disclosure that can be formulated in theological propositions, but it fails to appreciate that these propositions or doctrines are always historically conditioned human constructions subject to reinterpretation. Furthermore, in reducing revelations to "truths" coming from outside, such an approach leaves no room for the unfolding of the implications of the Christ event and for the development of doctrine.

Others see revelation in God's mighty deeds in history, miraculous or self-evident historical events such as the Exodus, the parting of the Red Sea, or the tearing of the Temple veil at the death of Jesus. While it is true that revelation takes place within Israelite history, this approach suggests an interventionist model; it pictures God as in some way intervening directly in the natural order. Unfortunately, those events claimed as divine interventions are not at all self-evident. What the believer sees as God delivering the children of Israel from bondage in Egypt, the historian or anthropologist sees as a migration of peoples as a result of adverse social and economic conditions. In addition, the interventionist approach creates further problems by suggesting that God acts in a way that suspends or overcomes the laws of nature.

Today many think it makes much more sense to see God's revelation, or more accurately, self-revelation, as something that comes not from outside but from within our world, where the transcendent God dwells in an immanent relationship with creation. This approach holds that we do not encounter God directly; revelation is always mediated by some experience in the world, some person, event, story, or natural phenomenon that becomes a symbol disclosing a deeper meaning. Our experience is a profound and complex reality. It includes things that happen to us personally, historical events in the life of our community, questions that trouble us, our desire for meaning, happiness, wholeness, our hunger for God.

From this perspective human experience itself and particularly the experience of the believing community becomes the locus for God's self-communication. In this way, what we call "revelation" represents a religious insight or vision emerging from a community of faith. The community discerns the divine presence and action through persons, events, and things; expresses it in language and story; and eventually formulates it as religious teaching. This is not to deny the mysterious working of the divine Spirit. It is precisely the Spirit that enables the believing community and its prophetic interpreters to come to a new awareness of God's presence and action through a wide variety of natural and religious symbols and particularly in the person of Jesus.

A sacred story or myth can be just as much a means of God's self-disclosure as a historical event or prophetic sermon. The biblical story of the fall of our first parents is a myth used by the biblical authors to explain their people's experience of evil and sin; the story of the serpent leading the man and woman astray in the garden teaches a profound religious truth in suggesting that the root of all sin is the failure of humankind to acknowledge human limits and to recognize God as God. From it Paul was to develop the theology of sin presented in his Letter to the Romans, and Augustine was to formulate what became the doctrine of original sin. Similarly, belief in life after death was not originally part of the Israelite tradition. But the hope that God might raise the dead to life begins to appear in the Hebrew Scriptures in apocalyptic writings such as the Book of Daniel, written around the time of Antiochus IV (ca. 150 B.C.), when pious Jews were being tortured and put to death for their faith. The resurrection of Jesus was evidence of God's power over death itself and is the basis for the doctrine of the resurrection of the body, so central to Christian faith. The chart on page 67 offers some examples of how the believing community moves from experience through interpretative symbols to what ultimately becomes its official beliefs or doctrines.

Thus revelation takes place within the history of God's people reflected in the Hebrew Scriptures and in the books of the New Testament and reaches its fullness in the life, death, and resurrection of Jesus. Or to put it another way, God's self-disclosure in Jesus can only be understood fully in the context of the people out of which Jesus came and the early communities of disciples who celebrated his presence among them. Their tradition is expressed in and preserved for us in Sacred Scripture. The expression "revelation comes to a close with the death of the last apostle" points to Jesus as God's definitive self-disclosure and to the normative quality of the Scripture of the apostolic Church. There can be no further revelation, for God's definitive word has been spoken and become flesh in Jesus.

EXPRESSIONS OF THE TRADITION

The faith experience of the community comes to expression both officially and unofficially. Unofficially it comes to expression in Christian art, music, and literature, in popular beliefs and the teachings of theologians, in various spiritualities and devotional traditions, in the efforts of parents to share their own faith with their children, in stories of the saints and the lives of individual Christians, and so on. Officially the living tradition of the

EXPERIENCE	SYMBOLS	DOCTRINES
ancient creation myth (*Enuma Elish* epic)	Genesis creation stories	creation
experience of evil	fall of Adam and Eve (Gen 3), Rom 4–8	original sin
Exodus—historically a social migration	crossing of the Red Sea, Sinai theophany, Decalogue	election, covenant, people of God, salvation
collapse of Davidic kingdom, social injustice, idolatry, prophetic preaching	prophetic images of salvation (messiah, Day of the Lord, etc.)	eschatology, messianic hope, justice of God
persecution under Antiochus IV, Jews dying for faith	apocalyptic literature with image of the resurrection of the dead (Dan 12:1-3)	resurrection of the dead taught by the Pharisees
death of Jesus, Easter experience of the disciples	Easter kerygma (Acts 2:32; 3:15; 5:31; Rom 10:9; 1 Cor 15:3-5) Easter stories (Mark 16:1-8; Luke 24; Matt 28; John 20, 21	resurrection of the dead taught by the early Church
Jesus: teachings, life, death	kingdom of God, parables, Gospels	divinity of Jesus, trinity, creed
John's baptism, community of disciples, table fellowship	ritual of initiation, *ekklesia, koinonia,* table fellowship trad., laying on of hands	baptism, Church, Eucharist, sacraments

Church comes to expression in the canonical Scriptures, in the creeds, in the liturgy and sacraments of the Church, and in the doctrinal formulations of the Church's teaching office, or magisterium.

Scripture

The books of the Bible are considered "sacred" writings, or Scripture, because in them the Church recognizes the voice of its Lord. According to the Dogmatic Constitution on Divine Revelation, the books of the Old and New Testament have been written under the inspiration of the Holy Spirit; they have God as their true author and "must be acknowledged as teaching firmly, faithfully, and without error that truth which God wanted put into the sacred writings for the sake of our salvation" (DV 11). Thus they have divine authority. They remain today the norm for Christian faith, preaching, and doctrine, and as the Word of God are a rich source for personal prayer.

At the same time, the Scriptures themselves are a product of tradition; they represent the written expression of the faith of Israel and of the primitive Christian communities. As a primary witness to God's revelation to Israel and in Jesus, the Scriptures are normative for the faith of the Christian community today and continue to be interpreted within the living tradition of the Church.

The Hebrew Scriptures represent a diverse collection, or canon, of sacred books written over a period of more than a thousand years. This collection is divided into three parts, the Law, the Prophets, and the Writings. The Law, traditionally attributed to Moses, consists of the first five books of the Hebrew Bible, Genesis, Exodus, Leviticus, Numbers, and Deuteronomy, also referred to as the Pentateuch. The Prophets, which includes more than the traditional prophetic books, embraces all the prophets, from Joshua and the Judges down through Malachi. The remaining biblical books—historical books, psalms, the Wisdom literature—are grouped together into the Writings.

The Catholic Old Testament canon contains all these writings plus six additional books and parts of books that had been preserved only in Greek (1 and 2 Maccabees, Tobit, Judith, Sirach, Wisdom of Solomon, Baruch, and some additional parts in Daniel and Esther). These books were part of the "Septuagint," the Greek translation of the Hebrew Scriptures, produced sometime after 250 B.C. at Alexandria in Egypt. They were used by many of the primitive Christian communities, which included large numbers of Greek-speaking Jewish and Gentile converts, but were not included in the Hebrew canon, drawn up by the Pharisees at Jamnia around A.D. 90, using the norm that a book had to be in Hebrew to be included. In the sixteenth century the Protestant Reformers returned to the Hebrew canon. By rejecting these deuterocanonical books, which they referred to as the "Apocrypha," the Reformers established a Protestant Old Testament canon slightly different from that traditionally followed by the Catholic and Orthodox Churches.

The New Testament canon consists of twenty-seven books written over a period of some sixty years. The earliest New Testament documents are the authentic letters of Paul, 1 Thessalonians, 1 and 2 Corinthians, Galatians, Philippians, Romans, and the short Philemon, written by Paul himself in the early fifties. The other letters attributed to Paul were most probably written by one of his disciples from one to three decades after his death (ca. 63). The first Gospel, that of Mark, appeared about 68, shortly before the destruction of Jerusalem, which marks the end of the Apostolic Age. Matthew and

Luke, based in large part on Mark but with access to another source of the sayings of Jesus known simply as "Q" (from the German *Quelle,* "source"), were written between 85 and 90, along with Luke's Acts of the Apostles. The Gospel of John appeared around 100, with the three Johannine epistles following slightly later. The last New Testament book, 2 Peter, was written sometime around or after 110.

Those books received into the biblical canon were recognized as being divinely inspired; that is, the early Churches saw them as expressions of their own faith and so as having divine authority. We can say they represent the living tradition of the community, or Church, coming to written expression. There are of course many other books, both Jewish and Christian, for which some individuals or communities, often Gnostic, claimed divine authority. These pseudoprophetic books, epistles, gospels, and acts of various apostles are known collectively as "apocryphal" writings; ultimately they did not pass the test of recognition and acceptance or "reception," which led to the emergence of the biblical canon. The Bible thus comes from the Church rather than the other way around.

In the sixteenth century Catholics and Reformers argued about the relation between Scripture and tradition.[5] The Reformers took up the cry *sola scriptura* (Scripture alone) as their standard. The Catholic Church continued to see Scripture as the book of the Church, interpreted within its living tradition.

Today both sides are much closer. Catholic and Protestant scholars often study in the same universities and divinity schools; they take courses from the same professors and read the same authors. Most Protestants recognize that the Bible is itself an expression of tradition and is always interpreted within a given community of faith that gives it life. Catholics acknowledge that Scripture remains the primary norm for the Church's faith and doctrine. Vatican II's Dogmatic Constitution on Divine Revelation says of the magisterium: "This teaching office is not above the word of God, but serves it, teaching only what has been handed on, listening to it devoutly, guarding it scrupulously, and explaining it faithfully by divine commission and with the help of the Holy Spirit" (DV 10).

Creeds

The faith of the Church also comes to expression in its creeds. A creed (from the Latin *credo,* "I believe") is an official profession of faith. One of the earliest Christian confessions was the expression "Jesus is Lord" (1 Cor 12:3). Similarly, the formula "If you confess with your mouth that Jesus is Lord and believe in your heart that God raised him from the dead, you will

---

[5]George H. Tavard's *Holy Writ or Holy Church: The Crisis of the Protestant Reformation* (London: Burns & Oats, 1959) is a classic study of this issue.

be saved" (Rom 10:9) may have been part of an ancient baptismal profession. Such formulas of belief were required of candidates for baptism from the very beginning.

It was from this baptismal context, particularly from the catechetical training that preceded baptism, that the historic creeds of the Church developed.[6] The Matthean formula, "baptizing them in the name of the Father, and of the Son, and of the Holy Spirit" (Matt 28:19), may have provided the Trinitarian model for subsequent creeds. In the second and third centuries candidates for baptism were asked three questions, enabling them to profess their belief in God as Father, Son, and Spirit. An example from the Roman Church of the early third century can be found in the *Apostolic Tradition* of Hippolytus (21.12-18). These interrogatory creeds gave way in time to declaratory creeds. The Apostles' Creed seems to have had its ultimate origins in the baptismal creed of the Roman Church, though the actual text is thought to have come from Gaul. It remains associated with baptism. The so-called Nicene Creed is actually a revision of Nicaea's creed (325) by the First Council of Constantinople (381). It is sometimes referred to as the "Ecumenical Creed." The Athanasian Creed may have been written in the fifth century by Caesarius of Arles, a student of Augustine. And there are others.

The Nicene Creed remains common to Catholic, Orthodox, and mainline Protestant Churches (though the Orthodox omit the *filioque* clause, which states that the Spirit proceeds from the Father *and* the Son, added to the creed in the West in the eleventh century). Unfortunately, many of us today are accustomed to rattling it off without much thought. But a little reflection reveals a wealth of Christian teaching, for the creed represents the Church's rule of faith, compressed into a relatively few "articles." Our belief in God as Father, Son, and Spirit, the virginity of Mary, the one, holy, catholic, and apostolic Church, the forgiveness of sins, the resurrection of the body, and life everlasting—all this is publicly confessed in this historic expression of the Church's faith. If you want to know what the Church believes, examine its creed. Then look at its life of worship.

Liturgy

The word "liturgy" *(leitourgia)* comes from the Greek *laos*, "people," and *ergon*, "work," thus "a work of the people." It refers to the official public prayer of the Church, the Eucharist, the other sacraments and official rites, and the Divine Office, now generally referred to as "the Liturgy of the Hours."

Liturgy represents the Church at prayer, not just as individuals or even the Church's official ministers but the whole people, or "assembly." When the Church initiates one into its community and so into Christ in the sacra-

---

[6]See J.N.D. Kelly, *Early Christian Creeds* (London: Longman, 1972) 50.

ment of baptism, when it gathers to break bread and share the cup in memory of Jesus, when it proclaims the forgiveness of sins in his name, the Church itself is becoming more fully what it is, the presence of the risen Christ in the midst of his people. In this way the Church's living tradition is again coming to expression.

Sacraments are symbols made up of ritual action and narrative; they "may be described as symbols of God's presence in world, life, history, and church."[7] Consider how much of Christian faith is compressed in each of the sacraments. Baptism initiates one into the Christian community. The baptismal formula is a profession of faith in the triune God; it requires a profession of faith on the part of the one to be baptized or, in the case of infant baptism, on the part of the parents and sponsors, who will be the primary Church the child will experience for many years. The waters of baptism are a sign of being cleansed from one's sins and rising to the new life that is ours through the death and resurrection of Jesus.

Similarly, notice how much is present when we unpack the sacrament of the Eucharist. When the Church gathers for Eucharist, it gives thanks to God in the great Eucharistic Prayer for the life, death, and resurrection of Jesus and asks God to pour out the gift of the Spirit. In sharing the bread and the cup in memory of Jesus the community recognizes the presence of the risen Jesus in its midst in the bread and wine, which become the sacrament of his body broken and blood poured out, the great sacrifice of Jesus, which frees us from our sins. Because we have been reconciled to God and to one another, the Eucharistic community is a sign of the unity of all humanity; whatever damages that unity is, as Paul says, a sin against the Body and Blood of the Lord (1 Cor 11:27). The Eucharist calls us to be reconciled with our brothers and sisters and to recognize our unity with all those who have been redeemed by Christ. At the same time, the Eucharistic banquet is a symbol of the great eschatological banquet in the kingdom of God.

The Jewish practice of praying three times a day, at morning, noon, and again at night, most probably lies at the root of what today is known as the Liturgy of the Hours. In the third and fourth centuries the Desert Fathers chanted the psalms alone in their cells or at their weekly gatherings and the "hours" of Morning and Evening Prayer were celebrated in major churches in both the East and the West from as early as the fourth century. Each hour of the Office would have included several psalms and canticles, some intercessions, and a final blessing and dismissal. The monastic communities built their religious life around the Divine Office, rising before dawn for Vigils and returning five more times to the Church for the other hours until the final Office of Compline brought the day to a close.

---

[7]Michael Downey, *Clothed in Christ: The Sacraments and Christian Living* (New York: Crossroad, 1987) 23.

Today monastic communities still chant the Office in choir. Diocesan priests and men and women religious from apostolic religious communities usually pray the Liturgy of the Hours privately, as do an increasing number of lay men and women. Ideally, however, the Liturgy of the Hours should be prayed in common.

Doctrine

Finally, the tradition of the Church comes to official expression in its doctrine. "Doctrine" (Latin, *doctrina*, "teaching") refers to more than mere beliefs or theological opinions. Doctrines are beliefs that have become official Church teachings, usually as a result of their being taught authoritatively by the Church's magisterium. "Dogmas" are teachings or doctrines considered to have been divinely revealed and taught with the Church's highest authority. As we saw earlier, they include the articles of the creed, the solemn teachings of the ecumenical councils, and the *ex cathedra* (infallible) teachings of the extraordinary papal magisterium.

The doctrinal tradition of the Church is a rich resource. But there is a often a fragile quality to our doctrines. Doctrinal statements represent an effort on the part of the Church to find the language and concepts to express what is intuitively grasped about its faith. Unless we prefer to remain in silence, we cannot escape the need to put our faith into words. Indeed, that is the nature of theology, finding the language to express what we believe so that we might better understand our faith and share it with others. According to St. Anselm (d. 1109), theology is faith seeking understanding (*fides quarens intellectum*).

But necessary as our theological language is, it remains imperfect. Our theological statements are always several levels of abstraction removed from the realities, human and divine, they seek to describe. As great an achievement as the doctrine of original sin is, it remains an inadequate expression of the mystery of evil, which has touched each of us in tragic and powerful ways from the first moments of our existence. Similarly, the language of grace is still far removed from the experience of life in the Spirit. Our language about God is at best analogical; it implies both affirmation and negation, since the transcendent God is beyond our ability to comprehend and to describe.

Doctrines can be true and still inadequate. As the Vatican's Congregation for the Doctrine of the Faith acknowledged in the instruction *Mysterium ecclesiae* (June 24, 1973), every "expression of revelation" (which includes the language of our creeds, our doctrines, dogmas, the teachings of the magisterium, even the Scriptures) is historically conditioned and therefore limited.[8] The CDF instruction noted that expressions of revelation

---

[8] "Declaration in Defense of the Catholic Doctrine on the Church Against Certain Errors of the Present Day," *Origins* 3 (1973) 97–100.

could be limited by the expressive power of the language used, by the limited knowledge or changeable conceptualities of the time, and by the specific concerns that motivated a particular teaching.

One of the tasks of theology is to reinterpret the language of the Church, even the language of its doctrines, so that it might more adequately reflect the faith it is intended to express. Even the dogmas of the Church are expressions of revelation, which can be subject to reinterpretation. For example, the Second Vatican Council (1962–1965) reinterpreted the dogmatic teaching of the First Vatican Council (1870) on papal infallibility, putting it in a new context by including the bishops in the exercise of the Church's charism of infallibility (LG 25).

THE CATHOLIC TRADITION

The Greek *katholikos* originally meant "whole" or "entire," as opposed to that which is partial or particular. Catholicism's understanding of Christian faith is "catholic" precisely in terms of its comprehensive approach to truth. "Catholicism is characterized, therefore, by a both/and rather than an either/or approach."[9] It is not the product of a single reformer or historical movement in post-New Testament Christian history. It does not find its identity in a single doctrine, confession, liturgical text, or theory of biblical interpretation. Thus it is able to include within itself a wide variety of theologies, spiritualities, liturgical rites, and expressions of the Christian life.

To be "catholic" is to be open to all truth, to whatever is genuinely human or naturally good. Protestant theologian Langdon Gilkey notes that there has been "a drive toward rationality" throughout Catholic history, but he also argues that Catholicism was slow to accept critical reason, particularly as it emerged in the Enlightenment and modern empiricism.[10] The official Church has at times inhibited the work of thinkers and scientists who challenged what was understood as Church doctrine; the case of Galileo remains an embarrassment to this day, and his is not the only one. As Hans Küng observes, "in the nineteenth century the writings of the modern scientists remained on the Index of books forbidden to Catholics alongside the Reformers and modern philosophy (from Descartes to Kant)."[11] But such moments or periods of repression, marked by a fear of what was new or different, are not typical. At its best, the tradition has recognized that truth is one and that science and the arts can also lead to God. From the Scholastic theologians of the medieval universities to the systematic theologians of

[9] Richard P. McBrien, *Catholicism: New Edition* (San Francisco: Harper, 1994) 16.
[10] *Catholicism Confronts Modernity* (New York: Seabury, 1975) 23.
[11] *Great Christian Thinkers* (New York: Continuum, 1994) 161.

today, Catholic thinkers have sought to integrate their faith with the knowledge that comes from philosophy and the sciences.

Faith and Reason

Catholicism sees no real discrepancy between faith and reason. Enlightened by faith, reason is able to ground the act of faith and attain a deeper understanding of faith's mysteries. The natural law tradition in Catholic philosophical ethics and moral theology reflects this confidence in the complementarity of faith and reason.

The Reformation in the sixteenth century tended to follow an either/or approach to Christian faith. Luther's fundamental insight, coming as it did out of his own struggle to make himself righteous before God through his monastic observance, was that we are justified by faith, not by works of piety or the law.[12] This great discovery from his study of Paul's Letter to the Romans (cf. 1:17) was formulated by the Reformation as the principle *sola fide,* faith alone. As a professor of Sacred Scripture, concerned that the medieval Church had substituted the philosophical theology of the Scholastics for the Gospel, Luther made Scripture the basis of all theology. From this came the cry *sola scriptura,* Scripture alone. Like Augustine, Luther was pessimistic in regard to what a damaged human nature could accomplish by itself; he stressed that access to God was through grace alone, *sola gratia.* Finally, he rejected what he understood as the medieval Church's teaching on the mediation of grace through saints, sacraments, priests, and devotions, teaching that we are saved through Christ alone, *solus Christus.*

Luther's theology emphasized what God has accomplished through the death of Christ; thus he was rightly devoted to a "theology of the cross" *(theologia crucis).* However, his rejection of any kind of philosophical theology as a species of the forbidden "theology of gloria" *(theologia gloriae),* along with his raising of the Scripture principle, was to lead to problems later in the Protestant tradition. The Reformers presupposed the clarity of Scripture when it was interpreted according to sound principles. But without a sense for the complementarity of faith and reason the Scripture principle ultimately collapsed, undermined by the rationalism of the Enlightenment in the eighteenth century and the triumph of the historical-critical method in the nineteenth. Since then, Protestant theology has not infrequently been left with the alternatives of philosophical rationalism or biblical fundamentalism.

The Catholic tradition prefers to say "both/and." Its approach is inclusive and comprehensive: not Scripture alone but Scripture and tradition, not

---

[12]H. George Anderson, T. Austin Murphy, and Joseph A. Burgess, eds., *Justification by Faith: Lutherans and Catholics in Dialogue VIII* (Minneapolis: Augsburg, 1985) offers in its supporting papers a contemporary review of the controversy over justification done by Lutheran and Catholic scholars.

grace alone but grace and nature, not faith alone but faith and works as well as faith and reason. The Council of Trent (1546–1543) was the Church's response to the challenges raised by the Reformers. Against the principle "Scripture alone," Trent taught those "truths and rules" that come from the Gospel "are contained in written books and unwritten traditions" (DS 1501). In other words, both Scripture and tradition witness to revelation. Trent's Decree on Justification sought to reply to the issues raised by Luther without canonizing one of the several schools of thought in the Church. It affirmed that faith is "the foundation and root of all justification," that the grace of justification could not be merited (DS 1532), and that justification is God's work in Christ from the beginning, since human beings without the grace of God are unable to move themselves to justice in God's sight (DS 1525). But Trent also insisted that faith cannot unite one perfectly to Christ without hope and charity, for "faith without works is dead" (DS 1531). One of its major concerns was to safeguard the role of human freedom in the process of justification. Thus it made clear that human beings are not merely passive; they must cooperate with God's grace (DS 1554).

Theological Anthropology

The Catholic tradition's theological anthropology, reflecting the incarnational perspective of patristic theology, takes both nature and grace seriously. Trent's insistence that we must freely cooperate with the grace of justification reflects this tradition. Protestant anthropology, heavily influenced by Augustine's theology and by Luther's soteriological interests, tends to be pessimistic. Protestantism sees human nature after the fall as totally corrupt. The image of God has been lost. Since the will was seen as being in a state of bondage, incapable of choosing or doing good, any human cooperation with grace was denied. Justification through faith is entirely God's work; the merits of Christ are "imputed" to us, sin is covered over, not taken away. The Calvinist doctrine of predestination is an extreme form of this pessimism. Similarly, for the Reformers the intellect was blinded by sin, unable to know anything of God apart from Scripture.

While Catholic theology has not been entirely free of a similar pessimism regarding nature after the fall, particularly when it has been influenced by Jansenism, its own theological outlook is more optimistic. The tradition continues to repeat that grace builds on nature, it speaks of fallen nature and redeemed nature. But a pure nature apart from grace does not exist; therefore nature is always graced nature, damaged but not radically corrupted by original sin.

Because the human person is created for union with God, the human faculties of intellect and will are ordered toward the divine. Augustine's famous line, "our hearts are made for you O God, and they will not rest until they rest in you,"[13] suggests that in some way the human spirit's reach exceeds its grasp or, more accurately, that it grasps more than it is able to know consciously. Thomas Aquinas saw a kinship between the human and the divine intellect; he taught that the "intellectual light" of the human intellect "is nothing more than a participating likeness of the uncreated light in which the divine ideas are contained."[14] In other words, the intellect is a dynamism grasping in some way the intelligibility of absolute being, for it participates in the uncreated divine light, in which infinite being and infinite intelligibility are identical. The transcendental Thomists developed this aspect of Aquinas' thought; for Karl Rahner, God is already apprehended in a nonexplicit way as the ground of the possibility of asking questions about being and desiring the good.[15]

According to the tradition, the existence of God can be known from the reflection of the divine in the works of creation, though we are dependent on revelation to know *who* God is. Justification is God's work, but human freedom is always involved because persons must cooperate with God's grace. Justification is not merely a juridical act; nature is genuinely transformed by grace. The body itself is seen as sacred; rather than being opposed to spirit, it is the medium through which spirit expresses itself. The tradition takes the Johannine theology of the divine indwelling seriously. God does not just "cover over" our sins but redeems us, offering us a participation in the inner life of the Trinity (John 14:16-23). The tradition of the Eastern Churches speaks of our share in the divine life as a progressive divinization *(apotheosis)*.

Emphasis on the Incarnation

The doctrine of the incarnation, with its sense for the divine immanence in creation, is at the root of Catholicism's appreciation for created reality, its reverence for tradition, its theological anthropology and sacramental imagination. Protestant theology tends to emphasize the sovereign transcendence of God, but at the cost of an adequate appreciation of the created order. While it is necessary to use the language of both transcendence and immanence in speaking of God, an incarnational perspective stresses that in Jesus God has entered definitively into space and time and human history. Because of the incarnation, created realities are graced; nature and grace can be separated conceptually, as we have seen, but creation itself is ordered by the incarnation. Christ is "the firstborn of all creation" (Col 1:15); "All things came to be through him" (John 1:3).

In the patristic tradition, which developed the notion of a *creatio ex nihilo,* God's creative work is dynamic and ongoing; it is not a one-time event in the

---

[13] *Confessions* 1.1.
[14] *Summa theologiae* I.84.5.
[15] *Foundations of Christian Faith* (New York: Seabury, 1978) 33–55.

past, for God continues to hold and sustain all things in being. The Scotist tradition, based on the teaching of the Franciscan John Duns Scotus (d. 1308), holds that the Word would have become flesh even if Adam had not sinned, in order to bring creation to its perfection. The Spirit of God is active in all creation, which reflects the glory of the Creator. St. Ignatius of Loyola saw this clearly in the sixteenth century. In the "Contemplation for Obtaining Love," a meditation at the end of his *Spiritual Exercises,* Ignatius invites the retreatant to consider how God gives us all created things, dwells in all created things, is working in them, and how all created gifts and blessings come down from above. In the twentieth century, Catholic theology has increasingly returned to this patristic notion that human nature is intrinsically ordered toward the divine and to a recognition of elements of divine truth in other world religions, without denying that the fullness of truth is revealed in Christ.

CONCLUSION

Catholicism has a deep respect for what is referred to simply as "tradition" (in contrast to "traditions"). This is more than a respect for what is ancient. Tradition represents the faith experience of the Church, received, lived, celebrated, and handed on; that tradition comes to official expression in the canonical Scriptures, in the creeds, the sacraments and liturgy of the Church, and in the teachings of the magisterium. Thus tradition bears for us and for future generations God's revelation in Christ through the community of the Church.

Revelation is God's personal self-disclosure. Mediated by persons, events, and things, revelation takes place within the story of God's people, reflected in the Hebrew Scriptures and the New Testament, and reaches its completion in the life, death, and resurrection of Jesus. The Scriptures are themselves a product of tradition; they are the normative expression of the lived faith of ancient Israel and the primitive Christian communities, and they remain today the norm for Christian faith, preaching, and doctrine. At the same time, Scripture continues to be interpreted within the living tradition of the Church with the assistance of the magisterium.

The Catholic tradition is comprehensive in its approach to truth. It embraces a rich diversity of theologies, spiritualities, and expressions of the Christian life. Believing that grace builds on nature, it seeks to integrate reason and faith. Its incarnational perspective leads it to value the human and to reverence creation, for the human was assumed by God in the incarnation, and creation reflects the presence and action of the Creator.

The tradition of the Church is not a dead letter; it is the handing on of the faith of a community that continues to live in the Spirit of Jesus. This tradition takes on concrete expression, both officially and unofficially, as we have seen. The expressions of the tradition in Scripture, creed, liturgy, and doctrine are important because they link and root the community today with God's revelation in history and especially in Jesus. Thus there is an intrinsically conservative dimension of tradition.

But precisely because tradition is a living reality, it continues to grow, to develop, to meet new challenges, even to change, as any historical study of the tradition would indicate. There are many challenges facing the Church of today and tomorrow. It must continue to carry out the renewal begun by the Second Vatican Council. Tensions remain between Rome and Catholic theologians. Lay people are asking for a greater share in the Church's liturgical life and in its processes of decision making and doctrinal formulation. Women are asking that their presence be more adequately recognized in the Church's language and ministry. Minorities are seeking greater inclusion. The Church in the United States is increasingly becoming a multicultural Church. The great wave of European immigrants has given way to a "second wave" of Hispanic and Asian peoples; it is estimated that Hispanic Catholics will constitute the majority of U.S. Catholics by early in the twenty-first century.[16] Many Catholic parishes today are already multicultural communities; they have distinctive African American, Filipino, Hispanic, and Vietnamese communities within them. The Church must find ways to bring these Catholics from the margins of the Church into its mainstream; they will certainly play a major role in shaping its future.

Tomorrow's Church should be a reconciled Church, one in which the different Churches can add their own unique traditions to the Church's catholicity. It will have to be able to hold universality and particularity—including expressions appropriate to particular cultures—together in one communion. It will have to enter into dialogue with the great world religions. It must find a new language for its faith, one that will bring the liberating message of the gospel to the millions of poor and suffering who make up the majority of the world's people. Issues such as these will continue to reshape the Catholic tradition. We will consider some of them in the final chapter.

Tradition is never static; it is at once a normative and a dynamic reality that embraces the sense of the faithful, the scholarly work of theologians, the witness of various prophetic voices, the pastoral leadership of the bishops, and the supreme teaching authority of the Church. It is difficult to say with any finality what the Church might or might not do in the future precisely because its tradition is a living one. The question is not just what has the Church done in the past but what is the Spirit calling it to today, as the Church confronts new challenges, so that it can continue to offer new life in Christ Jesus and communion in his Spirit.

[16]See Allan Figueroa Deck, *The Second Wave: Hispanic Ministry and the Evangelization of Cultures* (New York: Paulist, 1989) 12.

5. Sacraments and Christian Initiation

Each year I look forward to the celebration of the Easter Vigil. The assembly gathers in the dark of night outside the church doors to light the new fire, which in turn will be used to light the great Easter candle, the paschal candle, which symbolizes the presence of the risen Lord in the midst of his people. As the deacon begins to carry the candle toward the altar, all those present light their own candles from it, and its light begins to spread through and fill the darkened church. Three times the presider intones a joyous "Light of Christ," to which the people respond, "Thanks be to God." When the procession reaches the sanctuary, the deacon incenses the paschal candle and then sings the *Exsultet,* a great song of praise inviting all creation to witness and celebrate Christ's rising from the dead: "Rejoice, O earth, in shining splendor, radiant in the brightness of your King! Christ has conquered! Glory fills you! Darkness vanishes forever!" Then a series of readings beginning with the Genesis creation story reviews the history of salvation. As the choir begins the *Gloria,* the church's lights are all turned on while candles and flowers are brought to the altar.

After the homily those candidates who have been preparing for baptism are brought forth. We have been praying for them during Lent. Now a litany invokes the intercession of the saints of the Church. The candidates profess their faith, are baptized and confirmed, and are welcomed into the assembly. Finally, the whole assembly with its new members celebrates the joyous Easter Eucharist. This service—with its darkness and light, fire and water, bread and wine and oil, the sweet smell of incense, bees' wax, and lilies, its silence, music, and song—takes elements of our ordinary experience and makes them symbols of Christ's new life and mysterious presence among us. Our way of seeing is changed by them. To see a lily is to think of Easter. All this illustrates what has often been called the Catholic sacramental imagination.

THE SACRAMENTAL PRINCIPLE

This sacramental imagination is at the heart of the Catholic tradition. It reflects what can be called "the sacramental principle," a profound sense that the invisible divine presence is disclosed through created realities that function as symbols. As Langdon Gilkey has said, for Catholics the divine mystery is communicated "not merely through rational consciousness nor through ecstacy alone, but through a wide range of symbols related to all the facets of ordinary life."[1] Any symbol that suggests or allows us to intuit something of the mysterious depth of goodness, love, compassion, and presence that we call God can be sacramental.

Such symbols are not primarily intellectual; they speak as much to our feelings, intuitions, and affective natures as they do to our intellects. Some are natural symbols that can become religious through their evocative power. A brilliant sunset can communicate a sense of harmony and peace that suggests God's mysterious presence. Others are specifically religious. Prophetic figures like Moses, Isaiah, and Jesus himself disclose God's presence and action through their words and deeds. A story can help us recognize the deeper, religious meaning of some aspect of our ordinary lives. Religious symbols such as sacramental rituals, statues, crucifixes, icons, and churches raise our minds and hearts to God.

Catholics have a deep appreciation for such religious symbols. They adorn their homes and institutions with religious art, and their churches are rich in sacred images, statues, crucifixes, and stained glass. Holy water fonts flank the doors of the church, and a red lamp burns before the tabernacle. Catholic liturgies, with processions, lighted candles, incense, sacred music, and vested ministers, appeal unabashedly to the senses. Bishops and popes dress in attire and symbols centuries old. Religious feasts and holidays celebrate the mysteries in the life of the virgin Mary and the examples of the saints.

Catholic devotional life has frequently taken over symbols, customs, feasts, and rituals from the cultures in which the life of the Church has become inculturated.[2] Celebrating the birth of Jesus on December 25 most probably represents the Christianization of the Roman festival of the birth of the sun god (*Sol Invictus,* "the Unconquered Sun"); it became Christmas (Christ's Mass) in commemoration of the birth of the Son of God, who was confessed as Light of the World. The Celtic cross was originally an Indo-European fertility symbol.[3] Italian Catholics often process with a statue of

---

[1] *Catholicism Confronts Modernity* (New York: Seabury, 1975) 47.

[2] For a helpful explanation of popular Catholic traditions, see Greg Dues, *Catholic Customs and Traditions: A Popular Guide* (Mystic, Conn.: Twenty-Third, 1989).

[3] See Andrew Greeley, "Sacramental Experience," in Andrew M. Greeley and Mary Greeley Durkin, *How to Save the Catholic Church* (New York: Viking, 1984) 44–45.

their community's patron saint on the saint's feast day. Mexican Catholics revere the Virgin of Guadalupe; some seek to express their devotion by approaching her image on their knees. Filipino Catholics frequently act out the crucifixion as part of their observance of Lent.

The Sacraments of the Church

The concept of sacramentality is expressed in the New Testament and the early Church by the Greek word *mysterion,* "mystery," which in its secular usage meant something "secret" or "hidden." Paul used *mysterion* to describe the mysterious wisdom of God revealed through the death and resurrection of Jesus (1 Cor 2:7). In the post-New Testament Church *mysterion* was used of Christian rites, symbols, liturgical objects, blessings, and celebrations. The corresponding Latin word was *sacramentum.* It was only in the Middle Ages that the word "sacrament" was restricted to certain official acts of the Church. Peter Lombard (d. 1160) in his *Book of the Sentences* distinguished what he identified as "the seven sacraments" as *causes* of grace from other "sacramentals," which he described as *signs* of grace. The actual number of the sacraments is not particularly important. Protestant Christians have generally recognized only two sacraments, baptism and Eucharist, using a strict biblical norm of institution by the historical Jesus, which today neither Catholics nor Protestants would insist on. But sacramentality itself is extremely important.

How does the invisible God, who is spirit, become visible and tangible in our world of space and time? This is the question that the theology of sacramentality is concerned with. Contemporary sacramental theology, building largely on the work of Karl Rahner and Edward Schillebeeckx, sees Jesus in his historical ministry as the fundamental sacrament of God.[4] As the New Testament and subsequent Christian tradition would acknowledge, Jesus is God come in the flesh. In Jesus' healing of the sick and his driving out oppressive spirits from the afflicted, in his comforting of the sorrowing, his welcoming the outcast and offering forgiveness to the sinner, in the meals he shared with his disciples and the special love he showed for the poor, in his triumph over sin and death, in his resurrection to the right hand of the Father—in all of this God's infinite love and concern for human beings became visible and embodied in our human history.

The Church, "a kind of sacrament or sign of intimate union with God" (LG 1), continues to make that love and concern visible in the world. As the community of the disciples of Jesus, the Church lives from his Spirit and carries on his ministry. In proclaiming God's nearness, in healing and setting

[4]Edward Schillebeeckx, *Christ the Sacrament of the Encounter with God* (New York: Sheed & Ward, 1963); Karl Rahner, *The Church and the Sacraments* (New York: Herder & Herder, 1963).

free, in comforting, in gathering and reconciling, in anointing and blessing and sharing the bread and wine of everlasting life–in all of this the ministry of Jesus continues to be made manifest in space and time. Just as Jesus is the sacrament of God, the Church is the sacrament of Jesus. The Church makes visible God's love revealed in Jesus in a multitude of sacramental moments and particularly in those official signs of grace that it identifies as the seven sacraments.

How do sacraments "work"? Sacraments convey grace by symbolizing, by combining narrative and ritual action–washing with water, sharing bread and wine, anointing with oil, laying on hands, blessing, proclaiming forgiveness. As symbols, sacraments are polyvalent; they can convey several meanings. Sean McDonagh observes that sacraments "draw on elements of the natural world–water, food, oil, fire, light, darkness and wind"; they should "be able to draw us out of our false cocoon and reconnect us with God and creation."[5] They should be honest symbols. The waters of baptism should be a real washing with living water, not just a few symbolic drops. The bread of the Eucharist should look like real bread. The Eucharist itself is a symbol of unity, but for many women today it is experienced as a symbol of exclusion. As signs, sacraments lose much of their power if they are performed carelessly, without reverence and an expectant faith. As acts of the Church, sacraments express the Church's own nature as the body of Christ present in the world, sharing new life in the Spirit of Jesus (baptism), proclaiming the forgiveness of sins in his name (reconciliation), ministering to the sick (sacrament of the sick), celebrating human spousal love (marriage), appointing to leadership in the ecclesial community (orders), and recognizing his presence to his own in the Eucharistic meal (Eucharist).

Sacramentals

In addition to the seven sacraments there are many religious symbols, objects, rituals, and prayers that give expression to the Christian mysteries. Called "sacramentals," they are essentially signs of the sacred (SC 60). Many are ritual actions, the performance of which gives our faith bodily expression. There is also a social dimension to these sacramental actions; because they are done publicly, they witness to and remind others of God's presence in the midst of the human. Catholicism has a wealth of such sacramental ritual actions.

The sign of the cross, crossing oneself "in the name of the Father, and of the Son, and of the Holy Spirit," is a profession of our Trinitarian faith. It can be used to mark ritually the beginning and ending of a period of prayer. Making the sign of the cross with holy water recalls the grace of Christian

---

[5] *Passion for the Earth* (Maryknoll, N.Y.: Orbis, 1994) 148.

baptism; parents trace the sign of the cross on the foreheads of their infant children at their baptism. Receiving ashes on one's forehead on Ash Wednesday symbolizes the beginning of the season of Lent. Symbolizing both the Old Testament ashes of repentance (Jonah 3:6; Dan 9:3) and the dust to which we will one day return, they remind us of our mortality and invite us to open ourselves anew to the grace of the gospel. Similarly, processing with blessed palms on Palm Sunday invites us to a more personal participation in the mysteries of Holy Week. Many Catholics preserve their palms until the following year, tucking them under a crucifix or behind a religious picture as a reminder of their accompanying Jesus through the mysteries of his passion. Other sacramental actions include genuflecting before the Blessed Sacrament as a sign of reverence, bowing the head at the mention of the holy name of Jesus, sharing the sign of peace with another during the liturgy, giving a blessing, laying on hands in a prayer for healing, and lighting a candle to symbolize the holiness of the place where one prays. In Latin cultures many Catholics complete the sign of the cross by making and kissing a small cross with their thumb and forefinger.

The crucifix, the cross with the body, or "corpus," of Jesus upon it, is dear to Catholics as a sign of Christ's love and redemptive sacrifice. Religious statues remind us of the Church triumphant, the communion of saints, who are for us both examples and intercessors. It is difficult to imagine a Catholic church or chapel without a statue or image of Mary. Icons, so rich in the heritage of the Eastern Church, are stylized images of Christ, the virgin, and the saints, which invite us to contemplate the mysteries they represent.[6] Liturgical seasons such as Advent, Christmas, Lent, and Easter celebrate the mysteries of salvation, making time itself sacred. The paschal candle, lighted at the beginning of the Easter Vigil, is a powerful symbol of Christ and the light he brings to our lives. Wedding rings remind spouses of their promise of mutual love and fidelity. Liturgical vestments, religious habits, medals, crosses, candles, holy water—all are signs of the sacred present in our time and space and personal histories. They point to and allow us to participate in the invisible world of the spirit.

Sacramentals can be abused. They can become objects of superstition, like making the sign of the cross before shooting a free throw. They are not like talismans or amulets, magical charms that protect their possessors. Sacramentals invite our participation in the Christian mysteries; when they engage our faith, they can help us to see beyond the surface of things and raise our minds and hearts to God.

---

[6]For an introduction to this tradition see Henri J. M. Nouwen, *Behold the Beauty of the Lord: Praying with Icons* (Notre Dame: Ave Maria, 1987).

SACRAMENTS OF INITIATION

The sacraments of initiation—baptism, confirmation, and Eucharist—symbolize and celebrate the progressive incorporation of a person into Christ and his Church. In the early Church baptism and confirmation were separate moments in a single rite of Christian initiation, which was completed when the new Christians—baptized, anointed with oil, and dressed in white robes—were brought into the assembly, usually at the liturgy of the Easter Vigil on Holy Saturday, to share in the Eucharist with the community for the first time. The three sacraments of initiation celebrate the deepest realities in the life of a Christian: incorporation into Christ, life in the Spirit, communion in his body, the Church.

Baptism

The word "baptism" comes from the Greek *baptizo,* used of ceremonial washings or ablutions. In contemporary Christianity baptism has been too often understood as a sacrament for infants that washes them clean of the stain of original sin. But that is to reduce the rich symbolism of the sacrament to one of its dimensions. Baptism is primarily a sacrament for adults; it is a personal response of faith to the word that has been preached (Acts 8:26-40). Those Churches that continue to restrict baptism to adults ("believer's baptism") are a reminder to other Churches of this fact.

By baptism we are incorporated into Christ. Paul says that we are baptized into Christ's death (Rom 6:3), mystically incorporated into his passion so that we too might rise with him. "Baptized into Christ's death" means the forgiveness of sin; those baptized have been washed, sanctified, and justified in the name of Jesus and in the Spirit (1 Cor 6:11).

At the same time, to be incorporated into Christ is to be incorporated into Christ's body, the Church (1 Cor 12:13) and to receive new life in the Spirit (John 3:5). In a very early text with important ecclesiological implications, Paul states that by baptism we are "clothed" with Christ (symbolized in the early Church by dressing those baptized in white robes) to the extent that we become part of a new people that transcends differences of race, social status, and sex: "There is neither Jew nor Greek, there is neither slave nor free person, there is not male and female; for you are all one in Christ Jesus" (Gal 3:28).

How can we make greater sense of the meaning of baptism in terms of our experience? How does baptism "work" its transformation? Baptism unites us with Christ precisely because it incorporates us into the Church. Though the Spirit is not limited by the structures of the Church, it is the Church that mediates the risen Jesus to us. It is only through the Church—the historic community of believers that continues to proclaim his gospel, to celebrate in word and ritual the mysteries of his life, and to carry on his ministry of compassionate service—that we are able to come to know who Jesus is and to recognize his presence. Apart from the believing community the Scriptures remain at best pious stories.

Baptism makes possible a new life, a life "in the Spirit," or a life "of grace," precisely by bringing a person into a new community whose members try to live out in their own lives the paschal mystery of Jesus' death and resurrection. They have died to sin and seek to imitate the compassionate and self-sacrificing love of Jesus in the way they live. This is not to say that they never fall short or that the ideal of life in Christ Jesus does not sometimes grow dim. But their commitment to the Church is symbolic of their desire to live in the Spirit of Jesus. Theologically that Spirit is the divine Spirit poured out on the disciples of Jesus through his death and resurrection, the Spirit of truth, which testifies to Jesus in our hearts (John 15:26). Experientially, we come to recognize the Spirit's presence through its effects or "fruits" in the lives of the community members; Paul identifies the fruits of the Spirit as "love, joy, peace, patience, kindness, generosity, faithfulness, gentleness, self-control" (Gal 5:22-23).

We don't always grasp the importance of living in a community of faith because, in spite of so much talk today about "relationships," we don't take the network of relationships that shapes our lives seriously enough. Yet anyone who has ever really been in love knows from experience how creative and life-giving a relationship can be. Good relationships empower us. When we are loved, the whole world seems different; we discover a new freedom to be ourselves as well as a sense of well-being and security that enables us to try to accomplish things we would not otherwise have thought possible. Similarly, negative relationships can turn people in on themselves, making them angry and bitter. Often they do lifelong damage.

We know how important it is for a child to grow up in a home in which he or she is loved and cherished and how different is the development of a child whose environment is an abusive one. Such a child, lacking the love, security, and connection with others that it needs, is as fragile as a flower lacking good soil and water. He or she will probably spend a lifetime trying to compensate, searching desperately for affection and approval, often in inappropriate ways. Often the deprivation or injury suffered bursts forth years later in hostility or rage, and the abused child often becomes an abusing adult.

Adults need a supportive community as well, if only to help them realize their own ideals. We know also how difficult it is to live a simple lifestyle in a consumer culture driven by needs created by advertising, to value chastity in a society that trivializes it, to maintain integrity in a business environment where "everyone is doing it."

How much more empowering it is to live with men and women who are trying to live as disciples of Jesus, to model their lives on the gospel! It is to see new possibilities, to find the support for new efforts, to be able to live a different kind of life. Theologically, this community called Church shares with us the Spirit from which it lives, the Spirit of Jesus or "grace," which overcomes the forces of negativity and self-interest we call original sin, enabling us to live a new life, to rise again when we fall, to receive and offer to one another forgiveness. This life in the Spirit means that in a real sense we share in the life of the Trinity or, conversely, that God dwells within us sharing life and love through the Spirit.

If the grace of baptism is to be effective in the life of a person through his or her incorporation into the community of the Church, it becomes more apparent why it does not make much sense to celebrate the sacrament for an infant whose parents are not practicing and do not intend to practice their faith. In such cases of indiscriminate baptism, no matter how good the parents might be, there is no community of faith into which the child is received, no "domestic Church" to express and nurture the faith of the child as it grows. In a moment of candor the French philosopher Jean-Paul Sartre, perhaps the archetypal contemporary atheist, admitted that he was "led to disbelief not by the conflict of dogmas, but by [his] grandparents' indifference."[7]

Sacraments are not magical rites; they do not work "automatically," independent of our cooperation. As an old theological adage states, grace builds on nature. Unfortunately, indiscriminate baptism is widely practiced today, with the result that baptism becomes a cultural rite of passage rather than a sacramental celebration of coming to new life in Christ.

Confirmation

It has been sometimes said that confirmation is a sacrament in search of a theology. Originally the sign of confirmation, an anointing with oil accompanied by a laying on of hands, was part of the celebration of baptism. It still is in the Eastern Church, where the proper order of Christian initiation—baptism, confirmation, Eucharist—is preserved. Even infants are baptized, anointed with oil—which the Orthodox call "chrismation"—and given the Eucharist, usually by means of a spoon dipped in the consecrated wine. The ordinary minister of confirmation in the East is still the presbyter.

But in the Western Church the postbaptismal anointing was usually reserved to the bishop. As the Church grew and spread into rural areas and the number of candidates for baptism increased, the bishop could not always be present at baptisms. Gradually confirmation emerged as a separate rite. Though the bishop remains the original or ordinary minister of confirmation, priests are authorized to administer it when baptizing or receiving adults into the Church.

[7] *The Words* (New York: Fawcett, 1964) 63.

What is the meaning of confirmation? It should not be understood primarily as a bestowal of the Spirit, since the Spirit is given with baptism and indeed is already active in drawing a person to Christ before baptism. Nor should confirmation be conceived as a sacrament of Christian adulthood, a kind of Christian bar mitzvah, even though Thomas Aquinas gave support to this view by treating confirmation as a sacrament of spiritual maturity, preparing one for battle against the enemies of the faith. The "slight blow on the check" of the pre-Vatican II rite reflects this theology. Some theologians today see confirmation as a sacrament that expresses openness and submission to the Spirit. Certainly confirmation is a celebration of life in the Spirit of Jesus, and it remains true that for many Western Christians who were baptized as infants, confirmation is experienced as the sacramental moment in which the commitment made on their behalf long ago by their parents is affirmed personally as their own.

The 1983 Code of Canon Law states that confirmation should be conferred "about the age of discretion" (can. 891), though the code leaves considerable latitude to the bishops as far as choosing an earlier or a later time. At the present time in the United States the sacrament is generally conferred on young people in their early teens. It is not unusual today for a young adult, sensing a lack of readiness to make the commitment implied by the sacrament, to decide that he or she does not want to be confirmed. Such a decision makes sense. If one is not confirmed in infancy, the sacrament should be celebrated at an age when one knows what it means for one's life and for the life of the Church. I have often been impressed in hearing college students speak of their decision to be confirmed as a real decision made in their spiritual lives.

♣ *Eucharist* ♣

The Eucharist is "the central act of the Church's worship" and the celebration of its communion in the risen Jesus from which it lives.[8] In the Christian tradition it has been known by various names: the Holy Sacrifice of the Mass, the Lord's Supper, Holy Communion, the Divine Liturgy. According to the Second Vatican Council, the Eucharistic sacrifice "is the fount and apex of the whole Christian life (LG 11).

The origins of the Eucharist are complex. In the Hebrew Scriptures the image of the eschatological banquet appears as a sign of communion with God in the messianic age of salvation (Isa 25:6). Jesus uses this image in his parables about the kingdom of heaven (Matt 8:11; Luke 14:15-24). Certainly the table fellowship tradition in the ministry of Jesus, the meals he shared

---

[8]See the consensus statement on the Eucharist prepared by Catholic, Orthodox, and Protestant scholars in *Baptism, Eucharist and Ministry* (Geneva: WCC, 1982) 10.

with his disciples and with others, including the "tax collectors and sinners," is a part of the history of the Eucharist, as is the final meal that Jesus shared with his disciples on the night before he died. After his death his disciples continued to gather to break bread and share the cup in his memory, and in this context they came to recognize him as present with them in a new way. This is the import of the story of the two disciples on the road to Emmaus who come to recognize the risen Jesus "in the breaking of the bread" (Luke 24:35; cf. Acts 10:41; John 21:12). There is a continuity in being with Jesus at table, during his ministry, at the Last Supper, in the post-Easter meals of the disciples, and in the Church's Eucharist.

The structure of the Eucharistic liturgy consists of the Liturgy of the Word and the Liturgy of the Eucharist. The Liturgy of the Word derives from the Jewish synagogue service, which consisted of an opening prayer, two Scripture readings (one from the Law, another from the Prophets), followed by a homily or reflection and some prayers (cf. Luke 4:16-21). The Liturgy of the Eucharist, or Lord's Supper, was celebrated in the context of a communal meal in the earliest communities, though the separation of the two was already taking place by Paul's time. Paul rebuked the Corinthians for their disorderly Eucharistic assemblies, telling the members of the community to eat at home (1 Cor 11:22, 34).

✷   Like a diamond, the Eucharist is a multifaceted reality; it refracts the mystery of God's salvation in Jesus in a multitude of ways. The Eucharist is a sacramental meal, a communion in the Body and Blood of Christ, a memorial of his death and resurrection, a prayer of thanksgiving, a sacrifice, and a sign of the kingdom. ✷

Sacramental Meal

The Eucharist is first of all a sacramental meal. The sign or symbol of the Eucharist is the sacramental action of sharing in the bread broken and the cup blessed in memory of Jesus. Paul grounds the oneness of the community as the one body of Christ in its sharing or participation in the Eucharistic Body and Blood of Christ: "The cup of blessing that we bless, is it not a participation [*koinonia*/communion] in the blood of Christ? The bread that we break, is it not a participation in the body of Christ? Because the loaf of bread is one, we, though many, are one body, for we all partake of the one loaf" (1 Cor 10:16-17). It is in sharing the bread and wine of the Eucharist that the Church becomes more fully what it is, the body of Christ in the world.

Sign of the Kingdom

Reconciled to God and to one another in Christ Jesus, made one in his body, Christians become a sign that both anticipates and shows the union of all humankind. In this way the Eucharist is a sign of the kingdom. A beautiful prayer from the *Didache,* or "Teaching of the Twelve Apostles," a collection of instructions on morality and Church order written around A.D. 100, expresses this poetically: "As this broken bread was scattered upon the mountain tops and after being harvested was made one, so let Thy Church be gathered together from the ends of the earth into Thy kingdom" (9.4).

Thus the Eucharist is the most basic sacrament of reconciliation and calls each of us to be a sign of reconciliation in a divided world. Divisions within the Church, whether based on economic status, race, sex, or social position, vitiate the sacramental reality of the Eucharistic assembly; as Paul tells the Corinthians, to tolerate or introduce divisions within the community is to sin against the Body and Blood of the Lord (1 Cor 11:17-30).

As the memorial *(anamnesis)* of the sacrificial death and resurrection of Jesus, the Eucharist is a pledge of our own resurrection. Many Catholics experience this in the celebration of the Eucharist, particularly in the celebration of the Mass of Christian Burial as part of the funeral liturgy. Here especially our communion with the risen Jesus is a powerful symbol of our own hope of everlasting life.

Prayer of Thanksgiving

The Eucharist is also the Church's great prayer of thanksgiving *(eucharistia* in Greek means "thanksgiving"). The presider invites the assembly to give thanks with him in the opening dialogue of the preface and then prays on their behalf, thanking God for the great works of creation and redemption, remembering especially Jesus' offering his life for our salvation on the night before he died, his death and resurrection, and the gift of the Spirit. He invokes the Spirit on both the Eucharistic gifts of bread and wine and on the people (the *epiclesis*) and prays the concluding doxology, to which the assembly responds "Amen," making the prayer their own.

Memorial of Christ's Sacrifice

Catholics have traditionally referred to the Eucharist as "the Holy Sacrifice of the Mass." The sacrificial dimension of the Eucharist was recognized as early as the beginning of the second century, for the *Didache* speaks of the Eucharist as a sacrifice (14.1-3). Through narrative and ritual the Eucharistic Prayer makes present, or remembers, the sacrifice of Christ on the cross, so that in a very real sense the Church's Eucharistic worship makes present to God Christ's offering of himself. The concept of *anamnesis,* or memorial, is crucial here. In more traditional language Catholics have described the Eucharist as a repetition of the sacrifice of the cross "in an unbloody manner." Contemporary theology sometimes speaks of the Eucharist as the sacrament of the sacrifice of Christ, making Christ's sacrifice sacramentally—and therefore really—present in the Church's worship.

Real Presence

What Catholics refer to as the "real presence" of Christ in the bread and wine of the Eucharist has been recognized since the time of the New Testament (cf. John 6:52-60). But how to express this doctrine in theological language is a difficult question. From the second century Christian theology has spoken of a "change" of the bread and wine into the Body and Blood of Jesus. The language of "transubstantiation" was used in the Middle Ages to affirm that while the appearances of the bread and wine (the "species") remain the same, the substance of both really change. Through the action of the Holy Spirit in the liturgy, the bread and wine become the sacramental signs of Christ's presence; they are no longer bread and wine but the Body and Blood of Christ. But even this apparently very literal language still recognized that the presence of the risen Jesus was not physical; it was sacramental. That is to say, the risen Jesus is present in the sacramental action, not in his discrete flesh and blood understood in a physical sense but personally, in his glorified humanity.

If traditional Catholic language has sometimes spoken of the Eucharistic presence of Christ in an overly literal way, Catholics have long been taught that to receive "under one species" is to receive not just the Body or just the Blood of Christ but both; it is to encounter and receive the risen Jesus. As Nathan Mitchell has said so well: "The body of Christ offered to Christians in consecrated bread and wine is not some*thing* but some*one*. In the Eucharist Christ is present not as an 'object' to be admired but as a person (a 'subject') to be encountered."[9]

Eucharistic Devotion

From the early centuries the consecrated Eucharistic bread was reserved in the sacristy for the Communion of the sick, but it was not prominently displayed in the church itself until the Middle Ages. Beginning in the eleventh century worship of the Eucharistic presence of Christ became popular; Benediction of the Blessed Sacrament is an expression of this. The Council of Trent in the sixteenth century mandated that a tabernacle be mounted on the principal altar of every church, though after the liturgical renewal of the Second Vatican Council it has become more customary to reserve the Eucharist for private prayer in a special chapel. Other expressions of Catholic

---

[9] "Who Is at the Table: Reclaiming the Real Presence," *Commonweal* 122 (January 27, 1995) 12.

Eucharistic devotion include the daily celebration of the Eucharist, holy hours, forty hours devotions, Corpus Christi processions, and visits to the Blessed Sacrament.

The council and the liturgical renewal that preceded it have stressed the centrality of the Eucharistic liturgy in the Church's life and the importance of participating in it fully by receiving Holy Communion. This has effected a shift from devotion to the Blessed Sacrament apart from the Mass to full participation in the liturgy. Similarly, postconciliar teaching has insisted that worship of the Eucharist outside of Mass should be always related to the centrality of the celebration of the Mass itself. This has led in many places to a decreased emphasis on Benediction. At the same time, it is interesting to note that a number of contemporary Christian communities such as l'Arche, the Missionaries of Charity, and the Little Brothers and Little Sisters of Jesus make contemplative prayer before the Blessed Sacrament a regular part of their spirituality.[10] And visits to the Blessed Sacrament remain an important expression of Catholic Eucharistic devotion.

Intercommunion

Particularly painful for many Christians today is the inability to share together in the Eucharist because of the divisions in the Church. The question of Eucharistic hospitality, or intercommunion, is itself divisive. For many Protestants intercommunion is a sign of a growing unity and a means to its fulfillment. They emphasize that it is the Lord who invites baptized believers to the one table and that no Church has the right to restrict it.

Rome and the Orthodox take a different view, holding that Eucharistic communion is the sign of an already existing unity in faith, apostolic tradition, and ecclesial life. According to the new Roman Catholic *Ecumenical Directory* (1993), intercommunion is allowed only under certain limited conditions. With regard to the Eastern Churches, Eucharistic sharing is possible in principle, though it cautions Catholics that these Churches often have more restrictive disciplines that should be respected. For reasons of necessity or genuine spiritual advantage, Catholics may approach a minister of an Eastern Church for the sacraments of Eucharist, reconciliation, and the anointing of the sick, and Catholic ministers may give these sacraments to members of an Eastern Church who request them and are properly disposed, avoiding any suggestion of proselytism.

The rules for admitting those from other Churches and ecclesial communities are much more restrictive. A Catholic minister may administer these sacraments to a non-Catholic when there is danger of death or some pressing

---

[10]Cf. Thomas P. Rausch, *Radical Christian Communities* (Collegeville: The Liturgical Press, 1990).

need under the following conditions: that the person is unable to have re-course for the sacrament to a minister of his or her own Church or ecclesial community and that he or she asks for the sacrament and manifests a Catholic faith and proper disposition in regard to it. A Catholic who finds him- or herself in a similar situation may request the sacraments only from a minis-ter "in whose church these sacraments are valid or from one who is known to be validly ordained according to the Catholic teaching on ordination" (no. 132).

The time for restoring full Eucharistic communion does not yet seem to be here. While great progress has been made on a theological level in the ec-umenical dialogues, the resulting agreed-upon statements have not yet been received by their sponsoring Churches. Also, if the Churches are to share a common mission, they must find a way to cooperate effectively in the areas of teaching authority and social action, something they have not yet been able to do.

At the same time, it could be argued that the Catholic Church needs to find a way to be a little more flexible. As Adrian Hastings has written, the "sharing of communion is quite inappropriate where there is no common un-derstanding of the sacrament and no real ongoing sharing of church life. But both these are now increasingly a reality crossing formal Church/denomina-tional borders."[11] The liturgical movement has led to a renewed appreciation of the Eucharist in many Churches, and few Catholics today would raise the traditional questions about the "validity" of Eucharistic celebrations in other Churches when those celebrations reflect their own Eucharistic faith. The pre-sent discipline of the Catholic Church does not seem to be consistent with its own theology. Vatican II's Decree on Ecumenism teaches that "common wor-ship . . . may not be regarded as a means to be used indiscriminately for the restoration of unity among Christians. . . . Yet the gaining of a needed grace sometimes commends it" (UR 8). Some Catholic ecumenists today argue that a case could be made for *discriminate* intercommunion, for example, in an in-terchurch (mixed) marriage or in a stable ecumenical community in which a common Eucharistic faith is shared. Eucharistic hospitality in situations such as these could be a means for unity and a sign of hope for the future.

THE RITE OF CHRISTIAN INITIATION

How does one become a member of the Church? In the early Church an adult was sacramentally incorporated into the Church only after completing a process of preparation and instruction known as the "catechumenate" (from the Greek *catechesis,* "instruction"), which might last as long as three years.

---

[11]"How To Be Ecumenical in 1995," *Priests & People* 9 (January 1995) 6.

Basic to the process was the free, personal decision to ask for baptism. It presupposed a conversion to Christ, which was tested out by the individual and discerned by the community during the process of the catechumenate.

Each candidate, or "catechumen," had a sponsor, a member of the community who helped guide the candidate through prayer, a personal sharing of faith, and instruction. Early in the process the candidates were introduced to the bishop and community, and their names were entered into the baptismal register. On Sundays they would be present for the liturgical assembly, particularly for the instruction, which took place during the homily, though they would be formally dismissed by the deacon before the Liturgy of the Eucharist. The final weeks prior to Easter were given over to an intensive preparation for the candidates' sacramental initiation; they were examined through a series of interrogations, or "scrutinies," and they prepared themselves with prayer and fasting. This final preparation for the great feast of Easter became in time the liturgical season of Lent. Finally, when the community gathered to celebrate the Easter Vigil, after making their renunciation of Satan the candidates would be baptized, anointed with oil, dressed in white robes, and led into the assembly to share for the first time in the Eucharist.

The ancient rite of Christian initiation was a real spiritual journey, marked by clear symbolic stages such as the entering of the candidates' names into the baptismal registry, exorcisms, examinations by the bishop, and finally, the sacramental incorporation of the candidates into the Church. Unfortunately, the rite began to diminish in importance after Constantine's Edict of Milan in the fourth century put an end to the persecution of Christians in the West and granted the Church toleration. After this milestone in the Church's life the number of those seeking baptism began to increase enormously, and the baptism of infants became increasingly the norm. In time the rich process of the catechumenate was reduced to one of its elements, that of instruction. Prior to the Second Vatican Council, someone desiring to join the Church might be instructed privately by a priest or join an "inquiry" class. The basic text was usually the catechism. But the emphasis on personal prayer, spiritual growth, communal discernment, and ritual celebration of the process was largely missing.

Perhaps one of the most significant liturgical reforms of Vatican II was the restoration in 1972 of the catechumenate in what is known as the Rite of Christian Initiation of Adults, usually referred to simply as the RCIA. The new rite means that Christian initiation is now understood as a process of five stages, which generally extend over the period of a year or more.

Precatechumenate

The first stage is that period in which an individual begins to explore the possibility of joining the Church. It is the time in which a genuine conversion begins to take shape in a person's life. It also involves some kind of dialogue with the Church, often through friends whose own faith has awakened the person's interest in the Christian life. These friends can introduce him or her to the Church's life and teaching.

Catechumenate

The second stage is the period of formal instruction or catechesis, prayer, and discernment. The catechumenate begins with a ritual of entrance celebrated with the liturgical assembly, often on the first Sunday of Advent. Each candidate is presented to the community by his or her sponsor, and the community pledges to help the candidates in their desire to come to know Jesus. The Scriptures proclaimed in the liturgy should play an important part during the catechumenate process; so does the sponsor, who becomes a spiritual friend and shares the candidate's journey.

Period of Purification and Enlightenment

The last part of the catechumenate itself begins with the Rite of Election, usually celebrated on the first Sunday of Lent. The candidates are called forward after the homily, questioned as to their intentions, and officially admitted to the ranks of the "elect." The candidates intensify their preparation during this period. According to the ancient tradition of the Church, the gospel readings for the third, fourth, and fifth Sundays of Lent are, respectively, the story of the Samaritan woman (John 4), the cure of the man born blind (John 9), and the raising of Lazarus (John 11), with the themes of water, light, and life.

Sacramental Initiation

The period of purification and enlightenment culminates with the sacraments of initiation themselves, baptism, confirmation, and Eucharist, usually celebrated as part of the Easter Vigil.

Postbaptismal Catechesis (Mystagogy)

The final stage of Christian initiation is intended to continue the incorporation of those newly baptized into the life of the Church. Now that they have been sacramentally initiated into the Christian mysteries, they need to deepen their understanding of these mysteries for their own lives. The postbaptismal catechesis can take place during the Easter season or, as in the United States, be extended over the following year.

The RCIA seeks to be a more holistic way of initiating one into the Church; it is not just catechetical instruction but must involve prayer, shared reflection, and discernment. It is not intended to be a rigid process but should be tailored to the needs of the individual candidates. Today a typical RCIA group might include some who have never been baptized as well as some baptized Christians who have asked to become members of the Catholic Church. Rather than speaking of the latter as "converts," it makes more sense to see them as asking to come into full communion with the Catholic Church, since they are already in partial communion with it through baptism (cf. UR 3). Today it is also frequently the case that there will be some who have been baptized Catholics as infants but who have never made their First Communion, usually because their parents have not been practicing the faith. Thus their Christian initiation was never completed.

The celebration of the RCIA should distinguish between those seeking baptism and those who have already been baptized. Those asking for baptism will receive all three sacraments of initiation. Those asking to be received into full communion with the Catholic Church make a profession of faith, since baptism in other Churches is recognized as valid and is not to be repeated (unless there is reason to question the form or intention of the original baptism). If they are from the ecclesial communities of the sixteenth-century Reformation they are to be confirmed, since agreement has not yet been reached with those communities over the significance and sacramental nature of confirmation. Those whose Christian initiation was interrupted receive confirmation with the other candidates, and they share in the Eucharist for the first time. Though the bishop is the ordinary minister of confirmation, the pastor or priest who presides at the vigil Mass confers confirmation as part of the initiatory process.

CONCLUSION

Christianity is not an other-worldly religion. It does not disdain the material world but sees in it traces of the divine. God is encountered in the depths of our humanity, in our personal relationships and families, in moments of tenderness and our longing for communion, in facing the mystery of evil and of suffering, in the experience of the joy of love and friendship, the diminishments of age, the inevitability of death. It is precisely in and through these deeply human realities that our Christian life must be lived out.

Catholics perceive this world in a way that is profoundly affected by their sacramental imagination. The poet Gerard Manley Hopkins expressed this when he wrote, "The world is charged with the grandeur of God."[12] The sacramental imagination recognizes God's mysterious presence reflected in

---

[12]"God's Grandeur," *Poems of Gerard Manley Hopkins,* 4th ed., ed. W. H. Gardner and N. H. MacKenzie (London/New York: Oxford Univ. Press, 1967).

the wonders of nature and in religious rituals and art that give expression to the faith. It sees in the sacraments God's grace and presence becoming visible in the Christian community as it shares new life in the Spirit of Jesus, proclaims the forgiveness of sins, prays for the sick, celebrates faithful love in marriage and the presence of the risen Jesus in the Eucharist.

Those who ask for baptism and admission to the Church are often drawn to it because they have sensed that divine presence in the life of the community and the faith of its members. The rite of Christian initiation means a sharing in that faith through prayer and discernment, through reflecting on the Scriptures proclaimed and heard in the assembly, through sharing one's personal journey of faith with others and finally celebrating it in baptism, confirmation, and Eucharist.

The Eucharist stands at the very center of the Catholic understanding of Church. Most Catholics sense this, even if they cannot always explain why this is so or what exactly it means. They have been deeply shaped by the experience of communion with the risen Jesus and with one another in the breaking of the bread and the sharing of the cup in memory of his death and resurrection. As the locus of these sacramental actions, the Church itself is a sacramental expression of the presence of Christ in the midst of the people gathered in his name.

6. Christian Life and Discipleship

If our own century, now drawing toward a close, has witnessed human cruelty and suffering on a scale seldom before imagined, it has also seen some extraordinary examples of Christian discipleship. In the early 1930s Dorothy Day, a pacifist and convert to the Church, founded the Catholic Worker movement, the first expression of American Catholic social radicalism. Most of her life was spent feeding the hungry on New York's Lower East Side, speaking or demonstrating for peace, and supporting the growing network of Catholic Worker houses.

During the Second World War Franz Jäggerstätter, an Austrian farmer, was executed for his refusal to serve in the German army; he considered Hitler's war an immoral one. Dietrich Bonhoeffer, a German Lutheran pastor, also opposed the war. He thought about taking refuge in the United States but returned to Germany in 1939 after a brief stay in New York, explaining to his friend and sponsor Reinhold Niebuhr, "I will have no right to participate in the reconstruction of Christian life in Germany after the war if I do not share the trials of this time with my people."[1] Implicated in the July 20, 1944, attempt on Hitler's life, Bonhoeffer was executed by the Nazis on April 9, 1945, just a month before the war ended. A book he had published in 1937 is entitled *The Cost of Discipleship*.

Oscar Romero, a zealous if somewhat rigid priest of El Salvador, was reluctant to publicly challenge the government in his first years as a bishop. But his pastoral responsibilities brought him increasingly into contact with the country's people. After his appointment as archbishop of San Salvador in 1977, he became so outspoken an advocate of the poor that he was targeted for death by a right-wing political party and was assassinated in 1980 while saying Mass. Later that year four American women, Maryknoll sisters Maura Clark and Ita Ford, Ursuline sister Dorothy Kazel, and Jean Donovan,

[1]Eberhard Bethge, *Dietrich Bonhoeffer* (London: Collins, 1970) 558.

a lay volunteer, were murdered in that same country by government soldiers. After their deaths the U.S. ambassador to the United Nations, a Catholic herself, sought to play down their murder by saying, "The nuns were not just nuns, they were political activists."[2] In fact, the women had been working for the poor.

When we hear the extraordinary stories of men and women like these, we are moved by their courage and their faith. But they were people like ourselves, seeking to live out the discipleship to which each of us is called. In this chapter we will first consider that basic call to discipleship addressed to all Christians and then look at some of the different expressions of discipleship in the Christian life.

THE CALL TO DISCIPLESHIP

Jesus did not come to found a new religion. In his few brief years of public ministry he preached about the nearness of God's kingdom and called all who would listen to discipleship with him in its service.

Discipleship in the New Testament

The word "disciple" *(mathetes)* appears more than 250 times in the New Testament, mostly in the Gospels and Acts. The verb "to follow" *(akolouthe)* appears 70 times. Discipleship means following Jesus.

The concept of discipleship was not a new one; both the Pharisees and John the Baptist had disciples. But being a disciple of Jesus was unique in a number of ways. First, unlike the case of discipleship in Rabbinic Judaism,
• the disciples of Jesus did not choose the master; rather, the master chose and called the disciples. The initiative always comes from Jesus (Mark 1:17; 2:14).

• Second, there is an inclusive element to Jesus' call. He did not restrict it to the ritually pure and the religiously obedient; among those invited to follow him were the "tax collectors and sinners." He was often criticized for associating with them (Mark 2:16). Women also accompanied him as disciples (Luke 8:2).

• Third, Jesus' call to discipleship demands a radical change of heart *(metanoia)*, a religious conversion often symbolized by leaving behind one's possessions. The story of the rich young man in the Synoptic Gospels illustrates this theme. To this man, who had kept all the commandments since his youth, Jesus said: "You are lacking in one thing. Go, sell what you have, and give to the poor and you will have treasure in heaven; then come, fol-

---

[2]Jean Kirkpatrick, cited by Arthur Jones, "El Salvador Revisited: Special Supplement," *National Catholic Reporter* 30 (September 23, 1994) 23.

low me" (Mark 10:21). Thus discipleship means a clean break with one's past. In the Gospels those who followed Jesus "left everything" (Luke 5:11). They left behind jobs (Mark 2:14), parents, family, children (Luke 14:26). For some, discipleship also meant celibacy embraced for the sake of the kingdom (Matt 19:11-12).

• Fourth, being a disciple of Jesus means sharing in his ministry. Unlike the disciples of the rabbis who had to memorize their masters' teachings, the disciples of Jesus were called to minister as Jesus did. Jesus sent them out to teach and act in his name, to heal the sick, cast out demons, and proclaim that the kingdom of God was at hand (Mark 6:7-13; Luke 10:2-12). The disciples shared not just his ministry but his poverty and itinerant life as well (Matt 8:20). Their attitude toward authority was to be respectful but not uncritical (Mark 12:17; Matt 23:2-3). He warned them that they would be rejected by others, persecuted by religious and civil authorities, even alienated from their own families (Matt 10).

• Finally, being a disciple of Jesus means a willingness to love others with a love that is sacrificial and without conditions or limits. The disciples are to share whatever they have with others (Luke 6:30). They are to seek the last place and serve others (Mark 9:35). Nowhere is the ideal of discipleship as sacrificial love more clearly expressed than in John's Gospel, where Jesus says: "This is my commandment: love one another as I love you. No one has greater love than this, to lay down one's life for one's friends" (John 15:12-13).

Discipleship After Easter

After Easter the disciples understood that following Jesus included following him in his Easter passage from death to life. In his "way" section (8:27–10:52) Mark provides an extended instruction on discipleship. The way of Jesus means taking up one's cross and coming after him, taking the last place, even being willing to give up one's life (Mark 8:34-35). Mark joins the idea of following Jesus with martyrdom, a notion very popular in the early Church that saw martyrdom as the highest expression of discipleship. Acts uses the word "disciple" to identify the early Christians, though this usage did not long endure. But the idea of discipleship, expressed in different ways, was important in the early Church.

Thus discipleship in the Gospels means a personal and often costly following of Jesus that affects every dimension of human life. It shapes a person's attitude toward property and wealth, affects one's human and erotic relationships, gives a new meaning to love, changes the way one understands success and personal fulfillment, and finally, calls one to enter deeply into Jesus' paschal mystery, his passage through death to life. At its heart is what the Christian tradition came to call the *imitatio Christi,* the imitation of Christ.

Paul does not use the word "disciple" to describe the members of the Church, though the idea is certainly there. For Paul all of Christian life is a following of Christ; we are incorporated into Christ's death and resurrection by our baptism (Rom 6:3-5) and are called to model our own lives on his paschal mystery (Phil 3:8-11).

If each Christian is called to be a disciple of Jesus, to live a life of service using those gifts that he or she has received from the Spirit, then baptism, which incorporates one into the Church, becomes the basic sacrament of Christian service. An effective local community or parish is one that welcomes the contribution each member of the community might be able to make. Too often our parishes are so focused on families that those who don't fit into the pattern of the traditional family—whether they are single adults or parents, gay people, those in interchurch marriages, the divorced and remarried, the widowed—can feel left out. All Christians are called to discipleship and service. Some live out their discipleship through Christian marriage; others express it as ordained ministers. Some seek to follow Christ by becoming members of intentional Christian communities, while others choose the vocation of the single life.

MARRIAGE IN CHRIST

For most people marriage is the great school of love. Living in an intimate relationship with another human being, having to rearrange one's own priorities to accommodate the needs of a spouse, becoming a parent, taking time to play with one's children, dealing with conflict at close range, learning to forgive and to ask forgiveness for mistakes made, to accept forgiveness, to begin again each day without rancor over bruised feelings or past injuries, to share personal space, household chores, sensitivities, and faith—all this is part of the discipline of married life, which makes a promise of love that is not just empty words but a life-giving covenant.

The Sacrament of Marriage

The sacramental dimensions of married love have been recognized from the beginnings of Christian history. Paul includes marriage among the charisms, a manifestation of the Spirit's presence in the lives of two people for the building up of the Church (1 Cor 7:7). Paul's expectation of the imminent return of the risen Jesus leads him to make some rather negative-sounding remarks about marriage (1 Cor 7:27-29). But he also sees the transforming power of a marriage lived in faith; he argues that living with a Christian spouse could make holy the unbelieving partner as well as the children of their union (1 Cor 7:14). Later he speaks of the mutual love of husband and wife as a great *mysterion,* or symbol, of the intimate union of Christ and the Church (Eph 5:32). Augustine later used this text to speak of the sacramental nature of marriage. In the twelfth century Peter Lombard included marriage in his list of the "seven sacraments" in his *Book of the Sentences*.

Marriage is not so much a sacrament a couple receives as a sacrament they become. A couple who love each other with a love that is unconditional, forgiving, and life-giving become a sacramental embodiment of the unconditional, forgiving, and life-giving love of God—for each other, for their children, and for the Christian community. To live such a sacrament is not easy. Many single people, including many priests and religious, have difficulty understanding how much time and effort are necessary to be a good spouse and parent. Marriage is a full-time commitment. As people in the Marriage Encounter movement point out, love is not a feeling, it is a decision, something that must be lived out each day. Pledging such love to a spouse is a sacramental vocation precisely in mediating God's love and faithfulness to others. How many of us have come to appreciate something of the mystery of God's love for us through the love we have experienced from our parents!

As is the case with any charism, a desire to enter into a marriage needs to be discerned to see if it is truly a manifestation of the Spirit. The primary responsibility rests with the couple themselves. They need to test out their relationship, to see if they are really compatible and have a genuine community of interests, to find out if their love is genuine, if it is strong enough to overcome whatever obstacles or challenges may arise in their life together. The whole period of courtship and engagement is an important part of this period of discernment.

The Christian community has a great deal invested in the marriages of its members. Thus the Church seeks to assist couples in their discernment, though its attempts to institutionalize a process of discernment through its canon law for marriage and its prenuptial questionnaire remains at best imperfect. Since the Council of Trent sought to reform Catholic practice in the sixteenth century, Catholics have been required to observe "canonical form" for the validity of their marriage; that is, they are required to celebrate their wedding in a church before a priest or deacon and two witnesses.

Interchurch Marriages

Today the increasing number of marriages between a Catholic and a baptized Christian from another Church is resulting in a large number of interchurch families. According to the data collected by George Kilcourse, some studies suggest they may become more typical than exceptional.[3] The

---

[3]"Ecumenical Marriages: Two Models for Church Unity," *Mid-Stream* 26 (April 1987) 189; see also his *Double Belonging: Interchurch Families and Christian Unity* (New York: Paulist, 1992).

1993 Roman Catholic *Ecumenical Directory* has taken a number of steps to address the special concerns of Christians in these mixed or interchurch marriages.[4]

The directory stresses the need to respect the conscience of both Catholic and non-Catholic partners. The Catholic partner is expected "to promise sincerely to do all in his/her power to see that the children of the marriage be baptized and educated in the Catholic Church." But it also recognizes that the non-Catholic partner may feel a similar obligation toward his or her Church and therefore is no longer required to make a formal promise, either orally or in writing, to raise the children in the Catholic Church (no. 150), as was the case in the past. If in spite of the Catholic partner's best efforts, the children are not baptized and brought up in the Catholic Church, the Catholic partner does not fall under any censure of canon law (no. 151).

Mixed marriages are ordinarily celebrated outside the Eucharist, since the couple's Churches are not yet in communion with each other. However, the bishop may in certain cases grant an exception to this rule (no. 159). Catholics may also, for good reason, receive a dispensation from canonical form so that the marriage might be celebrated in the church (or synagogue) of the non-Catholic partner. An interchurch marriage service may with the agreement of both ministers be celebrated ecumenically. In such services one minister presides and receives the vows, while the minister of the other party may assist by offering a prayer, reading from the Scripture, giving a brief exhortation, or blessing the couple. What is not permitted is for the couple to have two separate religious services with the exchanges of consent.

When a Marriage Dies

One of the most painful questions the Church faces today is how to deal pastorally with those whose marriages for one reason or another do not work out. Certainly many Catholics find themselves in this difficult situation; there are as many divorces in the United States today among Catholics as among non-Catholics. In these cases the Church faces the dilemma of two values in conflict.

On the one hand, the Church is concerned to uphold and teach the value of the indissolubility of marriage in an age and culture in which many people enter and leave marriages without much thought. The Church's teaching on the permanence of marriage comes from Jesus himself, who prohibited divorce and remarriage (Mark 10:2-12), though it is interesting to note that both Paul (1 Cor 7:10-16) and Matthew (5:32; 19:1-2) admit exceptions to his prohibition. On the other hand, the Church recognizes the

[4]"Directory for the Application of Principles and Norms on Ecumenism," *Origins* 23 (July 29, 1993).

need of ministering pastorally to those who want to marry again after an unsuccessful marriage, or whose marriage after a divorce prevents them from participating in the Eucharist.

The traditional solution to this dilemma has been through the process of granting annulments. An annulment is the judgment of the Church, given through a Church court or matrimonial tribunal, that a canonically valid marriage never existed between the parties because something essential was missing at the time the couple entered the marriage. It does not mean that the couple was not legally married in the eyes of the state, or that their children are illegitimate.

Prior to the Second Vatican Council the conditions for an annulment were more strictly understood; a marriage was recognized as invalid if it was not freely entered into, or if one of the parties withheld consent to one of the "goods" of marriage such as permanence or children, or if some "impediment" such as a prior marriage bond stood in the way. Since the council those conditions have been more broadly understood. The Church has recognized more clearly that making the kind of commitment that marriage in Christ entails demands a maturity and careful judgment on the part of each person. Thus a couple might be granted an annulment on the basis of a "lack of due discretion."

Today it is much easier to gain an annulment than in the past. It is no longer necessary to apply to Rome, as annulments can be granted by the local Church. And the number granted each year has risen dramatically. In 1969 only seven hundred annulments were granted to Catholics in the United States. By 1979 the number had climbed to twenty-eight thousand, and by 1983 it had reached over sixty-six thousand. Still, the process for some people is not an easy one. One solution suggested by a number of canonists and moral theologians is to allow a couple whose second marriage gives evidence of a deeply committed love access to the Eucharist without formally celebrating the second marriage sacramentally. The Orthodox Churches, to mitigate the unintended harshness of the law, permit remarriage after a divorce by their principle of "economy" (similar to a Roman Catholic "dispensation").

The Catholic Church is trying to respond more pastorally to those who have married again without obtaining an annulment. Couples who enter such a marriage no longer incur excommunication, as was the case in the United States from 1884 until 1977, when Pope Paul VI removed the automatic penalty. Nor does the Church speak of such marriages as "adulterous unions," for most Catholics recognize that a second marriage may in time show all the signs of love and commitment that one expects in a sacramental marriage, even if the Church has not been able to officially recognize it as such.

PRIESTHOOD

The role of the priest in the Catholic community has changed considerably since the Second Vatican Council. Prior to the council the priest occupied a privileged place within the Catholic culture. The sacral understanding of the priesthood that emerged out of the Middle Ages defined priesthood almost exclusively in terms of the priest's role in the celebration of the Eucharist. Popularly, the priest was seen as a sacred person, equipped with sacramental powers so that he might offer the Holy Sacrifice of the Mass and "confect" the Eucharist. A priest was "another Christ." His role was clearly defined and protected by a clerical culture. The priest was a man apart, separated from the laity by clerical dress and privilege, titles of respect, a single-sex educational system, rectory living, even the Latin language used in the liturgy.

In the years after the council, with its emphasis on the Church as the people of God and its recovery of a broader concept of ministry, the sacral concept of priesthood was largely rejected. Hans Küng went so far as to suggest that even the word "priest" should be dropped, since the New Testament does not call Christian ministers priests.[5] Priesthood was understood in terms of ministry and service, not power and authority. In many ways this emphasis was important, given the one-sided sacral approach to priesthood prior to the council. Priests were servant-leaders, called to a ministry of humble service modeled on that of Jesus. But since popular theology tended to describe all Christians as ministers, the question was increasingly raised about what was unique to the ministry of the priest.

In the early 1990s a new, "representational" model for priesthood was suggested based on the priest's role in the celebration of the sacraments. The Church as the body of Christ represents and makes Christ present to the world, but to do this "it is also necessary for Christ to be represented by the official actions of the church as such."[6] This representational role is carried out by bishops and priests, who are authorized by their ordination as official ministers of the Church and are thus able to represent Christ in the Church's official actions, its sacraments. In language that has been traditional since the early centuries, the bishop or priest acts "in the person of Christ" *(in persona Christi)* (LG 28).

In Persona Christi

The concept is based on the bishop's role as leader of the local Church. As one who presides over the community, or Church, and has been or-

---

[5] *Why Priests?: A Proposal for a New Church Ministry* (Garden City, N.Y.: Doubleday, 1974) 42.
[6] See Avery Dulles, "Models for Ministerial Priesthood," *Origins* 20 (1990) 288.

dained, the bishop or priest acts *in persona Christi* in the Church's sacraments and particularly in its Eucharist. At the same time, the bishop or priest acts "in the person of the Church" *(in persona ecclesiae)* in virtue of his role as president of the liturgical assembly. The priest is able to act *in persona Christi* because he acts *in persona ecclesiae,* the body of Christ. Outside of the Church the priesthood has no meaning. Most diocesan or "secular" priests exercise a ministry of word, sacrament, and pastoral leadership within a local Church, usually by presiding over a local community of faith, or parish. Many monastic priests exercise a priesthood that is primarily cultic, focused on the praise of God through the liturgy. Priests belonging to apostolic religious communities generally exercise a ministry that extends beyond the confines of the local Church. Their ministry is often more prophetic or kerygmatic, as it involves a much broader range of the ministries of the word, giving retreats and doing spiritual direction, teaching and writing, devoting themselves to ministries of evangelization and social justice.

Celibacy

We will consider celibacy for the sake of the gospel when we look at the vocation to the single life. Here it should suffice to point out that although celibacy has been a value in the Christian life since the beginning, it was not always associated with the priesthood. In the early centuries many priests were married, though a considerable number chose celibacy. In the Eastern Church the tradition developed that bishops should be celibate, in large part because of the practice of choosing bishops from among the monks. That is still the Eastern tradition; a bishop must be celibate, but both the Eastern Orthodox and the Eastern Catholic Churches ordain married men. In a 1920 decree *(Qua sollerti)* Rome required the clergy of Eastern Catholic Churches in the United States and Canada to adopt the Western tradition of clerical celibacy with unfortunate results: "Up to 200,000 faithful, mainly of Ukranian Byzantine Rite . . . left the Catholic Church and joined the Ukranian Orthodox Church and some other Christian communities."[7]

In the West the tradition of mandatory clerical celibacy developed slowly. In the fourth and fifth centuries various local councils—in Spain (Elvira, 306), Africa (Carthage, 390, 419), Italy (Turin, 398), and France (Orange, 441)—sought to require sexual abstinence of married priests. Candidates for ordination had to take a vow of chastity. But many priests continued to marry and have children in spite of the protests of popes and the legislation of synods and councils. Nicholas II (1059) tried to prevent the laity from attending Masses celebrated by married priests. The First Lateran

[7]Petro B. T. Bilaniuk, "Celibacy and Eastern Tradition," *Celibacy: The Necessary Option,* ed. George H. Frein (New York: Herder & Herder, 1968) 60.

Council (1123) made celibacy mandatory for those in major orders; the Second Lateran Council (1139) declared clerical marriages invalid. Since then celibacy has been universally required in the Western Church.

It is important to note that celibacy is a matter of Church discipline, not doctrine, as the Council of Trent acknowledged (DS 1809). Though freely chosen celibacy can be a powerful sign of the kingdom, it is not intrinsic to the vocation of the diocesan priest. Thus it could conceivably be changed. However, for religious priests who live in community and profess the evangelical counsels of poverty, chastity, and obedience, celibacy is intrinsic to their vocation. Both Pope Paul VI and Pope John Paul II have strongly reaffirmed the tradition of clerical celibacy,[8] though many Catholics today argue that what is a free charism should not be made a matter of Church law, particularly in light of the diminishing numbers of unmarried male candidates for ordination. According to sociologist Richard Schoenherr, who has studied the statistics for years, "the full weight of history and social change is turning against male celibate exclusivity in the Catholic priesthood."[9] The priesthood has assumed a number of different forms in the past. What forms and expressions it might take in the future remains to be seen.

Priesthood Today

To proclaim the gospel in the face of widespread secularization and religious indifference, to witness to its social dimensions in the face of the crushing poverty that affects so many today, to be able to share one's personal faith experience with others struggling to clarify their own—all that is part of the challenge of being a priest today.

How does a priest speak to the young parents who have lost a child or are in danger of losing one because they are no longer able to communicate with a son or a daughter? How does he help a distraught parent accept and love a child who is gay or who discloses that he or she is HIV positive? How can he reach out to those women who are hurt and alienated because they feel discriminated against by their Church and help them to find a meaningful role within it? How does he help the elderly members of the community to be peaceful with their diminishing strength or disability? Such questions are easier to pose than to answer, but they are the kinds of questions that many priests face every day.

A priest can help only if he makes himself accessible; he cannot hide behind his status or role. The days when the priest was the most educated

[8]Paul VI, *Sacerdotalis coelibatus*, 1967; John Paul II, *Résurrection, marriage et célibat: L'Évangile de la rédemption du corps* (Paris: Cerf, 1985).

[9]"Numbers Don't Lie: A Priesthood in Irreversible Decline," *Commonweal* 122 (April 7, 1995) 13.

member of the parish are long gone. The image of a priest as a "man apart" is not very helpful today, nor is a clerical culture that erects artificial barriers between priest and people. A priest can take a leadership role in a community only if he is truly a part of it, involved with its members. This is especially true when the priest presides at the Eucharist.

The Eucharist stands at the center of the priest's ministry, for the community over which the priest is called to preside is created and sustained by the Eucharist. Through the celebration of the Eucharist the community becomes Church, while at the same time the priest, in virtue of his communion with the bishop, symbolizes and maintains the communion that exists between the local community and the worldwide communion of the Church. When the priest presides at the Eucharist, the nature of the Church as one, holy, catholic, and apostolic comes to expression.

In the final analysis, priesthood is a vocation, not a career. Those who seek the priesthood with the idea that it offers them security, status, or personal advancement will be disappointed. Prayer is particularly important in the life of a priest; Catholic people expect their priests to be prayerful so that they can carry out their ministry honestly and with some spiritual depth. Rightly lived out, priesthood is an expression of Christian discipleship—not the only one, but certainly one very close to that of Peter and Andrew and James and John and the other disciples called to be in Jesus' company and to share in his ministry.

CHRISTIAN COMMUNITIES AND RELIGIOUS LIFE

From the early centuries of the Church some men and women have tried to respond to the gospel's call to discipleship with Jesus by living with other Christians in communities gathered for prayer, evangelical ministry, and Christian service. In time some of these communities became religious orders and congregations, communities of monks or nuns, of priests, brothers, or sisters who live a common life and bind themselves by the "evangelical counsels" of poverty, chastity, and obedience. This manner of living, officially recognized by the Church, is referred to as the "religious life." Others are lay communities whose members share a common life and a common ministry. There are also canonically recognized secular institutes, societies of men or women who take the traditional religious vows privately and continue their "secular" lives in the world rather than in a religious community.

Monasticism

The Church has always recognized various groups, or orders, of Christians whose lives embodied gospel values in a particular way. The early Church honored women consecrated to virginity and martyrs who gave their lives for their faith as an expression of their discipleship. In the third and fourth centuries, when Christian life became not only legal but also respected and often prosperous, many men and women left the cities to seek God anew in the silence of the desert. They came to be called "monks," from their life alone *(monos)*.

St. Antony of Egypt, a third-century hermit, is considered the father of monasticism. Even if he was not the first monk, his story, the *Life of Antony,* written by St. Athanasius (d. 373), was to inspire thousands to follow his example. These men and women, following the evangelical counsels, stripped themselves of their possessions, lived celibate lives, and often promised obedience to a teacher, a spiritual father *(abbas,* hence "abbot") or mother *(amma)*.

Although there were thousands of monks living in the desert as hermits *(heremos,* "haunting the desert," "solitary") by the time of Antony's death (ca. 356), many of them lived in colonies grouped around a few common buildings. Pachomius (ca. 292–346) organized some of these colonies of hermits into monastic communities or monasteries whose members lived a common life of communal prayer, manual labor, and later, study under the direction of a leader. Basil of Caesarea (ca. 330–379) outlined a way of life that tempered personal asceticism with an emphasis on charity and works of mercy; his *Rules* helped secure the monastic movement firmly within the Church. Evagrius of Pontus (349–399) contributed to the development of monastic spirituality by dividing the spiritual life into two distinct stages, the "active" life, concerned with the purification of the senses and the acquisition of virtue, and the "contemplative" life, a disciplined kind of prayer that sought to quiet the mind and empty it of distractions so that the monk could be united with God.

Monasticism also flourished in the Western Church. Rome had men and women living a kind of urban monasticism as early as the fourth century. These "ascetics" (from *askesis,* used for athletic exercise) lived a celibate life and gave themselves to the study of Scripture and prayer. For women especially the monastic life provided an alternative to marriage and offered an independence from the roles dictated by their culture. Martin of Tours (317–397) and John Cassian (ca. 360–435) brought the monastic life to France. From there missionary monks brought it to the British Isles, particularly to Ireland, where a unique form of Celtic monasticism was to develop that shaped the Irish Church for centuries.

The most famous name in Western monasticism is that of Benedict of Nursia (480–550). Benedict was successively a student at Rome, a hermit at Subiaco, and the founder of a community of monks at Monte Casino, where he wrote his famous *Rule,* which was to establish the pattern for Western monasticism. Noted for its balance, the *Rule* of Benedict sought to integrate a life of work and prayer, solitude and community, personal responsibility and authority.

The monks lived in a virtually self-contained community under the direction of an abbot. Their buildings, a church, dormitory, chapter house for community meetings, and refectory, were grouped around an open courtyard, or cloister. The monks worked, studied, and walked in the covered passages, which formed the sides of the cloister. Their day was divided into three parts. Seven times a day they assembled in the church for the monastic Office, known as the *opus Dei,* or "work of God," chanting the psalms in praise of God. Several hours each day were given to a prayerful reading of the Scripture, the *lectio divina,* which nourished their life of prayer. Finally, six or seven hours were given to the manual labor, *labora,* that supported their life.

In the early Middle Ages the monasteries provided a network of important social services. They provided hospitality for travelers and food, clothing, and shelter for the indigent. They became centers of learning and art. Many families sent their children to live in monasteries, where they obtained an education. At the same time, it was not always easy to maintain the idealism that first drew men and women to the monastic life. When one studies the history of monasticism, a recurrent pattern emerges. A way of life that began as a communal search for God in solitude, poverty, and self-denial would gradually become settled, secure, and prosperous. Celibacy was a factor here. Since the monks did not have children to inherit the wealth that their industry produced, the monastic community itself gradually gained a corporate wealth. Many Benedictine monasteries became quite wealthy.

But always new groups emerged to start again, seeking through solitude and prayer the hidden God for whom the human heart hungers. The tenth and eleventh centuries saw a number of new beginnings. Romuald of Ravenna (ca. 950–1027) and Bruno of Cologne (1032–1101) helped establish new communities of hermits. Romuald founded the Camaldolese, who derived their name from their hermitage at Camaldoli in the Tuscan hills. Bruno helped found the Carthusians, who called their monastery in the French Alps La Grande Chartreuse. In France a group of monks left the monastery of Molesme in 1098 in the hopes of restoring the simple life of work and prayer that characterized the *Rule* of St. Benedict. They chose isolated areas for their monasteries, stripped the elaborate liturgy of the Benedictines to its basic forms, and tried to banish from their churches the rich art, statuary, colored glass, and great towers of the Benedictines. Known as the Cistercians, from their new monastery at Citeaux *(Cistercium),* these "White Monks" were to become the most influential monastic order in the twelfth century.

Evangelical Communities and Apostolic Orders

In the turmoil and upheavals that reshaped the life and geography of Europe in the twelfth and thirteenth centuries, new communities emerged that were influenced by an evangelical awakening sweeping across Europe. These communities sought to live a life of evangelical poverty and apostolic preaching modeled on the gospel in an increasingly urban culture.

Many of these were lay movements. Some, such as the Humiliati, the Waldensians, and the Poor Catholics, were mixed communities of men and women. Others, communities of lay women like the Beguines, can be seen as representing for the first time a genuine movement of women within the Church. The efforts of these communities to develop and live an evangelical lay spirituality were to give rise to a number of tensions between themselves and the official Church, particularly over the issue of lay preaching. Some, like the Waldensians, ultimately became heterodox and lost communion with the Church.

Other communities became new religious orders, most notably the Franciscans and the Dominicans. Dominic de Guzman (1172–1221) was a cathedral canon of the Diocese of Osma in Spain. His order grew out of a group of missionaries who joined him in his ministry of preaching against the Albigensians in southern France. Francis of Assisi (1182–1226) was the son of a wealthy Italian cloth merchant. After a conversion experience that took place over several years, Francis gathered around him a group of companions with whom he began wandering the Umbrian countryside, preaching in the town squares, working with the peasants in the fields, and begging to provide for their own needs.

Both Francis and Dominic were moved by the new evangelical spirit that influenced so many of their contemporaries. The notion of an apostolic community, free to go where there was need, preaching the gospel in the towns and cities, living in poverty and simplicity of life, did not originate with either of them. Indeed, their communities at the beginning were sometimes confused with other, more radical and heterodox groups. Dominic and some of his early companions went barefoot until the Council of Constance ordered that shoes be worn to distinguish orthodox preachers from the heretics who identified the right to preach with going barefoot. The early Franciscans were at times mistaken for members of other suspect evangelical fraternities, particularly the condemned Waldensians, while their lack of education left some in danger of accepting heretical ideas for themselves.

But both Francis and Dominic were successful in finding ways to incorporate their vision of the apostolic life into the structural life of the Church. Dominic's companions constituted a clerical community from the beginning, assisted by lay brothers and a "second order," a group of women some of whom had been converted themselves from the Albigensians. Pope Honorius III recognized Dominic's community as an Order of Preachers *(Ordo Praedicatorum)* in 1217. The "lesser brothers" *(fratres minores)* of Francis, originally a lay community, became increasingly clericalized in order to accommodate their emphasis on preaching. Francis wrote several rules before his "Second Rule" *(Regula Bullata)* was approved by Honorius III in 1223. Francis himself apparently was ordained a deacon.

Franciscan women, led by Francis' friend Clare, sought to live the same kind of life as the lesser brothers, particularly in serving the poor, but gradually they were obliged to accept the obligation of a cloistered life, which curtailed their apostolic lifestyle. The Church was not quite ready to accept an apostolic community of women. The "Poor Clares" became a monasticized, contemplative community.

Post-Reformation Communities

Although the Reformation in the sixteenth century dealt religious life in Europe a serious blow, the spirit of reform that was awakened in the Catholic Church produced a number of new religious communities. In Spain Teresa of Avila, assisted by John of the Cross, carried out a reform of the Carmelites that was to revitalize the contemplative life. In 1526 a reform movement within the Franciscans produced the Capuchins. The sixteenth century also saw the founding of a number of apostolic communities of priests, "clerks regular" such as the Theatines (1524), the Somaschi (1528), the Barnabites (1533), and the Piarists (1597).

Perhaps the most successful of these new communities of men was the Society of Jesus, or Jesuits, a group of former students from the University of Paris led by Ignatius of Loyola. Their way of life was different from that of other religious orders of the time; they had no distinctive habit, no prescribed fasts and penances, no obligation of choir—a radical departure from the tradition. The religious life of these "friends in the Lord" was based not on a rule but on the common experience of the *Spiritual Exercises,* a series of considerations and meditations on the gospel designed to bring one into a new relationship with God, which had grown out of Ignatius' months of prayer at Manresa in 1522. Their way of life was approved in 1540 when Pope Paul II approved the "Formula of the Institute" drawn up by Ignatius. By the time Ignatius died in 1556 the Jesuits were working as missionaries in India, Japan, Brazil, and Africa and were conducting forty-six colleges.

The centuries that followed the Reformation were to see a succession of apostolic communities of men and women. Vincent de Paul founded the Vincentians in 1625 and with Louise de Marillac established the Daughters of Charity to work with the sick and the poor. John Baptist de la Salle founded the Christian Brothers in 1681 to educate the sons of the working class. The eighteenth century saw the foundation of the Passionists (1725) and the Redemptorists (1735). Some sixty-five congregations and societies of priests were founded in the nineteenth century.

Though women of faith had sought to devote themselves to charitable and apostolic works even before the time of Clare, they had to struggle against a Church that could not conceive of women religious living in community without the protection of monastic practices such as distinctive habits, enclosure, cloister, and choir. The Ursulines, founded by Angela Merici in 1535, began as an uncloistered community of apostolic women; originally they lived at home with their families, but gradually they were required to live in communities, which became increasingly monastic. The Sisters of the Visitation, founded by Francis de Sales and Jane Frances de Chantal in France in 1610 was similar; they began as a community dedicated to the care of the sick but before long were transformed into a strictly enclosed order of cloistered nuns. More than four hundred congregations of apostolic women religious were founded in France between 1800 and 1880. From these communities of dedicated women—communities such as the Sisters of Mercy, the Sisters of Saint Joseph, the Sisters of the Immaculate Heart of Mary—came the sisters who made the social and educational ministries of the Church concrete for millions of people throughout the world. They did missionary work, staffed hospitals and schools, and cared for the sick, the orphaned, the elderly, and the disadvantaged.

New Religious Communities

The impulse toward Christian community life has been equally strong in the twentieth century. New communities have appeared, both lay and religious, that seek to make possible for their members a way of life rooted in the gospel.

The Little Sisters and Little Brothers of Jesus trace their inspiration to Charles de Foucauld, the French hermit-monk who lived among the Berber people at Tamanrasset in the Sahara trying to model in his own life the hidden life of Jesus in Nazarcth. Foucauld was murdered in 1916 by a fifteen-year-old tribesman. His example of solidarity with the poor was to influence a number of contemporary religious communities. The Little Brothers and Little Sisters seek to share their lives with the poor, working like ordinary working people in factories, farms, and shops, returning at the end of the day to their "fraternities" to spend an hour of adoration before the Blessed Sacrament. They are contemplatives whose monastery is the everyday world of the poor.

Much better known are the communities of Mother Teresa, the Missionaries of Charity. The Missionary Sisters practice a very severe poverty and take a fourth vow of charity. Their day begins about 4:30 A.M. with meditation and Mass and is spent in care of "the poorest of the poor." The Missionary Brothers, though smaller in number, follow the same rigorous life. After meditation and Mass they go to their works of charity, returning at the end of the day for Evening Prayer and a meditation before the Blessed Sacrament. The Missionaries of Charity are not the only modern community whose ministry is to the poor. Many communities of men and women religious are involved in this kind of ministry. They staff inner-city parishes, run shelters and hospices, and provide a network of services for the disadvantaged.

Religious Life After Vatican II

The Second Vatican Council called for a twofold renewal of religious life: "(1) a continuous return to the sources of all Christian life and to the original inspiration behind a given community and (2) an adjustment of the community to the changed conditions of the times" (PC 2). In the years that followed, the religious life changed immensely, both in its appearance and in the way it was understood.

Many of the changes involved externals. For a considerable number of active communities of men and women, the religious habits, common order, required devotions, corporal penances, restrictive rules, cloister, and other external symbols that had defined religious life disappeared. Monastic communities pruned a host of practices that had been added to their way of life over the centuries.

Other changes were more substantive. The challenge to return to the sources was a fruitful one. Monastic communities began to rediscover the contemplative dimension of their vocations. Many rethought the separations between ordained and unordained members of their communities as well as the general assumption that a monk should be a priest. Apostolic communities sought to recover the charisms of their founders. The Franciscans focused on St. Francis' simplicity of life and solidarity with the poor. The Jesuits rediscovered the individually directed retreat, the way in which the early Jesuits gave the *Spiritual Exercises*. For many communities of women religious a "return to the sources" meant recovering an original flexibility, which had been lost in the monasticizing of their way of life by the Church. They set about the revision of their constitutions and a reconsideration of their ministries. Many communities, inspired by the council's Pastoral Constitution on the Church in the Modern World and its challenge to scrutinize "the signs of the times" (GS 4), began to direct more of their energies toward social justice and the service of the poor.

For many religious communities the process of renewal was costly. As communities rethought the meaning of religious life, some of its underlying "myths" or rationales were reinterpreted. For centuries the religious life had been spoken of as superior to the lay vocation; it was described as a "state of perfection" and considered "objectively higher." Too often personal sanctification was presented as its primary end, while service or ministry was considered secondary. For some religious the council's stress that all Christians were called to holiness had seemed to undercut one of the primary reasons for living a religious life. In the decade after the council thousands of religious left their communities. Within thirty years "the number of religious has decreased by 45 percent for brothers and sisters and 27 percent for religious priests."[10] Some communities will probably disappear or reaffiliate with other communities.

If the process of renewal has been a painful one, it has also been one of genuine renewal and purification. Religious life will survive, as it has in other periods of turmoil and change in the Church, but religious communities will probably not have the great numbers they had in the middle of the twentieth century. There are today too many other expressions of Christian discipleship and service, particularly for women.

Contemporary religious communities face a number of challenges. They will continue to struggle to find a balance between individualism and community, spontaneity and structure, fidelity to tradition and adaptation. They must find ways of witnessing to simplicity of life in an age of affluence. They need to attract new members. But they have also been strengthened by a new emphasis on community, a new appreciation of prayer and contemplation, and a new commitment to social justice and solidarity with the poor. The Church is richer for the presence of these religious communities in its history, not because their way of life is higher or more perfect than that of other Christians but because their very existence symbolizes the primacy of the gospel and the discipleship to which all Christians are called.

Lay Communities

The twentieth century has also seen a great variety of lay communities where men and women, both single and married, strive to live a life of discipleship. Catholic Worker communities have fed and clothed the poor and homeless of our desolate inner cities and worked for social justice since 1933 when Dorothy Day and Peter Maurin began publishing the *Catholic Worker,* a radical Catholic newspaper, in New York City. Since then, Catholic Worker soup kitchens and houses of hospitality have become a standard feature of many of our poor inner cities. There are over eighty Catholic Worker communities in the United States today.

L'Arche (the ark), a movement founded by Jean Vanier at Trosly-Breuil in France in 1964, provides homes where developmentally disabled people can live in community with other men and women, called "assistants," who devote themselves to caring for them. These alternative communities follow a simple way of life centered around prayer and the Eucharist; their spirituality is based on the Jesus of the Beatitudes, who identifies himself with the poor and the

---

[10]David Nygren and Miriam Ukeritis, "Future of Religious Orders in the United States," *Origins* 22 (1922) 257; in 1965, the year the council ended, there were 22,707 religious priests, 12,271 brothers, and 179,954 sisters in the United States. By 1994 the numbers had fallen to 17,116 religious priests, 6,510 brothers, and 94,431 sisters.

suffering. Those who come to l'Arche know that when we open ourselves to the poor and the disadvantaged, we come to know the presence of Christ and to experience his peace. Today there are more than one hundred l'Arche communities around the world. Some are ecumenical or interreligious.

In many Third World countries today small groups of Christians, often neighbors and most often poor, are forming Basic Christian Communities (BCCs); they come together weekly to share their concerns and their faith. The Bible holds pride of place in a BCC; its members ponder the biblical text so that it might illumine their own experience with the living Word of God. The BCCs have helped to empower the poor in many Third World countries and developed a new group of effective pastoral leaders (in Latin America, many of them women) from the grass roots, or "base." They have done much to renew the Church.

Covenant communities took their origin from the charismatic renewal movement, which began in the Catholic Church shortly after the Second Vatican Council. They represent groups of Christians who commit themselves to one another in a shared life of faith. Basing themselves on Acts 2:42-47, they agree to share their lives, their faith, and usually their financial resources. Their members generally meet daily for a period of common prayer. Covenant communities have been particularly strong in the United States and also in France, where the charismatic renewal has been perhaps the major force for renewal in the French Church. They have helped many Christians, Catholic and non-Catholic, to develop a more loving image of God and to become comfortable with a more spontaneous and affective style of prayer.

SINGLE LIFE

The single life can also be a vocation, that is, a call from God to Christian discipleship and service. There are many men and women in the Church who are single, either by choice or by circumstance.

Though celibacy was not generally esteemed in the Old Testament, the idea of giving up marriage for the sake of the kingdom is clearly a gospel value. Jesus himself is the primary model of such a dedicated single life, and he teaches that others are called to give up marriage "for the sake of the kingdom of heaven" (Matt 19:12). The phrase "for the sake of the kingdom," however, is key. A single life can be chosen for any number of self-serving reasons. A person might choose a single life because he or she does not want the responsibility of married life, or out of fear of intimacy and commitment, or to make possible a lifestyle centered on one's self and one's own needs.

To choose celibacy for the sake of the kingdom means that a single life becomes the expression of a life given over to the love of God and to some specific way of sharing that love with others. Paul reflects this understanding when he speaks of both marriage and the single life as charisms, gifts of the Spirit for the building up of the Church (1 Cor 7:7). For some a vocation to the single life might mean the life of a hermit, given to contemplation, prayer, and solitude. For others it might be expressed through ministry and service in the Church. Or it might reflect a passionate commitment to a gift that has been received and can be used to give glory to God and assistance to God's people. Excluding those called to religious life, Christian history is full of examples of men and women who have chosen a single life in order to dedicate themselves to art, music, scholarship, theology, medicine or nursing, education, or social justice—not just as an interest or a career but as an expression of faith and discipleship.

What about those who are single not by choice but by circumstance? There are many people who would have preferred to be married but have not been able to find a partner. Others have lost a spouse through death or separation or divorce. For some marriage is not an option because of disability or sexual orientation or physical circumstance. This is not to suggest that marriage is the norm and single life second best but to acknowledge that sometimes our dreams don't work out. None of us is as free as we would like to be, and our choices are often limited. Thus a vocation can be embraced as well as chosen.

What is most important is that a person respond to God's gracious presence and invitation to intimacy in the concrete and particular circumstances of his or her life. It is here especially that our range of choices opens up. We can become closed in on ourselves and embittered because of events and circumstances in our lives beyond our control. We can seek to fill up our emptiness and the aloneness that is a part of every person's life with possessions or power over others or fleeting gratifications of various sorts. Or we can open ourselves to the God who is always with us to draw hope out of disappointment, good out of evil, life out of death. It is precisely here that each of us must encounter the cross and embrace the paschal mystery of Jesus' dying and rising to new life, which remains the pattern for all those who choose to follow Jesus (Mark 8:34-35; Phil 3:10; John 12:24-25). A single life, even if one is single by circumstance, can become a vocation, a choice of God in the mystery of our own lives and a joyful celebration of faith. Embracing it as a vocation is to allow ourselves be transformed by grace.

A vocation to the single life, like any other, needs to be nourished by prayer and worship and expressed in some kind of concern for the wider community.[11] If it is an authentic celebration of God's presence in one's life, it should open one up to others. Single people are free to love with a nonexclusive love that welcomes and cherishes all those they meet. They are more

---

[11]See Susan A. Muto, *Celebrating the Single Life: A Spirituality for Single Persons* (New York: Crossroad, 1989).

available for ministry. This should be true even for hermits. Hermits are different from recluses; "the virtues characterizing a true hermit are compassion and hospitality."[12]

CONCLUSION

In chapter 3 we saw that the Church is confessed as "holy" in part because it is the assembly of God's holy people, the baptized who have been regenerated in Christ and anointed by the Holy Spirit. Unfortunately many Christians continue to assume that holiness of life is something that belongs to the saints alone, or that it is reserved for those who live public "religious" lives in the Church, such as priests and religious brothers and sisters. This is not the case at all.

In an important chapter of the Dogmatic Constitution on the Church entitled "The Call of the Whole Church to Holiness," the bishops at the Second Vatican Council emphasized that all Christians are called to holiness, not in virtue of their status or position in the Church but precisely through cooperating with God's grace in the concrete circumstances of their everyday lives (LG 41). Not just religious but all Christians—bishops, priests and deacons, married couples and parents, single people and those who have lost their spouses, laborers, the sick and infirm, the poor—are called to sanctity and holiness of life, not by embracing some kind of artificial religiosity but by living lives marked by "prayer, self-denial, active brotherly service, and the exercise of all the virtues"—in short, by living the love the Spirit of God pours into our hearts (LG 42).

In this chapter we have considered the call of all Christians to holiness in terms of Jesus' call to discipleship; the following of Jesus, which is at the heart of the Christian life; and some of the different expressions of discipleship in the life of the Church. "Discipleship" in the Gospels is not something that takes us out of the world. Rather it is an invitation to change the way we perceive the world, to join Jesus in his ministry on behalf of God's reign, to love with an unconditional and self-sacrificing love. After Easter, discipleship took on the added meaning of following Jesus in his paschal mystery. All are called to follow Jesus, and there are many expression of discipleship and Christian service in the Christian life.

Many Christians live out their discipleship through the sacrament of matrimony. It is a sacrament that is not so much received as it is lived out, for the vocation of a couple married in Christ is to image the unconditional love of God in their love for each other and for their children.

[12]Karen Karper, "'By No Worldly Logic': To Be a Hermit in the 1990s," *America* 171 (September 10, 1994) 28.

Priests express their discipleship through a ministry of word, sacrament, and pastoral care for God's people. Particularly in celebrating the sacraments for the community of faith, priests act in the person of Christ, showing Christ's presence and faithfulness to his people in the sacramental actions of the Church.

Throughout Christian history some men and women have sought to follow Christ through the religious life. In the tradition, the religious life, whether monastic or apostolic, has been described as a sign of the kingdom. The Second Vatican Council reaffirmed this understanding (PC 1). But this function cannot be restricted to canonical religious communities.

Any Christian community, lay or religious, Catholic, Protestant, or ecumenical, whose members seek to live Christian discipleship in a public way stands as a sign of the kingdom.[13] As communities whose lives are rooted in the gospel, they are signs of compassionate service of the poor, reconciliation of people, holiness of life, and communion with Christ, all of which are characteristics of the kingdom.

Finally, many men and women live out their following of Jesus as single people. Their way of life is no less a vocation because it is lived without a spouse or community, since they are free for a number of nonexclusive friendships and often participate in several different communities. Nor is it lacking in sacramental expression, since the grace of baptism gives rise to this and to all vocations. And the commitment to Christ as a single person is affirmed in the regular celebration of the sacrament of the Eucharist.

The public vocations we have considered are only particular expressions of the call to discipleship, which is addressed to all those who claim to follow Jesus.

---

[13]For more on Protestant and ecumenical communities, see Thomas P. Rausch, *Radical Christian Communities* (Collegeville: The Liturgical Press, 1990).

7. Sin, Forgiveness, and Healing

Recently a colleague at the university was telling me about his young son's preparation for his first confession and first Holy Communion. He was quite impressed with the catechesis his son was receiving and with the boy's understanding of the Eucharist. Then he said, a little taken aback, "You know, they don't talk about sin any more; they talk about making poor choices."

Why is it that in a world in which there is so much evident evil we are so reluctant to talk about sin? Psychiatrist Karl Menninger raised this question more than twenty years ago in a book entitled *Whatever Became of Sin?*[1] Or as Kathleen Norris observes of the contemporary human potential movement, "if I'm O.K. and you're O.K., and our friends (nice people and, like us, markedly middle class . . .) are O.K., why is the world definitely not O.K.?"[2]

It is probably easier to define evil than sin. The presence of evil in our world is self-evident. We know of horrendous examples of evil in this century now drawing to a close. We read about it daily in our newspapers and see examples of it each evening when we watch the news on television. Evil has often touched our own lives or the lives of those dear to us. But it remains something outside of us. Sin is more subtle. Sin is the personal side of evil; it does have to do with our choices, with our own involvement in the mystery of iniquity, an involvement we are often reluctant to acknowledge.

A sense of guilt is often a sign of the presence of sin in our lives. Unfortunately, in our therapeutic culture guilt is too often dismissed as a neurotic problem rather than being recognized as a healthy response to some wrong we have done. Although there is such a thing as neurotic guilt (for example, in the case of the scrupulous), the experience of guilt can also be the sign of a healthy conscience. As Bill O'Malley has said, "What you get in a world without guilt is Auschwitz, gang rapes, pushers, saturation bombing, toxic

---

[1] *Whatever Became of Sin?* (New York: Hawthorn, 1973).
[2] *Dakota: A Spiritual Geography* (Boston: Houghton Mifflin, 1993) 97–98.

waste dumps, drive-by shooters, terrorism. . . . Our society—and religious education—desperately need to stop suppressing legitimate guilt."[3]

We know that we do things that are wrong, that we act out of self-interest in a way that is damaging to others, that we sin. But we also sometimes have the sense that sin is something greater than those "sins" we commit, that it is a far more comprehensive reality, that it goes beyond poor choices and wrong actions. In his Letter to the Romans St. Paul captures this existential sense of sin as a power that subverts our intentions and limits our freedom:

> What I do, I do not understand. For I do not do what I want, but I do what I hate. . . . So now it is no longer I who do it, but sin that dwells in me, . . . that is, in my flesh. The willing is ready at hand, but doing the good is not. For I do not do the good I want, but I do the evil I do not want. Now if [I] do what I do not want, it is no longer I who do it, but sin that dwells in me (Rom 7:15, 17-20).

Sometimes we gain a glimpse of this destructive power of sin, which can capture and overpower another, leaving tragedy and heartbreak in its wake. How often have we read the report of some horrifying crime in which an innocent victim has been brutally murdered. Our reactions are visceral; we want the criminal to suffer the maximum penalty. But frequently, when we learn more about the case, read an in-depth report, we discover that the one who committed the crime has also been a victim, was the product of an abusive home, never had loving parents or a normal childhood. Suddenly we see the story in a new light; the person's crime is not excused, but the rage that erupted into tragedy is no longer a total mystery; it has a history and probably a record of warning signs over the years.

SIN IN THE BIBLICAL TRADITION

In the biblical tradition sin and its correlative, evil, enter the story of humankind in its opening chapters. The first Genesis creation account (Gen 1:1–2:4a) stresses over and over again that God's creation is good; in fact, God's creative work is precisely one of bringing a world of order, light, and life out of the dark and formless primordial chaos. In more philosophical terms the myth of the Garden of Eden says that evil is absent from the world in which God places man and woman; they enjoy dominion over the earth, equality with each other, and intimacy with their Creator.

But the story of the fall (Gen 3) suggests that our first parents were not content with their status as creatures; they easily succumb to the serpent's temptation to eat the forbidden fruit, which will make them like gods them-

---

[3]William J. O'Malley, "A Sane Sense of Sin," *America* 172 (April 8, 1995) 11.

selves. The result is that their innocence is lost forever; their sin turns creation upside down, and they experience a threefold alienation. They find themselves alienated from each other, from the natural world in which they live, and from God (Gen 3:7-19). There is great insight in this story. Adam and Eve's refusal to acknowledge the one who alone is God in their desire to become gods themselves is catastrophic; if one reads the following chapters carefully, it is evident that there is now something new in the world, an evil that is the direct result of this egotism on the part of humankind. The very next story is of fratricide, and before long the increasing human wickedness brings about the Great Flood. Only through God's direct intervention is the story of humankind able to continue.

The Ten Commandments

The Genesis prehistory shows how sin and its disastrous effects enter the world; because of sin the intimacy with God enjoyed by our first parents is lost. But Genesis and the other books of the Pentateuch also serve as introduction to God's saving work. The great themes of election and covenant show God choosing and entering into relationship with a people. The Ten Commandments, the first expression of the covenant and the basis of the Jewish Law, spell out what it means to live in covenant relationship with Yahweh (Deut 5:6-21; cf. Exod 20:2-17):

> I, the LORD, am your God who brought you out of the land of Egypt, that place of slavery. You shall not have other gods besides me. . . .
> You shall not take the name of the LORD, your God, in vain. . . .
> Take care to keep holy the sabbath. . . .
> Honor your father and your mother. . . .
> You shall not kill. . . .
> You shall not commit adultery. . . .
> You shall not steal. . . .
> You shall not bear dishonest witness against your neighbor.
> You shall not covet your neighbor's wife.
> You shall not desire your neighbor's house or field, . . . nor anything that belongs to him.

These commandments are not understood simply as ethical norms. They represent the terms of the covenant. Failing to observe them was to step outside this covenant relationship with God. Thus there is a very personal dimension to this Hebrew understanding of sin; it means the rupture of a relationship. The two passages containing the Decalogue describe sin as a hatred of God (Exod 20:5; Deut 5:9). But since the Decalogue demands respect for others as the condition for being in relationship with God, it is clear that hatred of God and abuse of others amounts to the same thing. In the Hebrew

Scriptures some sins are particularly offensive, sins that "cry out to heaven," among them fratricide (Gen 4:10), oppressing the alien, the widow, or the orphan (Exod 2:20-22), or taking advantage of the day laborer (Deut 24:15).

Jesus

Jesus took sin for granted. He taught his disciples that sin comes from the human heart: "For from the heart come evil thoughts, murder, adultery, unchastity, theft, false witness, blasphemy" (Matt 15:19). He implied in the story of the woman taken in adultery that all are sinners, challenging those so quick to condemn the woman that whoever among them was without sin should cast the first stone (John 8:7).

St. Paul

The most systematic New Testament treatment of sin is St. Paul's Letter to the Romans. In the first half of the letter Paul presents a great drama in which the stage is the entire history of salvation. The *dramatis personae* include Adam, Sin, Death, the Law, and Christ. Adam introduces Sin into the world, and with Sin comes a companion, Death. Death is a result of Sin, indeed, it is part of that rupture of the right order of creation so evident in the Genesis story of the fall.

In Paul's theology, Sin brings about a threefold death; first, there is that temporal disintegration or death that sin brings about in our relationships. Sin alienates us from one another; it introduces divisions into the human community (Rom 3:13-17; cf. Gal 5:20). Second, Paul attributes physical death to sin. He writes that death comes to all "inasmuch as all sinned" (Rom 5:12). In other words, death comes to all not just because Adam sinned but, more precisely, because all men and women live in a world into which sin has entered and have themselves sinned personally, and so they have fulfilled the conditions for death. Sin has become part of the human condition. And finally, because sin alienates us from God, it brings about eternal death (1 Cor 6:9-10).

The fourth major character in Paul's drama, the Mosaic Law, comes on stage with Moses. What was the function of the Law? The Jews had an advantage not enjoyed by the Gentiles, for the Law served to reveal to them their sinful state. This theme was first developed in Galatians where Paul speaks of the Law as a "tutor" or "disciplinarian" (Gal 3:24) prior to the coming of Christ. He says clearly that "through the law comes consciousness of sin" (Rom 3:20) and "I do not know sin except through the law" (Rom 7:7). The Jews living under the Law were made aware of their sins, for the Law made explicit their violation of the inner law written by nature on the hearts of all people, both Jews and Gentiles (Rom 2:14-15). But Paul insists that both Jews and Gentiles have sinned.

The Law reveals sin for what it is, but it was unable to deliver the Jews from sin for it was incapable of breaking sin's power. That was the work of Christ, the one for whom Adam, the first man, was the type (Rom 5:14) in Paul's theology. If sin and death entered the world through the disobedience of one man, then it is through the obedience of Christ that the many will be made righteous and grace will reign (Rom 5:19-20).

In Romans 8 the focus of the drama has shifted; the theme is no longer sin and death but grace and life in the Spirit, not bondage and slavery but freedom, the "firstfruits" of Christ's death and resurrection (Rom 8:23). If the world has not yet been returned to the ideal order of its beginning, nonetheless justification, grace, and salvation are now available to all through Jesus Christ and in his Spirit. Prior to Romans 8 the Spirit has been referred to only five times; in chapter 8 it occurs twenty-nine times. In his First Letter to the Corinthians Paul can speak of Christ as the "last Adam" or the "second man" (1 Cor 15:45, 47). In a real sense, with Christ the human race has been re-created; hence Christ is the new Adam. Grace is Paul's word for God's gracious salvific action on our behalf and, at the same time, for the new life that comes to us as a result of God's salvific action. In its essential reality grace is our sharing in God's own life through Christ and in the Spirit.

Paul is realist enough to recognize that even for the baptized there is a continual struggle between our efforts to live in the Spirit and the desires of the flesh. In his Letter to the Galatians his distinction between the "works of the flesh" and the "fruit of the Spirit" provides a principle of discernment in terms of the quality of our lives:

> Now the works of the flesh are obvious: immorality, impurity, licentiousness, idolatry, sorcery, hatreds, rivalry, jealousy, outbursts of fury, acts of selfishness, dissensions, factions, occasions of envy, drinking bouts, orgies, and the like. I warn you, as I warned you before, that those who do such things will not inherit the kingdom of God. In contrast, the fruit of the Spirit is love, joy, peace, patience, kindness, generosity, faithfulness, gentleness, self-control (Gal 5:19-23).

To summarize, for Paul sin in its deepest meaning is much more than a question of wrong actions, of "lawbreaking." It is an existential state or ontological condition-in-the-world that affects all people because all people have sinned. Martin Luther saw this clearly. In his commentary on Psalm 51, part of which was a reflection on Romans 7, he wrote: "Two kinds of sin can be distinguished. There is, first, the whole nature corrupted by sin and subject to eternal death. There is, second, a kind of sin which a man who has the Law can recognize when such things as theft, murder, and adultery are committed. Even civil laws talk about this latter kind, though not very precisely."[4]

---

[4]"The Psalm Miserere," *Luther's Works*, ed. Jaroslav Pelikan (St. Louis: Concordia, 1955) 12:307-08.

From the Catholic perspective, Luther probably went too far in speaking of our "whole human nature corrupted by sin." Nevertheless, his fundamental insight here was correct. For Paul the real evil of sin was its existential effect, its disordering of humankind's natural orientation toward God. Sin as a state or condition means that the dynamic structure of the human person becomes increasingly directed toward the self and thus toward death rather than toward God and life. The word Paul uses for sin, the Greek *harmartia,* means "to miss the mark" or, more generally, "to go wrong." It confirms this view of sin as a radical disordering of the person's relationship to God given in creation.

THE DOCTRINE OF SIN

In its deepest sense sin is much more than breaking rules or laws. Paul's personification of sin as a malevolent power let loose in the world is extremely apt; it is very much in the biblical tradition, which has an implicit sense of the unity of the human community and of what it means to be part of a sinful people. Our own sinfulness is in part explained by the sinful human community to which we belong. There is a solidarity in sin, just as there is a solidarity in salvation. We readily recognize the corrupting power of evil habits and that "violence breeds violence." So sin breeds sin, affecting the families into which we are born, the people with whom we come in contact, the societies in which we live. The effects of sin are dynamic; like ripples made by a pebble thrown into a pool, they radiate out from the source, affecting those around the sinner.

Original Sin

If Paul had a good sense that the sin that came into the world with Adam is a power that disorders our intentions and limits our freedom, it was Augustine (d. 430) who formulated what has come to be called "the doctrine of original sin." In large part Augustine was reacting to Pelagius (d. ca. 418), an ascetical teacher from Britain who maintained that Christians were called to a life of perfection (cf. Matt 5:48) and, once baptized, were fully able to live such a life because of the gift of free will. Pelagius' emphasis on free will seemed to make human nature itself an expression of grace. He denied that Adam's sin had any real effect on those who came after him, beyond the fact that many sinned by "imitation." One consequence of this for Pelagius was a rejection of the tradition of infant baptism, already being widely practiced. Perhaps we can best understand Pelagius as a humanist who presupposed the fundamental goodness of human nature or as a spiritual director who wanted to encourage others to strive for a life of perfection.

Augustine, who had come to Christianity late in his life and only after considerable struggle (his famous prayer, "Lord, give me chastity, but not yet," is well known),[5] had a much greater sense of the mystery of sin. His most basic experience was of the sovereign power of God's grace, which had finally freed him from his own disordered existence. Thus his personal experience greatly affected his theology. He taught that Adam's sin had not just damaged human nature but radically corrupted it, rendering the will incapable of choosing good apart from the grace it so much needed. But Augustine went considerably beyond Paul's sense of the solidarity of the human race in sin; according to Augustine, Adam's sin was passed on to each human person through sexual intercourse at the time of conception, by "generation." Thus even infants were stained by this first or "original" sin and were in need of baptism to cleanse them of this sinful condition. Augustine's theology helped explain the practice of infant baptism. It was made official Church doctrine by the provincial Synod of Carthage (418) and the Second Council of Orange (529).

In the sixteenth century both the Reformers and the Catholic theologians were strongly influenced by Augustine's theology of original sin, but they interpreted it differently. Taking Augustine at his word, the Reformers taught that human nature had been radically corrupted by Adam's sin and that the *imago Dei,* the image of God reflected in human intellect and will, had been lost. The intellect, blinded by sin, is unable to know anything of God apart from Scripture. Without the possibility of a natural knowledge of God through philosophical reflection, a split hitherto unknown opened up between reason and faith. The will is in a state of bondage, incapable of choosing good on its own. It cannot even cooperate with God's grace; justification is entirely God's work. Calvin carried this line of argument to its logical conclusion and, like Augustine, ended up with the doctrine of predestination.

In 1546 Trent reaffirmed Augustine's teaching that the sin of Adam "is passed on by propagation not by imitation" (DS 223), without necessarily embracing his negative view of sexual intercourse. It taught, against the Reformers, that baptism removes the guilt of original sin, even if "concupiscence," an inclination toward sin, remains in the lower faculties. In the Catholic view human nature is damaged by original sin but not radically corrupted; if we have lost the "likeness" of God, we are still created in God's "image."

A Contemporary Approach

How can we best understand the Church's traditional teaching on the sin of Adam today? The doctrine of original sin is rooted in the radically

---

[5] *Confessions* 8.7.

social nature of the human person. It says that each of us is born into a world or, more concretely, a network of human relationships already damaged by sin. We are constituted by our social relationships. Even prior to birth each of us has developmental needs that must be met if we are to someday fully realize our human potential. We need to be welcomed and cherished as infants if we are to be happy and secure. We need to be caressed, cuddled, and loved if we are to be able one day to love and express affection ourselves. Without a human community, with its language, culture, and personal relationships, none of us would be able to develop the ability to speak, to think abstractly, even to be self-aware. We learn to live and function as *human* beings from the human communities of which we are a part, and to a large extent we are shaped and formed by the relationships with our parents, siblings, and those who are closest to us.

Because those relationships have themselves been damaged by the egotism, the disordered affections, the alienation that sin introduces into the world, each human being is deprived, damaged, and weakened by the sinful world into which he or she is born. Our history bears the scars of the violence, war, and injustice that embitters members of the human family against one another. Our cultures often include prejudices against those who are different from us. They teach us social roles based on gender, which are functional but also limiting. Our languages condition the way we perceive reality. Each of us has been formed, affected, and in many ways limited by our concrete historical and social circumstances, by our family, race, culture, religion, sexuality, personal environment, and interpersonal relationships. Since all of these are touched by sin, so is each of us in ways we seldom suspect. We experience ourselves often as broken; we sense that our relationships are disordered; we regret our inability to love.

This social nature of original sin, which limits human freedom even prior to its exercise, can be seen in the countless stories of children who grow up in dysfunctional homes, the victims of childhood physical or sexual abuse, the adult children of alcoholics, the youngsters in the inner-city ghetto or barrio forced by peer pressure and the insecurity of their neighborhoods into joining gangs. Not long ago a friend sent me a story written by one of her students, a seventeen-year-old Mexican American girl, written for the school newspaper. Her school was a poor one, an inner-city Catholic high school with an all-minority population, but her short story stressed how different it was from the constant threat of violence in the public schools:

> Personally, I believe that at this point in our lives we shouldn't have to deal with shootings during school or confrontations between gang members. That is something nobody should have to be exposed to.
>
> In a private school, I feel safe. Bottom line. When I walk in I don't feel afraid or intimidated. I feel like I can do anything I want—all without fear. This is the best thing about going to a private school—you are allowed to be yourself.

The point of the story is not to hold up private schools against public ones but to emphasize how much we are shaped by our environments. Original sin means that we find it very difficult to be ourselves. We all know stories of personalities damaged and lives broken, often irreparably; and even if some manage to rise above their personal histories through good fortune, character, and grace, most of those who have been the victims of sin go on to sin against others. So the pattern continues; we understand this dynamic implicitly even when we fail to see the same pattern at work in our own lives.

Though it has not always been well understood, the doctrine of original sin remains one of the greatest achievements of Christianity, one of the few doctrines, as has often been said, for which there is empirical evidence. It expresses in language that is not always adequate what today we take for granted, the radically social constitution of the human person, the infectious power of evil, the presence in our lives of negative factors prior to our own deliberate choices, our radical need for God's saving power. It is only when we can recognize ourselves as sinners that we can open ourselves to God's healing touch and accept God's forgiveness.

The Sins We Commit

The New Testament recognizes that sin leads to death (Rom 6:16; 1 Cor 6:9-10), but it is also aware that not all sin is "deadly" (1 John 5:16-17). The tradition has identified seven deadly or "capital" sins: pride, avarice, envy, anger, lust, gluttony, and sloth. It has also distinguished between "mortal" (i.e., deadly) sin and "venial" sin: mortal sin is an offense that destroys our relationship with God, while a venial sin damages that relationship without completely severing it.

The distinction is a helpful one. Obviously there are less serious sins, or serious sins that are lessened through ignorance or a diminished freedom, what the tradition calls "lack of full consent." We fail many times a day in our relationships with one another, both by commission and by omission. Yet we have not separated ourselves from God's grace and can open ourselves to God's life within us in new ways. At the same time, there are sins of such gravity that they break our relationship with God, or perhaps more accurately, so consume us and focus our attention on ourselves and our own desires that God is effectively excluded from our lives. To commit such a sin, the matter must be serious and our freedom must be fully involved. In language still current in the Church, Thomas Aquinas taught that a mortal sin is one that involves grave matter, sufficient reflection, and full consent of the will.[6]

---

[6] *Summa theologiae* I–II.88.2.6.

If the distinction between mortal and venial sin is useful, it is also true that it tends to trivialize lesser sins by making them seem unimportant, as though someone might say, "It's only a venial sin." Traditional theology taught that no number of venial sins could ever add up to one mortal sin. But what such an approach overlooks is that repeated sins tend to weaken our will and deepen within ourselves destructive habits that can gradually and subtly change our primary orientation from God to ourselves. When we become completely focused on ourselves, we have died spiritually.

Some contemporary theologians have used the term "fundamental option" to describe the process through which a person's basic moral stance emerges and is shaped by all the decisions made in the course of one's life. From this perspective it is difficult to say at which point or in which particular decision one's basic stance toward God and others has been determined, though over the whole of a person's life a pattern or direction is clearly evident. Each choice of good or evil is significant, even if some sins are more serious than others. For example, it is difficult to say that deliberately missing Mass on a particular Sunday would be equivalent to breaking one's relationship with God. But a habit of missing Mass or an attitude that does not take seriously one's need to worship God regularly and to take one's place within the community gathered in prayer might lead to a gradual erosion of that relationship to the point where it ceases to exist. We all know too well how easy a relationship with someone we love can die from lack of attention.

Neither the concept of a fundamental option nor the distinction between mortal and venial sin provides a completely satisfactory explanation of our own involvement in the mystery of evil. The distinction has a long history in the Catholic tradition. It recognizes that some acts are objectively evil and some sins so grave that they include a rejection of God's love. Its emphasis on the need for sufficient reflection and full consent respects the complex nature of our motivation and the often diminished capacity of our freedom. At the same time, it can easily lead to a legalistic attitude (how much? how far?), to trivializing lesser sins, and to scrupulosity.

Fundamental option language is less objective and juridical, more psychological. It recognizes the complex nature of moral consciousness and the importance of choice and behavior in personal development. It represents a more personal, biblical understanding that sees sin not primarily in terms of rules but in terms of relationships. Sin alienates us from God and from one another. Both approaches have much to contribute in our efforts to understand our own frailty and our capacity to do wrong, to sin.

Social Sin

In recent years terms such as "sinful structures," "institutionalized violence," and "social sin" have become part of the vocabulary of moral theology.[7] Liberation theology in particular has contributed to this, but the notion that social structures could be affected by the sin present in the world and in turn contribute to destructive or sinful conduct on the part of others is already present in Vatican II's Pastoral Constitution on the Church in the Modern World (GS 25). The Latin American bishops at Medellín (1968) spoke of "a situation of injustice that can be called institutionalized violence."[8] We could add racism, sexism, militarism, and environmental pollution as further examples of social sin.

Pope John Paul II recognizes social sin in a qualified sense; in his apostolic exhortation *Reconciliatio et paenitentia* he states that social sin must be understood as "sin by analogy" (no. 16). In his encyclical *Sollicitudo rei socialis* he uses the term "structures of sin," but he stresses that these structures are always rooted in the personal sins of individuals; as the network of these structures grows and spreads, they become the source of new sins on the part of others (no. 36).

In what sense can we speak of social sin? In the strict sense an institution or structure cannot be the subject of a moral act, since only persons are capable of moral decisions. But insofar as structures embody the decisions and reflect the interests of sinful human beings, they can be moral or immoral, and the power for evil they can exert is considerable. The Church has not hesitated to direct its social teachings not just to individuals but also to groups and social systems.[9] Laws, social structures, economic systems, and states can embody the narrow self-interest of individuals and power groups within a society; if they violate human rights, victimize the powerless, or institutionalize an unjust distribution of goods, they can be said to be sinful or unjust. What is perhaps most destructive about evil structures is that because of our social nature we are necessarily implicated in them. We either take them for granted as the way things are or because we benefit from them, or we may in desperation react violently against them. From this perspective of passivity or complicity in the face of evil, or of becoming involved in evil oneself in reacting against it, the truly destructive power of sinful structures becomes more evident.

Here is where social sin comes in. According to Joseph McKenna, social sin entails "a morally culpable, irresponsible accommodation to a structural evil, an evil that should rather be resisted."[10] We often have a sense of our complicity in social evil and of our need to be cleansed of the accompanying guilt. We feel tainted by the violence and racism in our society, but unlike the people of Israel, who had their rituals and days of atonement (Lev 4:13-29; Num 29:7-11; Ps 106), we lack sacramental rituals to cleanse ourselves of our

[7]See Mark O'Keefe, *What Are They Saying About Social Sin?* (New York: Paulist, 1990) 13–17.

[8]CELAM II, "Peace," no. 17.

[9]See Peter J. Henriot, Edward P DeBerri, and Michael J. Schultheis, eds., *Catholic Social Teaching: Our Best Kept Secret* (Maryknoll, N.Y.: Orbis, 1988).

[10]"The Possibility of Social Sin," *The Irish Theological Quarterly* 60 (1994) 130.

complicity in such sin. Perhaps the Church might someday celebrate a communal penance service with general absolution for the social sins of which we as a people are so obviously guilty.

FORGIVENESS AND RECONCILIATION

Jesus talked much more about forgiveness than about sin. He proclaimed the forgiveness of sins in his preaching, illustrated it in his parables, and enabled others to experience it through his table fellowship (cf. Mark 2:15). The command to proclaim the forgiveness of sins was part of the Easter message (John 20:23).

Penance and Reconciliation

The early Church was slow to develop a ritual celebration of forgiveness beyond the sacrament of baptism. Perhaps the early Christians assumed naively that those who had found new life in Christ and had been baptized would be able to live lives that were free from sin. Nevertheless, from the beginning the Christian community was aware of the damaging effects of sin upon its members and provided ways for dealing with serious offenders. At Corinth Paul ordered that a man living in an incestuous relationship with his stepmother be excluded from the community (1 Cor 5:1-13). In another case he urged the community to forgive and welcome back a member who had been disciplined for some offense (2 Cor 5:5-11). Matthew's Gospel sees the community's leaders as having the final authority of "binding and loosing," that is, excluding sinners and readmitting those who had repented, as in the synagogue tradition (Matt 18:15-18). A few communities refused in certain cases to welcome back repentant sinners (Heb 6:4-8).

Some early post-New Testament documents *(1 Clement; Didache)* spoke of postbaptismal forgiveness and reconciliation, though the *Shepherd of Hermas* spoke of it as a "second chance," which was interpreted to mean only once. By the late second and early third centuries a penitential discipline similar to that of the catechumenate began to appear. Those guilty of serious sin—apostasy, murder, adultery—entered an order of penitents; they were excluded from the assembly after the Liturgy of the Word and could only be readmitted to the full liturgy by the bishop after a period of prayer and penance. In some Churches those entering the order of penitents received ashes on their foreheads as a sign of repentance, from which was to develop the celebration of Ash Wednesday, which marks the beginning of the season of Lent.

This process of "canonical penance," sometimes described as a "second and more laborious baptism," was a rigorous one, particularly in the Western

Church. First, since those in the order of penitents were segregated from the rest of the congregation, it was public. Second, a person could seek this reconciliation only once. By the sixth century it had fallen into disuse; most people chose to wait for sacramental reconciliation until they were on their deathbeds, despite various efforts on the part of popes and councils to revive the practice.

From the sixth century on, a new celebration of forgiveness, introduced to Europe by the Irish monks, began to grow in popularity. The practice had its roots in the monastic tradition, where a monk seeking direction and guidance would confess his sins to another member of the community—not necessarily a priest—and would receive an assurance of God's forgiveness. What this represented was private confession rather than public penance, and a person could practice it repeatedly. In place of the lengthy period of public penance, the "confessor" would assign a particular penance such as abstaining from certain foods for lesser sins, or from marital intercourse or the use of weapons for more serious sins such as adultery or the shedding of blood. The practical Irish monks collected these penances in books called "penitentials" as an aid for confessors.

The Church on the continent reacted to this practice as an abuse; various councils and synods tried to proscribe it. But it obviously met a real pastoral need, and by the tenth century it had become almost the universal practice. Acknowledging this, the Fourth Lateran Council decreed in 1215 that every Christian who had committed a serious sin should confess it within the year. Note that the law, which still remains in effect, requires that one should go to confession yearly *only if* he or she has a serious sin to confess; there are many who still mistakenly believe that one has to confess prior to receiving the Eucharist. Thus private confession was no longer to be considered an abuse; it had become the rule.

For many American Catholics who grew up in the years prior to the Second Vatican Council, frequent confession was the norm. Behind this practice lies the overemphasis on sin so much a part of the preconciliar American Catholic ethos or worldview, which historian Jay Dolan has described by its four central traits: "authority, sin, ritual, and the miraculous."[11] This "devotional Catholicism," strongly influenced by Augustine's pessimism, saw the threat of sin everywhere. Prayer books and devotional guides, lengthy examinations of conscience, the Sacred Heart devotion with its emphasis on reparation for sin, parish missions with sermons on hell and vivid descriptions of the torments of condemned sinners, a suspicion of the secular world, and most of all, the practice of frequent confession were all a part of what Dolan calls a "culture of sin."[12]

[11] *The American Catholic Experience* (Garden City, N.Y.: Doubleday, 1985) 221.
[12] Ibid., 226–27.

One effect of this culture of sin was that many Catholics imagined God as a stern judge, keeping careful records and waiting for a person to make a mistake. Many devout Catholics went to confession several times a month, or even weekly. In Catholic schools children were excused from class to go to confession prior to the "First Friday" of each month, when of course they were expected to attend Mass. Today this practice of frequent confession is spoken of as "confessions of devotion" (as opposed to confessions of oblig-ation), since most people went to the sacrament even though they did not have serious sins to confess. Like so much in devotional Catholicism, the practice of frequent confession did not long survive the council.

Reconciliation Today

Many Catholics today find sacramental reconciliation difficult. Some who grew up with the practice of frequent confession still feel the need to list all their failings, no matter how insignificant. Some have given up sacra-mental reconciliation because they don't find these "laundry lists" of sins, real or imagined, especially meaningful. Others are uncomfortable because they are not really sure how one "goes to confession" today. I have often had the experience of a student who knows me primarily as a teacher asking, "Do you *do* confessions?"

The fact that for many centuries in the life of the Church a person could receive ritual sacramental reconciliation only once and then only for certain very serious sins is clear evidence that the Christian community then, as now, recognized a number of ways of experiencing the grace of forgiveness. The New Testament teaches us that our sins are forgiven when we acknowl-edge them honestly (Luke 18:9-14; 1 John 1:9) or confess them to one an-other (Jas 5:16). We can ask God humbly for forgiveness in prayer. The penitential rite at the beginning of the liturgy can be a rich experience of for-giveness when we enter into it with sorrow for something for which we are especially regretful.

Sacramental reconciliation can be a particularly healing grace, for it en-ables us to hear God's assurance of forgiveness from one authorized by the Church to act in its name and thus in the person of Christ. It is not so hard to say in a general sense that we are sinners. We can do this without any per-sonal disclosure and so with less personal investment. But to acknowledge that I have been dishonest or damaged another's reputation or taken ad-vantage of a friend is much more difficult; it demands that we look at our behavior honestly, that we acknowledge before our confessor that we have fallen far short of the life of holiness to which we are called.

In its essential nature sacramental reconciliation is a dialogue between two people, the penitent, whose sins have diminished the community and raised an obstacle in the penitent's relationship with God, and the priest, who represents both Christ and the Church. The penitent acknowledges that he or she is a sinner, confesses those sins most on their mind, and asks for absolution. The confessor listens carefully, suggests a penance, often prays with the penitent, and assures him or her of God's forgiveness through the Church's formula of sacramental absolution. The dialogue between priest and penitent and the sorrow and purpose of amendment it expresses are far more important than any formula or "right words." Someone unfamiliar with the rite or overwhelmed with confusion or sorrow only has to ask for help.

New Rite of Penance

The new Rite of Penance, issued by the Sacred Congregation for Divine Worship in 1973, provides three forms of the rite. The first is for individual confession and absolution. The second provides for a communal penance service with individual confession and absolution. The third allows for general absolution, but only in certain situations; the number of people present must be too great for individual confessions and those who receive it "must resolve to confess in due time each one of the grave sins" he or she was unable to confess (no. 33). In this new rite the emphasis is much more on healing and reconciliation than on a juridical remission of sins; thus it is usually referred to as "the sacrament of reconciliation."

For the individual rite of reconciliation the whole atmosphere is different. Most churches now provide a reconciliation room, a room comfortably arranged with a table holding the Scripture and often a candle, for the celebration of the sacrament. Although the penitent still has the option of confessing anonymously, most choose now to sit facing the confessor.

The priest welcomes the penitent with some greeting or word of encouragement, usually from Scripture. The priest may read—if time permits— a short passage of Scripture, after which the penitent confesses his or her sins, beginning by saying something like "Bless me father, for I have sinned" or "I accuse myself of . . . and ask for God's pardon and for absolution. . . ." The priest then suggests a penance, some prayer, work of mercy, or symbolic action done as a sign of sorrow and reparation. Then he invites the penitent to pray for forgiveness and healing. Many Catholics are accustomed at this time to say the Act of Contrition, but any prayer asking God's help and forgiveness, whether said aloud or in silence, would suffice. Finally, the priest extends his hand and prays the prayer of absolution, and the penitent responds by saying "Amen."

The new Rite of Penance makes possible more of a dialogue between priest and penitent than the old rite did. Many of those who take advantage of the sacrament find it to be an opportunity for some brief spiritual conversation; they receive the sacrament less frequently but with greater preparation and reflection.

HEALING AND THE ANOINTING OF THE SICK

The sacrament of reconciliation is a sacrament of healing. When we acknowledge our sins and failings, we open ourselves to God's transforming grace. Grace reconciles us to God and begins the process of healing the negative effects of evil and sin in our lives and the lives of others, enabling us to become involved in healing the hurt that our sins have brought about between ourselves and others. The Eucharist is also a sacrament of healing, renewing the covenant God has made with us (SC 10).

Healing grace, however, is not limited to these sacraments. From New Testament times the Church has invoked God's healing grace on the sick with prayer and ritual. The author of the Letter of James writes: "Is anyone among you sick? He should summon the presbyters of the church, and they should pray over him and anoint [him] with oil in the name of the Lord, and the prayer of faith will save the sick person, and the Lord will raise him up. If he has committed any sins, he will be forgiven" (Jas 5:14-15). The Church prays that the healing grace of Christ might touch the whole person, not just for physical healing, but that the one sick might find forgiveness and hope.

Sacrament of the Sick

Evidence for this sacrament is sparse in the early centuries. Hippolytus speaks of the bishop blessing oil with a prayer, that it might "give strength to all that taste of it and health to all that use it" (*Apostolic Tradition* 5). In the early centuries the oil blessed by the bishop was used in a number of ways for healing. Sometimes the sick would drink it, or they might anoint themselves with it. Or family members would anoint them, accompanying the anointing with a "prayer of faith." The time of the Carolingian reform (740–840) saw the appearance of ritual books that included rites for anointing the sick and Viaticum, the Eucharistic "food for the journey." These books were to be used by priests in administering the sacrament of penance to the dying. From this time on, the anointing of the sick was restricted to priests, and the rite became increasingly associated with a preparation for death and the forgiveness of sins.[13] In the twelfth century Peter Lombard included this "last anointing" in his list of the seven sacraments. Hence the unfortunate name "extreme unction," by which the sacrament was known up to the time of Vatican II.

In its renewal of the sacrament, the council pointed out that extreme unction could also and more fittingly be called "anointing of the sick," stressing that it "is not a sacrament for those only who are at the point of death" (SC 73). Today it is understood as a sacrament for health and healing; it is

[13]See John J. Ziegler, *Let Them Anoint the Sick* (Collegeville: The Liturgical Press, 1987) 68–70.

celebrated for the seriously ill, the aged, those preparing for major surgery, and sometimes for those suffering from psychological trauma. It can be a powerful experience for all these people, helping them find God's grace precisely in their illness or disability or nearness to death.

The revised rite specifically situates sacramental anointing in the broader context of the pastoral care of the sick.[14] Among its most important elements are the proclamation of the word, the prayer of faith, the laying on of hands, and the anointing of the forehead and hands with oil. Particularly important is the human touch. Jesus cured the sick by touching them (Mark 1:41; 8:23; Luke 4:40). The human touch in the laying on of hands helps bridge the isolation so often experienced by the sick, especially the terminally ill. Think of the isolation so often experienced by people with AIDS. The sick need to know that they are not alone, that friends, loved ones, and the Church are with them. For the same reason, the sacrament should be celebrated communally; it can be done at the Eucharist or, in the case of someone confined to bed, in the presence of family members who add their prayers to those of the priest. Pastoral care of the sick involves more than the priest. Anointing with the oil of the sick recalls one's baptismal anointing and thus his or her incorporation into Christ and his paschal mystery.

CONCLUSION

Contemporary thinkers often use the presence of so much suffering and evil in the world as an argument against the existence of God. So much suffering, particularly of the innocent, is an obstacle to belief. How could a good God create such a world, how could an all-powerful God permit such suffering? Why does God remain silent?

The mystery of evil is not easily understood. From the very beginning the biblical tradition insists that creation is good. The first creation story celebrates God's victory over the forces of chaos to create a world of beauty and order (Gen 1:1–2:4a). The problem lies not in the created world but in the hearts of the creatures God placed at its center, man and woman, created in the divine image, capable of receiving and responding to love but also capable of rejecting this gift. Because we are created in freedom, God cannot force our love; God can only invite us to respond in freedom. With freedom comes the possibility of sin, which enters the world by the free choice of human beings. The biblical tradition emphasizes the pervasive reality of sin; it is a force let loose in our world that brings suffering, death, and destruction in its wake.

---

[14] The revised rite was originally called the *Rite of Anointing and Pastoral Care of the Sick;* it was revised and translated as *Pastoral Care of the Sick: Rites of Anointing and Viaticum* (Washington: ICEL, 1982).

But rather than acknowledge the destructive power of sin, we tend to blame suffering and evil on God.

Part of the problem is a natural tendency to overemphasize the power of God. We frequently think of God in philosophical terms, speaking of God as "omnipotent." In fact, as Pope John Paul II suggests, God's very creation of a universe of freedom can be understood as a self-limitation of the divine power: "In a certain sense one could say that *confronted with our human freedom, God decided to make Himself 'impotent.'*"[15] God cannot *not* respect our freedom. Therefore, rather than seeing God as the immediate cause of every event, it makes more sense to image a long-suffering and compassionate God mysteriously at work bringing good out of evil, victory out of defeat, life out of death. Nowhere is this shown more clearly than in the death and resurrection of Jesus.

The view of sin that emerges in the Bible is thus a personal one; sin ruptures our relationship with God and alienates us from one another. The ultimate malice of sin is revealed in its overcoming Jesus, the "Righteous One" (Acts 3:13; 7:52), bringing about his death. Yet his death and resurrection reveals God's great victory over sin, breaking its power once and for all and establishing a new covenant in Christ's blood (Luke 22:20). In writing to the Corinthians, Paul speaks of the mystery of the cross as "the weakness of God," which is stronger than human strength (1 Cor 1:25).

It was only in the fifth century that Augustine formulated what was to become the doctrine of original sin, but its roots are to be found in St. Paul, and we can experience its effects in our own lives. Each of us is affected by our birth into a sinful world and stands in need of God's mercy; we are aware of our own sinfulness, that we are broken, that we need to be healed and set free. We can sin by omission as well as by commission, as Jesus taught in his parable about the day of judgment: "I was hungry and you gave me no food, I was thirsty and you gave me no drink, . . ." (Matt 25:31-46).

Penance and the anointing of the sick are sacraments of healing. Preaching the forgiveness of sins was central to the ministry of Jesus, and the Church has continued to proclaim forgiveness in his name (John 20:23). In Church history sacramental reconciliation has taken different forms. If Catholics today take part in the new Rite of Penance less frequently than in the recent past when the practice of confessions of devotion was so widespread, many find more fruit in the sacrament, with its emphasis on prayer, healing, and reconciliation. Many parishes today have communal penance services with the opportunity for individual confession as part of their observance of Advent and Lent.

The healing ministry of Jesus continues to be made visible in the sacrament of the anointing of the sick. This sacrament too has taken on various

---

[15] *Crossing the Threshold of Hope,* ed. Vittorio Messori (New York: Random House, 1994) 61.

forms and emphases in its history. The new rite stresses healing of the sick from the effects of evil and sin, that is, from sickness, suffering, and our fear of death. It brings Christ's healing grace and strengthens those close to death with the promise of the resurrection.

8. Sexual Morality and Social Justice

Christian discipleship should inform both our interpersonal and our social lives. Sexual morality is concerned with the appropriate expression of the drive for intimacy, love, and generativity, which plays such an important role in our interpersonal relationships. Social justice describes what happens when our societies are organized in such a way that each person is respected and all are able to participate in the social, political, and economic life of the community. The issues raised by both of these areas touch us personally. Both have been addressed extensively by the teaching authority of the Church, and both are areas of controversy that generate considerable emotion, concern, and very different reactions to Church authority.

Some Catholics today disagree with Church teaching on questions of birth control, divorce and remarriage, sexual relations outside of marriage and between committed homosexuals, and (to a lesser extent) abortion. Other Catholics, who accept the Church's teachings on these issues, have considerable difficulty accepting its teaching in the areas of social justice, for example, on the right of peoples to immigrate, the question of using nuclear weapons as a deterrent, and the implications of the principle of distributive justice, which affirms the right of all members of a national community to participate equitably in its economic life. Similarly, in the past some Catholics disagreed with the Church's teaching on the right of workers to join unions or with its condemnation of the evil of racism and segregation. In this chapter we need to consider both sexual morality and social justice.

SEXUAL MORALITY

It is only honest to acknowledge that the Catholic Church has been profoundly ambivalent in its attitude toward human sexuality. On the one hand, it has always recognized sexuality as a good, a gift of God given to our first parents for their mutual love and for bringing new life into the world. This has remained the deepest conviction of the Catholic tradition. On the other hand, the Church has often seemed fearful of sexuality's mysterious power. Echoing Augustine's pessimism, it has too often narrowed the meaning of sexual union to procreation, barely tolerated the pleasure in each other that accompanies it, and developed around it a moral theology that has tended to view sexuality in terms of disembodied acts rather than complex human relationships.

The Catholic view that human sexuality is a divine gift that finds its appropriate genital expression in a loving and exclusive relationship, open to new life, is rooted in Scripture. The Book of Genesis teaches that sex is for procreation (1:28) and mutual love (2:18-24). The Song of Songs, a frankly erotic poem, celebrates the physical love of man and woman. Jesus presupposed the divine institution of marriage and affirmed its permanence. By rejecting the provision of the Mosaic Law that allowed a man to divorce his wife but not the reverse, he taught a mutuality in sexual relationships that had not been honored in the tradition. Paul recognizes marriage as a charism, a gift of grace for the building up of the Church (1 Cor 7:7). The Letter to the Ephesians sees the intimate union of husband and wife as a great mystery *(mysterion)* that images the union of Christ and the Church (Eph 5:31-32), an intuitive understanding of what the later Church would recognize as the sacramentality of marriage.

Lisa Sowle Cahill emphasizes that the Bible sees sexuality not in isolation but always in relation to the community. Still, there are biblical texts condemning certain types of sexual acts that are considered deviant from the general norm of heterosexual, monogamous, permanent marriage. These include

> adultery (Lev 20:10; Gen 39:9; Prov 2:17; Sir 23:16-21; Exod 20:14; Deut 5:18; Mark 7:22; Matt 5:28; 15:19; 1 Cor 6:9); fornication (Sir 42:10; Deut 22:13-21; Lev 19:29; *porneia* or "sexual immorality" as including fornication, Mark 7:21; Matt 15:19; 1 Cor 5:9-11; 7:2; 2 Cor 12:21; Gal 5:19; Eph 5:3, 5), homosexual acts (Lev 18:22; 20:13; Rom 1:27; 1 Cor 6:9).

Cahill presents these texts not to suggest that the Bible offers a systematic reflection on sexuality but because these acts are seen by the biblical authors as being incompatible with the life of faith in the religious community. Much more important is the nature of the community and the characteristics of the life of its members.[1]

[1]"Humanity as Female and Male: The Ethics of Sexuality," *Called to Love: Towards a Contemporary Christian Ethic,* ed. Francis A. Eigo (Villanova, Pa.: Villanova Univ. Press, 1985) 87.

Certainly the expectation is present from the beginning that those who have been baptized into Christ and into the community of his disciples should live in a way that reflects those two fundamental Christian realities. Paul instructs the community at Corinth to excommunicate one of its members who has been living in an incestuous relationship with his stepmother; his concern is not just for the individual but for the well-being of the community (1 Cor 5:1-13). Similarly, in the case of some Christians who are involved sexually with prostitutes, he argues that a union already exists between each of them and Christ, and therefore, any sexual union should reflect the holiness of this relationship (1 Cor 6:15-20). He is suggesting here a theology of sexual relations.

Development of Moral Theology

The early Christians, formed in part by the great conflict in Paul's time over circumcision and the Mosaic Law, did not understand their life in Christ in terms of a new moral law. They knew the teaching of Jesus that love of God, inseparably joined to love of neighbor, sums up at the commandments (Mark 12:29-31; Matt 22:37-40). They sought to internalize the gospel call to conversion. They were conscious of discerning the Spirit's presence in their communities and in their lives. Thus a post-New Testament Christian author, writing about how Christians lived among their neighbors but were different from them, pointed out that they didn't expose their children or share their wives with one another (*Ad Diognetus* 5).

How then did Catholic teaching on sexuality become so legalistic in its expression, so concerned with sin? John Mahoney, in his fine study of the development of Catholic moral theology, points especially to the legacy of Augustine and to the preoccupation with sin that developed in conjunction with the practice of auricular confession.[2]

Few thinkers have had a greater influence on Christian theology in the West than Augustine (354–430), bishop of Hippo. The doctrines of God, Trinity, grace, original sin, Church, sacrament, the Roman primacy—to mention just a few—bear his influence to this day. But as many have observed, there was a dark side to Augustine's thought, a profound pessimism evident in his view of the damage done by original sin to human nature and in his preoccupation with the problem of sin and evil.

This dark side was to mark Catholic theology in at least two significant ways. First, his principle that God does not command the impossible, formulated to stress the sovereign power of grace against Pelagius' emphasis on what human freedom could accomplish on its own, was to impart a rigorist di-

---

[2] *The Making of Moral Theology: A Study of the Roman Catholic Tradition* (Oxford: Clarendon, 1987).

mension to Catholic moral teaching that has carried down over the centuries. Pius XI appealed to this principle in his condemnation of contraception in *Casti connubii* (1930),[3] and John Paul II cited it in his 1993 encyclical on the principles of moral theology, *Veritatis splendor* (no. 103).[4] Some today would see this same rigorist reasoning in the Church's teaching that the only moral option for a person who is homosexual in orientation is a life of celibacy.

Second, no doubt affected by his own long and difficult struggle for chastity, Augustine saw human sexuality after the fall as so dominated by lust that the only moral end of intercourse was procreation. This Augustinian doctrine also was to have a long history in Catholic theology. In the Middle Ages theologians following Augustine continued to teach that marital intercourse for pleasure rather than for procreation was sinful—mortally according to the rigorists, or at least venially in the view of the greater number of moral theologians.[5]

Another major factor that contributed to moral theology's preoccupation with sin was the introduction in the sixth century of the practice of auricular confession. Before that, sacramental reconciliation was reserved for apostasy, adultery, and murder; it was a public ritual and could be received only once in a person's lifetime, as we have seen. But the introduction of private confession, a practice borrowed from the monastic tradition, led to the development of the penitentials, books designed as an aid to priest confessors in discovering and classifying sins and assigning their proper penances. The first penitentials, simple and unsophisticated theologically, gave way later to more systematic *summas* for confessors, particularly after the Fourth Lateran Council (1215) mandated yearly confession and Communion during the Easter season. These summas continued to proliferate—summas for confessors, summas of moral cases (particularly favored by the Jesuits), summas of moral theology—down into the mid-twentieth century. From this tradition a moral theology developed that was designed for confessors. Unfortunately, it was a moral theology cut off from dogmatic and spiritual theology. Trent's emphasis on the *judicial* role of the priest in confession contributed to its legalistic tone. Its preoccupation with sexual sins was heightened by a seventeenth-century declaration of the Vatican's Holy Office that "classified every transgression in matters of sexuality as objectively serious matter constituting mortal sin."[6]

The traditional teaching on sexuality coming from this moral theology was presupposed by Catholics—if not always honored—down to the time of

[3]Ibid., 53–54.
[4]*Origins* 23 (October 14, 1993).
[5]John T. Noonan, *Contraception* (Cambridge, Mass.: Harvard Univ. Press, 1965) 251–52.
[6]Mahoney, *Making of Moral Theology*, 33.

the Second Vatican Council. But after the council the credibility of that teaching began to erode. In this process Church teaching on artificial contraception played a key role. Many had hoped that the council's reforms would soften the Church's strict approach to questions regarding sexuality. There were some encouraging signs. The council, in avoiding the traditional language of the "primary and secondary ends of marriage," finally moved away from the subordination of the mutual love of the spouses to procreation, which had been the Church's position since at least Augustine's time (GS 48–50).

In 1963 Pope John XXIII appointed an international committee to investigate the Church's traditional ban on contraception, particularly in response to the anovulant "birth control pill" developed by Dr. John Rock and others in the late 1950s. But in 1967 Pope Paul VI rejected contraceptive methods in his encyclical *Humanae vitae*. Commentators on Catholic theology have made the point that *Humanae vitae* dealt the teaching authority of the magisterium a blow from which it has yet to recover.[7]

But there were other factors as well that contributed to a loss of confidence in the Church's sexual doctrine, among them the so-called sexual revolution in the late 1960s and early 1970s, helped by the wide availability of contraceptive pills, the women's movement, and an increasing dissent from the magisterium's sexual doctrine (particularly after *Humanae vitae*) on the part of Catholic theologians.

In 1976, concerned that even faithful Christians were "unsettled," the Congregation for the Doctrine of the Faith published a "Declaration on Certain Questions Concerning Sexual Ethics."[8] The declaration reaffirmed the Church's traditional teachings in no uncertain terms. These teachings, it argued, are based on certain precepts of the natural law that have "an absolute and immutable value" (no. 4). According to Christian doctrine, "every genital act must be within the framework of marriage" (no. 7); thus any sexual acts outside of that context are forbidden. The declaration singled out masturbation, premarital sex, and homosexual acts for special consideration and reaffirmed the tradition that there is no "parvity of matter" where sex is concerned: "The moral order of sexuality involves such high values of human life that every direct violation of this order is objectively sinful" (no. 10).[9]

It is not the place in a book such as this to enter into an involved discussion of all the questions raised today in regard to the Catholic Church and sexuality. It will have to suffice to present the Church's official teaching

---

[7]See, for example, George Gallup Jr. and Jim Castelli, *The American Catholic People: Their Beliefs, Practices, and Values* (Garden City, N.Y.: Doubleday, 1987) 51.

[8]*Origins* 5 (1976) 485–94.

[9]For a survey of reactions to the declaration, see Richard A. McCormick, "Notes on Moral Theology," *Theological Studies* 38 (1977) 100–14.

and, at the same time, to point out some of the questions that are being raised today by Catholic moral theologians. We will consider birth control, abortion, masturbation, premarital sex, and homosexual relations.

Birth Control

Although contraception by any means had been condemned by theologians since at least the fourth century, it did not become a critical question until the end of the nineteenth, when the practice of birth control began to become more common in Europe. After a number of statements against contraception by national hierarchies and a qualified approval of contraceptive methods by the 1930 Lambeth Conference of Anglican bishops, Pope Pius XI condemned any form of contraception in his encyclical on marriage, *Casti connubii* (1930). Pius XII moved Catholic teaching forward a step in 1951 when, in his address to the Italian Society of Catholic Midwives, he approved periodic abstinence during a woman's fertile period for the purpose of avoiding conception, provided there was sufficient reason. This was the so-called rhythm method.

With the appearance of contraceptive pills in the 1950s, the question of artificial contraception was raised with a new intensity. Paul VI did not want the Second Vatican Council to enter into the discussion of the question; instead, he expanded to sixty-nine members the international commission set up by John XXIII to study the Church's teaching on contraception.

In 1967 the commission voted sixty-four to four (Archbishop Karol Wojtyla—later Pope John Paul II—did not attend the meeting) in favor of changing the traditional teaching that all use of contraceptives was immoral. Nevertheless, after an agonizing consideration of the issue, Paul VI reaffirmed the traditional ban in his 1968 encyclical, *Humanae vitae,* arguing that "each and every marriage act must remain open to the transmission of life" (no. 11) because of the inseparable link between the unitive and procreative meanings of the sexual act (no. 12).

Few questions have been as divisive for contemporary Roman Catholicism as this papal teaching against contraception. The encyclical represents an authoritative but noninfallible exercise of the magisterium, as the Vatican pointed out at the time it was released. Episcopal conferences in as many as thirteen countries showed a tendency to mitigate the papal position in their responses.[10] Charles Curran, a moral theologian at that time at The Catholic University of America, authored a statement dissenting from the pope's position; Curran argued that spouses could responsibly decide according to their conscience that artificial contraception in some circumstances

[10]See Vincent J. Genovesi, *In Pursuit of Love: Catholic Morality and Human Sexuality* (Wilmington: Glazier, 1987) 237–38.

is permissible and indeed necessary to preserve and foster the values and sacredness of marriage. Over six hundred theologians, priests and academics, signed his statement. Today many theologians take the position that the unitive and procreative meanings of sexuality need to be kept together in principle, but not necessarily in every act of intercourse.

The debate sparked by *Humanae vitae* has continued over the years.[11] At the 1980 Synod of Bishops on the family in Rome, Archbishop John R. Quinn of San Francisco spoke for many—laity, clergy, and no doubt a number of bishops—when he observed that there was widespread opposition among Catholics to the encyclical's teaching on the intrinsic evil of each and every use of contraceptives. He cited a study that indicated that 76.5 percent of American Catholic women were using some form of birth control, and 94 percent of these were using methods condemned by the encyclical. Quinn suggested that the Church try to create a new context for its teaching on contraception emphasizing what the Church has said about responsible parenthood; that it begin a dialogue with theologians on the problems raised by dissent from the teachings of *Humanae vitae;* and that careful attention be given to the way in which encyclicals are written and communicated.[12]

Abortion

If the traditional teaching of the Church against contraception has not been widely received by the Catholic faithful, the situation in regard to abortion is quite different. Most Catholics today believe that to directly terminate life in the womb is a serious moral evil, even if not all of them are agreed on how best to address the problem of abortion in a pluralistic society such as the United States.

From its earliest days the Catholic tradition has been against abortion.[13] The *Didache,* which dates from the early second century, teaches that "you shall not kill a child by abortion, nor kill it at birth" (2.2). It was only in the second half of the twentieth century that this tradition began to be challenged by an increasingly secular world, giving rise to a number of papal and episcopal statements concerned in part with the relation between law and morality.[14] On January 22, 1973, the U.S. Supreme Court handed down its *Roe v. Wade* decision on abortion, permitting the direct termination of pregnancy up to the end of the third trimester. The Congregation for the Doctrine of the

[11]For a survey of reactions to the encyclical see Richard A. McCormick, "Notes on Moral Theology," *Theological Studies* 30 (1969) 635–44; 40 (1979) 80–97.

[12]"New Context for Contraception Teaching," *Origins* 10 (1980) 263–67.

[13]See John Connery, *Abortion: The Development of the Roman Catholic Perspective* (Chicago: Loyola Univ. Press, 1977).

[14]Richard A. McCormick, "Notes on Moral Theology," *Theological Studies* 35 (1974) 325.

Faith issued its *Declaration on Procured Abortion* in November 1974. The 1983 revised Code of Canon Law states that "a person who procures a completed abortion incurs an automatic excommunication" (can. 1398). Pope John Paul II's 1995 encyclical *Evangelium vitae* reaffirmed in the strongest terms the Church's teaching on abortion, stressing that all are called to a greater responsibility to protect innocent human life.

Although the Church has not determined officially when human life actually begins, it has taken the course of maintaining that human life is present from the moment of conception or fertilization. This means that it considers any intervention such as an I.U.D. (intrauterine device) or a "morning after" pill, which prevents a fertilized ovum from becoming implanted in the wall of the uterus, as an abortifacient.

A number of Catholic theologians such as Richard McCormick, Charles Curran, Bernard Häring, and Karl Rahner suggest that discoveries in reproductive biology make it unlikely that an individual human life can be present until two or three weeks after fertilization. "Hominization" requires two changes to take place in the early embryo. First, it must pass the stage of "twinning," the stage during which the embryo can divide into two or more, after which there is the certainty that the individuality of one or more embryos has been established. Second, it must change "from a cellular form of human life to a form which begins to display the differentiation characteristic of the human organism."[15] This argument leaves a limited period of fourteen to twenty-one days, a gray area within which, for serious reasons such as rape or incest, an early embryo might be terminated. Others, however, argue that human life is so sacred that even potential human life must be protected. Indeed, it is important to note that Church documents "generally place the fight against abortion in the larger context of respect for life at all stages and in all areas."[16]

A therapeutic abortion, removing a fetus for medical reasons such as an embryo that has become lodged in the fallopian tube and thus cannot develop to term (ectopic pregnancy) or in the process of removing a cancerous uterus, is a different question. Such procedures would constitute an indirect abortion; they are permissible and necessary to save the life of the mother.

How can the Church win a greater hearing for its position on the sanctity of life? In a recent article Todd David Whitmore has made the case that the Church's position would be much stronger if it subsumed the language of "right to life" under its traditional notion of the "common good," and if it set abortion in the context of the issue of gender roles in society. Using a survey that lists as the most common reason for having an abortion the inability to

---

[15]See Carol A. Tauer, "The Tradition of Probabilism and the Moral Status of the Early Embryo," *Theological Studies* 45 (1984) 5–6.

[16]McCormick, "Notes on Moral Theology," 35 (1974) 490–91.

continue work or education if the pregnancy were brought to term, he argues that the Church needs to more adequately recognize women's rights to participate in the public realm, so that "reproductive freedom" is not perceived as the only way to guarantee that right.

At the present time, despite some helpful steps in this direction on the part of the American bishops, the Church continues to treat social roles along gender lines, stressing women's role in the home and family without adequately recognizing their right to participate equally in the public realm. One way to do so would be to teach that men also have responsibilities in the domestic realm, so that the question of child care would be a joint discernment within a family and not merely the responsibility of the woman. In the case of single women, the Catholic community as an eschatological community should be willing to provide support for raising a child that is at least commensurate with the sacrifices it expects of the woman. Since raising a child is an eighteen-year commitment, that means much more than offering one year of support.[17]

Masturbation

Magisterial pronouncements against masturbation occur as early as the eleventh century.[18] The doctrine of no "parvity of matter" where sexual sins are concerned has contributed to masturbation assuming an inflated importance in Catholic moral theology and probably in the lives of many Catholics as well. Today opinions vary widely on the subject. Many see masturbation as a normal part of adolescent sexual awakening and maturing. In such cases there is often a diminished freedom and thus a lessening of responsibility. A compulsive habit of masturbation suggests that a healthy integration of one's sexuality has not yet taken place; it would seem to have different meanings in an adolescent and an adult, a married person and someone who is single.

Most Catholic moralists are reluctant to take the view that masturbation is merely a neutral form of sexual release. They point out that phenomenologically it suggests an expression of sexuality that is self-centered, solitary, and hedonistic rather than relational, mutual, and giving and thus is a frustration of the integrative dimension of our sexual nature. To engage in masturbation knowingly and deliberately is to inhibit the integration and personal transformation that is the fruit of life in the Spirit. Vincent Genovesi wisely observes that the fact that many people who experience periods of regular masturbation that alternate with periods of abstinence suggests that these people do not accept masturbation as a good; they see it as a sign of weak-

[17]Todd David Whitmore, "Notes for a 'New, Fresh, Compelling' Statement," *America* 171 (October 8, 1994) 14–18.

[18]See John P. Dedek, *Contemporary Sexual Morality* (New York: Sheed & Ward, 1971) 51–55.

ness, an embarrassment. "But a person's very lack of complacency, the unwillingness to grant masturbation a permanent and undisputed place in one's life, argues strongly that in such circumstances masturbation may more inspire a person to humility than be an expression of basic and serious sinfulness."[19]

Premarital Sex

One of the most difficult topics to raise in a homily with undergraduates today is the subject of premarital sex. Instantly one senses a chilling of the atmosphere; heads go down, eyes are averted, the chapel becomes uncomfortably tense. Some of the couples sitting side by side are living together. As they leave the chapel at the end of the liturgy, most will look the other way rather than greet the presider. It is clear that the Church's teaching on premarital sex for many of them is unwelcome; they are not interested and some will say so explicitly.

Nor do they receive very helpful guidance from the colleges and universities they attend. At most, including Catholic ones, responsible administrators and professionals presume that students are sexually active. They are more concerned with respecting the diversity of their students than with giving anything that could be interpreted as narrowly "confessional." "Sexual responsibility" for eighteen- to twenty-two-year-olds means that sex be consensual and safe. As Michael Hunt, a Paulist priest with many years experience as a university campus minister, observes, the message is usually something like this: "We don't care how you behave sexually as long as you don't force yourself on anyone and you use a condom for safety."[20]

Catholic theologians "always and everywhere" have held that premarital intercourse is a grave sin.[21] Yet Catholics have been as much affected by changing societal attitudes toward sex as anyone else. According to Andrew Greeley, "at the present time only one out of six American Catholics thinks that premarital sex is always wrong."[22]

The Church's deepest vision in regard to human sexuality is that the unitive and procreative meanings of sexual intercourse are intrinsically related, and thus it sees an inseparable relationship between matrimonial fidelity and sexual expression. Sexual intercourse represents the total gift of each to the other; if it is loving it implies commitment. But if the outward or physical sign is not the manifestation of an inner, spiritual reality that includes an unconditioned love and gift of self, if the union of a couple's bodies is not

[19]Genovesi, *In Pursuit of Love,* 318.
[20]*College Catholics: A New Counterculture* (New York: Paulist, 1993) 52.
[21]Dedek, *Contemporary Sexual Morality,* 36.
[22]"Sex and the Single Catholic: The Decline of an Ethic," *America* 167 (1992) 345.

the symbol of the union of their spirits, their sex easily becomes exploitative. Without this self-gift and faithful commitment of each to the other, there is no community of love into which new life can be received and nurtured. The tragedy of abortion, some 1.5 million every year in the United States, occurs most often because couples enter into a sexual relationship before they are ready to welcome the new life to which it is ordered.

Today many young people use the term "relationship" to describe an exclusive but nonbinding sexual friendship. Because such relationships are essentially temporary, they are not able to realize either the unitive or the procreative meaning of sexuality. According to Richard McCormick, the Christian view is just the reverse: "It has been a Christian conviction that it is a relationship lived in the promise of permanency that prevents the collapse of sexual expression into a divisive, alienating, and destructive trivialization."[23] Or as Greeley has observed, "sex without public commitment is fraught with dangers of deception, self-deception and exploitation, particularly of women by men"[24]

Some moralists today distinguish preceremonial from premarital sex, suggesting that once the commitment is there, sexual expression might be in some cases appropriate. But others ask, is the commitment really there if it is not yet able to be made publicly? And isn't it possible that consummating their union before they are ready to make that public commitment is to cut short a process of discernment—the whole point of a period of engagement—as to whether each is able to make that commitment?

One of the reasons so many marriages fail today is that too many couples short-circuit this discernment process. Rather than letting their sexual union be the seal and expression of a love that has grown to the point where they are deeply committed to each other, they begin living together before they have learned how to talk to each other, to share their innermost feelings, to be comfortably quiet in each other's presence, to be intimate with each other in various ways short of genital expression. It is easy to confuse "good sex" with genuine love, and when the sex is no longer new or exciting, they find out that the love it was supposed to express is not there. Unfortunately, this discovery often comes too late.

A different case is presented by the adult who is neither married nor given the charism of celibacy but who may be in an intimate relationship in which there is sexual expression. Lisa Cahill raises this question; she observes that our traditional framework for evaluating sexual relations is not particularly helpful here and suggests that in such cases the Christian community must take itself as a source of moral insight. Her argument is clearly challenging the tradition. But it is difficult to disagree with her comment that

[23]McCormick, "Notes on Moral Theology," 35 (1974) 461.
[24]Greeley, "Sex and the Single Catholic," 343.

"responsibility in sexuality is no more an either/or, black-and-white matter than it is in other spheres of human moral existence, such as economics, war and peace, or respect for life. Exercises of sexuality which fulfill or depart from the norm are not all equally good or equally bad."[25]

Homosexual Relations

One of the most difficult questions facing the Christian community today is posed by its official inability to recognize faithful and exclusive relations between those who are "constitutionally homosexual" or homosexual in orientation as appropriate expressions of intimacy and love.

There are a number of explicit condemnations of homosexual relations in both the Old and New Testaments, but many contemporary commentators and biblical scholars do not see in them a condemnation of homosexual relations as such, as the concept of the constitutional homosexual was unknown until modern times. In their judgment the biblical texts are concerned with participation in idolatrous worship by consorting with male and female temple prostitutes (Lev 18:22; 20:13; Deut 23:18; cf. 1 Kgs 14:24; 15:12), a common practice in the ancient Near East, or with violation of the duty of hospitality (Gen 19:4-8), or with pederasty (1 Cor 6:9-10; 1 Tim 1:10). A more difficult text is Romans 1:24-31, where Paul is clearly talking abut homosexual relations in themselves; but the fact that he sees those he is condemning, both men and women, as giving up natural relations and choosing homosexual ones is taken as evidence that he did not understand homosexuality as a condition.[26] Other scholars of course do not agree with this interpretation, or they judge it irrelevant to the biblical condemnation.

It is clear today that a person does not choose to be homosexual, even if we are not yet sure just what causes a homosexual orientation. The *Catechism of the Catholic Church* acknowledges that a homosexual orientation is not a matter of choice (2358). Thus the term "sexual preference" is inaccurate. The Church distinguishes between homosexual orientation and homosexual activity; it is only the latter that is considered immoral. The American Catholic bishops have stated that "homosexuals, like everyone else, should not suffer from prejudice against their basic human rights. They have a right to respect, friendship and justice. They should have an active role in the Christian community."[27]

Irresponsible, promiscuous, or violent homosexual acts are as morally evil as heterosexual ones. The moral dilemma facing the Church today is

[25]Cahill, "Humanity as Female and Male," 91.

[26]For a review of this discussion see Genovesi, *In Pursuit of Love*, 262–73. See also Jeffrey S. Siker, *Homosexuality in the Church: Both Sides of the Debate* (Louisville: Westminster/John Knox, 1994).

[27] *To Live in Christ Jesus: A Pastoral Reflection on the Moral Life* (Washington: USCC, 1976) 19.

what it might say to gays and lesbians who are in stable, exclusive, and faithful relationships and who want to express their love sexually. The official Church has not been able to move beyond its traditional condemnation of homosexual acts. But many moral theologians are questioning this position today. They ask, why cannot the question be seen in a broader context, so that it includes not just the act, but the quality of the relationship? Is it realistic to insist that the only moral possibility for homosexuals is celibacy, particularly given the recognition that the charism for celibacy is precisely a charism, given to some and not to others? Should not true homosexuals be encouraged to form stable and lasting relationships, even if these relationships may sometimes involve sexual expression? These are difficult questions that will continue to trouble the Christian community.

Veritatis Splendor

Recently Pope John Paul II, himself a moral philosopher and former professor of ethics at the Catholic University of Lublin in Poland, intervened in the conversation over fundamental moral theology and its applications. In his encyclical *Veritatis splendor* (1993) his concern was to reaffirm the traditional teaching of Catholic moral theology that the negative precepts of the natural law are universally valid (no. 52). Showing a remarkable familiarity with the contemporary debate, he specifically rejected teleological, proportionalist, and consequentialist ethical theories for holding "that it is never possible to formulate an absolute prohibition of particular kinds of behavior" that would in every case be in conflict with the moral values indicated by reason and revelation (no. 75). Thus he was reaffirming the existence of "intrinsically evil acts," actions that are always wrong in themselves apart from the circumstances and intention of the one acting (no. 80). He also reaffirmed the traditional concept of mortal sin, maintaining that one's fundamental option or orientation toward God can be radically changed by particular acts (no. 70).

Veritatis splendor is a powerful restatement of the tradition. It deserves careful consideration, the religious respect, and the obedience *(obsequium religiosum)* that is owed to an authoritative teaching of the ordinary papal magisterium (LG 25). But Catholics and other Christians will probably continue to raise questions of their tradition and the teaching of their Churches as they seek to integrate their personal and sexual lives with the gospel call to discipleship.

SOCIAL JUSTICE

Perhaps one of the Second Vatican Council's most significant documents was its Pastoral Constitution on the Church in the Modern World, *Gaudium et spes*. This document, with its vision of the Church at the service of the world (GS 3) and its call for Christians to come to the relief of the poor (GS 69), was to inspire many Catholics to play an active role in the various liberation movements that have marked the latter part of the twentieth century.

But it is by no means the only example of recent Catholic magisterial teaching on social justice and human rights. The roots of the Church's social teaching are to be found in the prophetic writings of the Hebrew Scripture and in a rich tradition of Catholic social thought that includes over the centuries thinkers such as Augustine, Aquinas, Suarez, von Ketteler, Maritain, and John Courtney Murray as well as a tradition of papal social encyclicals reaching back over the last hundred years.

The Social Encyclicals

The social encyclicals of the popes represent the most recent ecclesial expression of the Church's social teaching. From Leo XIII's *Rerum novarum* (1891) on the rights of workers, these social encyclicals have expanded in focus to embrace issues of development and economic justice between nations, technology and the arms race, the widening gap between the rich and the poor, and a critique of both communism and capitalism. At the heart of this social teaching and grounding its pro-life stance is Catholicism's profound conviction of the preeminent value of every human person created in the image of God (GS 12). It is, unfortunately, a tradition too little known to most contemporary Catholics.[28] Richard P. McBrien distinguishes three periods in this tradition.[29]

Stage I: 1891–1939. Leo XIII's *Rerum novarum* (1891) was set in the context of the Industrial Revolution, which in both Europe and the United States allowed the laws of the marketplace to completely dominate the rights of workers. Wages were miserable, child labor was taken for granted, and any attempt of workers to form protective associations was resisted, often with force. *Rerum novarum* focused on those rights, particularly the right to a just wage that would support the workers' families and the right to join unions. The encyclical affirmed the right of private property but stressed that it must serve the common good; in other words, it was not an absolute right. It stressed that governments should intervene to prevent harm to individuals or to the common good.

---

[28]See Michael J. Schultheis, Edward P. De Berri, and Peter J. Henriot, *Our Best Kept Secret: The Rich Heritage of Catholic Social Teaching* (Washington: Center of Concern, 1987).

[29]See *Catholicism,* rev. ed. (San Francisco: Harper, 1994) 913–14. For the texts, see Michael Walsh and Brian Davies, eds., *Proclaiming Justice and Peace* (Mystic, Conn.: Twenty-Third, 1991); Joseph Gremillion, *The Gospel of Peace and Justice: Catholic Social Teaching Since Pope John* (Maryknoll, N.Y.: Orbis, 1976) covers from 1961 to 1975 and includes the more important documents from Medellín.

According to Donal Dorr, by defending the rights of workers to join associations, including "workingmen's unions" (no. 36), Leo was moving beyond a call to conversion of the oppressors to address the problem of what would today be called the structural level of injustice. Yet the pope's approach was still quite conservative. Suspicious of the emerging trade-union movement because of its secularist and sometimes anti-Catholic character, he encouraged Catholic workers to form their own associations, with the result that the Church was not able to influence or support the labor movement as much as it might have.[30] Nevertheless, in calling attention to the issue of justice in the social order, Leo was raising the voice of the Church on behalf of the poor. His encyclical provided a firm foundation for Catholic social teaching, one that would continue to function as a standard and a point of reference for subsequent popes.

Forty years later Pope Pius XI developed Leo's social teaching in his *Quadragesimo anno* (1931), formulating for the first time the principle of subsidiarity (nos. 79–80), the idea, based on the priority and rights of the individual and the family, that larger social bodies should not take over the responsibilities of smaller groups or associations. He also introduced the concept of social justice *(iustitia socialis)* as a "directing principle" or norm for public institutions and the economic order (nos. 88–90).

In 1937 Pius XI issued *Mit brennender Sorge,* an encyclical sharply critical of the Nazi government for violating the rights of the Catholic Church; it was read from all Catholic pulpits in Germany. In the last year of his life he was preparing an encyclical on the unity of the human race. A major section of the document, reportedly analyzing and condemning anti-Semitism in Germany and racism in the United States, was prepared at the pope's request by the American Jesuit John LaFarge. Unfortunately, someone in Rome thought the document, with its specific condemnation of anti-Semitism, inopportune, given the inflammatory political situation in Europe, and the completed draft was prevented from reaching the pope's desk. Pius XI died in 1939, without publishing what was to be his encyclical on racism.

Stage II: Post-World War II. The period after the Second World War saw an internationalization of Catholic social teaching. The documents appearing in this period dealt with the organization of the international community, the demands of social justice on the international level, and the moral issues raised by warfare in a nuclear age.

John XXIII's first encyclical, *Mater et magistra* (1961), called attention to the widening gap between the rich and the poor. The encyclical stressed the social function of private property and called for a reconstruction of social re-

---

[30]Donal Dorr, *Option for the Poor: A Hundred Years of Vatican Social Teaching* (Maryknoll, N.Y.: Orbis, 1983) 26–27.

lationships. *Pacem in terris* (1963), his encyclical on peace, was an appeal to all people of good will. The pope called for a ban on nuclear weapons and stressed the responsibility of each individual to protect life: "If civil authorities legislate for, or allow, anything that is contrary to . . . the will of God, neither the laws made nor the authorizations granted can be binding on the consciences of the citizens, since 'we must obey God rather than men'" (no. 51).

The social teachings of the Second Vatican Council were contained in two documents that appeared in 1965. *Gaudium et spes* (Pastoral Constution on the Church in the Modern World) treated the practice of social justice as part of the mission of the Church.[31] *Dignitatis humanae,* the Declaration on Religious Freedom, was one of the most controversial of the council's documents. It was drafted by John Courtney Murray, the American Jesuit who had been silenced by Rome in the 1950s but was invited to the second session of the council at the insistence of Cardinal Francis Spellman of New York.

Pope Paul VI's *Populorum progressio* appeared in 1967. Besides repeating the traditional teaching that the right to private property is not absolute, the pope addressed the issue of land reform: "If certain landed estates impede the general prosperity because they are extensive, unused or poorly used, or because they bring hardship to peoples or are detrimental to the interests of the country, the common good sometimes demands their expropriation" (no. 24). He also rejected liberal capitalism as "a system . . . which considers profit as the key motive for economic progress, competition as the supreme law of economics, and private ownership of the means of production as an absolute right that has no limits and carries no corresponding social obligation" (no. 26). A nervous *Wall Street Journal* denounced the encyclical as "warmed-over Marxism."[32]

Justice in the World (1971), the document of the Third Synod of Bishops, linked evangelization with a commitment to the transformation of the world: "Action on behalf of justice and participation in the transformation of the world fully appear to us as a constitutive dimension of the preaching of the Gospel, or, in other words, of the Church's mission for the redemption of the human race and its liberation from every oppressive situation" (no. 6).

Stage III: 1971– . The most recent stage of Catholic social teaching has dealt with the widening gap between the rich and the poor, the problems caused by technology, the arms race, torture and oppression, and includes a critique of both communism and capitalism.

Octogesima adveniens (1971), a letter sent by Paul VI to Cardinal Maurice Roy, president of the Pontifical Council on Justice and Peace, deals with problems stemming from urbanization, including the condition of women, youth,

[31]See Timothy G. McCarthy, *The Catholic Tradition: Before and After Vatican II* (Chicago: Loyola Univ. Press, 1994) 251.

[32]March 30, 1967.

and the new poor. Gregory Baum notes three significant points in the letter. First, it recognizes that socialism was an option for Catholics. Second, it takes a more nuanced approach to Marxism, rejecting it as a complete philosophical system and as a political form of government associated with dictatorship but acknowledging its usefulness as a form of social analysis, though one that must be used with the greatest care. Finally, the encyclical manifests an appreciation of the critical function of "utopia," a notion borrowed from the revisionist Marxist philosopher Ernst Bloch that is able to provoke a vision of an alternative society.[33]

Pope Paul's apostolic exhortation on evangelization, *Evangelii nuntiandi* (1975), stresses that evangelization has a social dimension as well as a personal one. The former involves human rights, family life, peace, justice, development, and liberation (no. 29). The pope sees profound links between evangelization and liberation because the person "who is to be evangelized is not an abstract being but is subject to social and economic questions" (no. 31). He notes that though some base communities are characterized by a bitter criticism of the Church and its hierarchy, others cause the Church to grow and can be a place of evangelization (no. 58).

Evangelization belongs to the very mission of the Church; it is the responsibility of local Churches as well as of the universal Church. All Christians, clergy and laity alike, have an important role to play in evangelization.

Pope John Paul II's first social encyclical, *Laborem exercens,* appeared in 1981. It has been praised for being a genuine teaching document, one that seeks not just to instruct but to clarify and explain. Stressing the priority of labor over capital and of people over things, it offers an evenhanded critique of both liberal capitalism and Marxism. Developing a spirituality of labor, the pope sees work as necessary for human dignity and for the development of the kingdom.

A key concept for the pope is solidarity (no. 8). Its frequent appearance in the encyclical at the time when the Polish solidarity movement was engaged in its struggle with the country's Communist government "undoubtedly had the effect of giving a certain discreet aura of Vatican approval to the Polish Workers Movement."[34]

Sollicitudo rei socialis (1987), John Paul's encyclical on the social concerns of the Church, was designed to celebrate and develop further Pope Paul VI's *Populorum progressio.* It emphasized the widening gap between the developed countries of the Northern Hemisphere and the underdeveloped countries of the Southern, attributing much of the blame for this situation to the existence

[33]Gregory Baum, "Faith and Liberation: Development Since Vatican II," Gerald M. Fagin, ed., *Vatican II: Open Questions and New Horizons* (Wilmington: Glazier, 1984) 90–93.

[34]Donal Dorr, *Option for the Poor: A Hundred Years of Vatican Social Teaching* (Maryknoll, N.Y.: Orbis, 1983) 248; Dorr notes that the pope first analyzed solidarity as a concept in 1969 when he was archbishop of Cracow; see p. 245.

of two opposing blocs, liberal capitalism in the West and Marxist collectivism in the East. The Church's social teaching is critical of both systems.

The pope makes it clear that the Church does not have a solution for the problem of underdevelopment, some "third way" between the two competing systems. Echoing liberation theology, he calls for "the option or love of preference for the poor," a concern for the poor that must condition "our daily life as well as our decisions in the political and economic fields" (no. 42). The encyclical represents the pope's strongest challenge to the affluent countries and is noteworthy for calling attention to ecological concerns (no. 39).

Centesimus annus (1991), marking the centenary of *Rerum novarum,* was published after the collapse of Communism in Eastern Europe and the Soviet Union. The encyclical is more positive toward capitalism, with its recognition of the positive role of business and its allowance for human creativity in the economy. Yet capitalism has its own inadequacies. It cannot be simply the goal of Third World and developing countries, where there is need to circumscribe freedom in the economic sector within a juridical framework that respects a more comprehensive notion of freedom rooted in ethical and religious values (no. 42).

Evangelium vitae, John Paul II's lengthy encyclical on human life, appeared in 1995. Taking as his point of departure "the sacred value of human life from its very beginning until its end" (no. 2), the pope calls on all people of good will to affirm "a new culture of human life" (no. 6). Examples of the contemporary lack of respect for life include the unjust distribution of resources that leads to poverty, malnutrition, and hunger for so many millions, the violence of wars and the scandalous arms trade, the reckless tampering with the world's ecological balance, the spread of drugs, and the promotion of certain kinds of sexual activity that present grave risks to life (no. 10).

In particular the encyclical concentrates on "attacks affecting life in its earliest and in its final stages" (no. 11). The encyclical breaks new ground in speaking out so strongly against the death penalty, arguing that today, "as a result of steady improvements in the organization of the penal system," cases in which the death penalty would be justified in order to protect society "are very rare if not practically nonexistent" (no. 56).[35] It reaffirms the Church's position that "abortion willed as an end or as a means, always constitutes a grave moral disorder" (no. 62) and condemns "the use of human embryos or fetuses as an object of experimentation" (no. 63). Though it rejects euthanasia, suicide, and "assisted suicide" as contrary to God's law, it respects a patient's decision to forgo "aggressive medical treatment" that "would only secure a precarious and burdensome prolongation of life, so

[35]At the release of the encyclical (March 30, 1995), Cardinal Ratzinger announced that the reservations on the death penalty present in the *Catechism of the Catholic Church* would be reformulated in light of the pope's teaching; see *Origins* 24 (April 6, 1995) 690.

long as the normal care due to the sick person in similar cases is not interrupted" (no. 65). In the final chapter the pope calls for the creation of a new
culture that respects and protects each human life. Christians should show special concern for the poor and the disadvantaged; their communities should
support single mothers, marriage and family counseling agencies, treatment
and care programs for those with drug addictions, minors, the mentally ill, persons with AIDS, and the disabled (nos. 87–88).

The Church and the Environment

Though *Evangelium vitae* includes the abuse of the environment among
the modern threats to life, the Catholic Church has been late in incorporat-
ing a concern for the environment into its official teaching.[36] The bishops at
Vatican II did not raise the issue and the council documents reflect what is
today called a "domination theology," one that sees the natural world as existing for the exclusive use of humankind (cf. GS 34). This theology can be
found in Paul VI's 1967 *Populorum progressio,* which quotes the command in
Genesis 1:28 to "fill the earth and subdue it" (no. 22). The second creation
story in Genesis suggests a greater responsibility toward the natural world;
according to this account the Lord God "took the man and settled him in
the garden of Eden, to cultivate and care for it" (Gen 2:15). The image here
is not domination but stewardship.

Pope Paul's 1971 letter *Octogesima adveniens* expressed a concern for the
environment (no. 21), and Pope John Paul II made several references to the
exploitation of the earth in his first encyclical, *Redemptor hominis* (nos. 8, 15, 16).
But his report on the 1984 Synod of Bishops on reconciliation, *Reconciliatio et
paenitentia,* missed a great opportunity to include the growing alienation of
human beings from the environment that sustains them as among those relationships in need of reconciliation. His 1988 encyclical *Sollicitudo rei socialis*
was the first to include a strong emphasis on environmental concerns. And
his January 1, 1990, message for the World Day of Peace, "Peace with God the
Creator, Peace with All Creation," was entirely devoted to the environment.

The World Council of Churches has had environmental concerns on its
agenda since at least 1975. In 1983 at its Vancouver Assembly, it broadened
a concern for a "sustainable" society to include a concern for "justice, peace,
and the integrity of creation."[37] Regrettably, the Catholic Church declined an
invitation from the WCC to cosponsor a 1990 world conference on justice,
peace, and the integrity of creation held in Korea.

[36]Sean McDonagh, *The Greening of the Church* (Maryknoll, N.Y.: Orbis, 1990) 175; see
"The Environment in the Modern Catholic Church," 175–203.

[37]According to Sean McDonagh, Pope John Paul II's January 1, 1990 document, mentioned above, is heavily dependent on the WCC JPIC program, though this is not acknowledged in the text; see his *Passion for the Earth* (Maryknoll, N.Y.: Orbis, 1994) 106.

Documents of Episcopal Conferences

Since the council some national and regional conferences of bishops have produced a number of important documents and pastoral letters on social issues. Even if these documents do not represent an official exercise of the magisterium, they have already played an important role in the development of the social conscience of Catholics.

CELAM

The first postconciliar meeting of the Episcopal Conference of Latin America (CELAM II) took place at Medellín, Colombia, in 1968. The meeting marked a turning point for the Church in Latin America as the bishops began to reflect on the reality of life in their countries in light of the council, the social teaching of the Church, and the new theological reflection taking place in their Churches, which would be known as liberation theology. The sixteen documents of Medellín locate the problems of Latin America not in underdevelopment itself but in "a situation of injustice that can be called institutional violence."[38] They call for a solidarity with the poor on the part of the Church, one that will include a redistribution of resources, and for "conscientization" of the poor so that they will begin to take responsibility for their own lives. The word "liberation" appears frequently, and Jesus is spoken of as a liberator from sin, hunger, oppression, misery, and ignorance.[39]

This "turn toward the poor" was recognized immediately by government officials in the United States. In 1969 Nelson Rockefeller in a report prepared for President Nixon warned that the Catholic Church in Latin America had become "a force dedicated to change—revolutionary change if necessary," pointing to the Medellín documents as an example. Somewhat condescendingly comparing the new spirit in the Church to youthful idealism, he argued that it was "vulnerable to subversive penetration."[40]

CELAM III took place in Puebla, Mexico, in 1979. Reviewing the situation in Latin America, the bishops found that it had worsened; most of their countries faced greater poverty, more foreign debt, a growing urban

---

[38]CELAM II, "Peace," no. 17; the Medellín documents can be found in Gremillion, *The Gospel of Peace and Justice*, 445–84.

[39]See Edward L. Cleary, *Crisis and Change: The Church in Latin America* (Maryknoll, N.Y.: Orbis, 1985).

[40]"Rockefeller Report on the Quality of Life in the Americas," *The Department of State Bulletin* 61 (December 8, 1969) 504. For a fascinating report on the Church's struggle for human rights in Latin America and the conflict with U.S. policy, see Penny Lernoux, *Cry of the People* (New York: Penguin, 1982). Her book was finished shortly before some of the worst periods of violence began.

underclass as the greater percentage of their populations shifted from rural areas to the cities, and an increase in repression.[41]

The conference lacked the unanimity experienced at Medellín; it was more divided between progressives and conservatives. Nevertheless its final document supported the vision that had emerged at Medellín; it called for liberation without violence and for lay participation in the work of evangelization, and it encouraged the movement for Basic Christian Communities. The expression "preferential option for the poor," appearing as a chapter title in the document, has come more than anything else to symbolize the direction taken by the Latin American Church since Medellín.

CELAM IV, timed to coincide with the 1992 quincentenary of the arrival of Columbus and thus of Christianity in the "New World," was held in Santo Domingo, Dominican Republic. The spirit at Santo Domingo was even more divided that at Puebla. The majority of the bishops, many of them appointed by Pope John Paul II, were more conservative. A new concern was the number of Catholics in many Latin American countries being lost to proselytism by the Evangelical and Pentecostal Churches. Still, the conference reaffirmed the direction taken at CELAM II and III.

U.S. Catholic Conference

In the 1980s the U.S. bishops published two pastoral letters to assist Catholics in the formation of their consciences on the issues of peace and the economy. Each letter was the product of a broad consultative process involving conversations with theologians, representatives of business, the defense department, and other government officials. Three separate drafts of each letter were published before a final document was approved by the bishops. The entire process models an exercise of the episcopal teaching office, which allows for input from other important voices in the Church.

The Challenge of Peace (1983) is concerned chiefly with the question of nuclear war.[42] It argues that neither the use of nuclear weapons against population centers, the threat to so use them even as a deterrent, nor the initiation of nuclear war can be justified morally. The bishops give no more than "a strictly conditioned moral acceptance of the principle of nuclear deterrence" (no. 186); they reject the concept of "prevailing" in a nuclear war and the quest for nuclear superiority; and they state that nuclear deterrence should be used as a step toward nuclear disarmament.

Economic Justice for All (1986) is an attempt to apply the principles of Catholic social teaching to the U.S. economy.[43] Its thesis is that the morality

---

[41]McCarthy, *The Catholic Tradition*, 275.

[42]*The Challenge of Peace: God's Promise and Our Response* (Washington: USCC, 1983).

[43]*Economic Justice for All: Pastoral Letter on Catholic Social Teaching and the U.S. Economy* (Washington: USCC, 1986).

of every "economic decision and institution must be judged in light of whether it protects or undermines the dignity of the human person," regardless of that person's social or economic status (no. 13). The bishops are careful to distinguish between the principles they enunciate, having behind them the authority of the Church's social doctrine, and the concrete but admittedly controversial recommendations they offer (no. 22).

Both letters were widely read and much discussed. The letter on peace was more positively received; the one on the economy was more controversial, but it also might be the more prophetic. In 1992 the bishops abandoned an effort to write a letter on women after a number of interventions from the Vatican. Among their other efforts are pastoral letters on African Americans, Hispanics, and persons with disabilities.

Catholic Social Principles

While Catholic social teaching is built on the principle of the dignity of the human person, its approach is communitarian rather than individualistic. In this way it stands in stark contrast to the individualistic ethos of contemporary American and Western culture. A systematic review of Catholic social teaching would uncover the following basic principles:

1. *The dignity of the human person.* Each human being is created in the image of God, and therefore each human life is sacred and may never be treated as a means. A consequence is that everything in the economic and political realm must be judged in light of whether it protects or undermines human dignity. This is the foundational principle of Catholic social thought.

2. *Priority of community and the common good.* The person is social by nature and must be seen in relationship to the community, which is necessary for the person's full development. Human rights must be protected if individuals are to participate in society. Individual rights have correlative responsibilities and must be exercised with a view toward the common good. The family is the basic unit of society.

3. *Distributive justice.* Of principal concern to the common good is just distribution. Without it the right of each person to have access to what is considered essential to a dignified standard of living cannot be realized. The purpose of the economy is to serve the common good (rather than the maximization of profit).

4. *Priority of labor over capital.* Persons are more important than things. Material goods are not the sole reason for the economic community, for the dignity of persons is primary, and work must serve this dignity. Work has an inherent dignity, and the person's dignity is inseparable from his or her work. Through work the person becomes more human.

5. *Right to participation.* All people have a right to participate in the economic life of a society. This includes the right to work, given that work is

essential to human dignity. Full employment is a primary goal. Unemployment cannot be allowed as a means to some other goal, for then capital has priority over labor. Work is the primary means to participate in the economic order, and workers should not be denied access. Workers should also be given the opportunity to participate in the day-to-day decisions of the organization. Work is not merely an economic function but also an activity that influences the psychological and spiritual character of the person.

6. *The principle of subsidiarity.* Whenever possible decisions should be made at local levels rather than by higher bodies, thus giving primacy to individual initiative. Intermediate associations (families, local communities, unions, societies, etc.) should be free to perform operations proper to themselves without interference from the state.

7. *Limited right to private property.* The right to private property is not absolute; it cannot be separated from one's obligation toward the common good.

8. *Obligation to the poor.* Both individuals and civil societies have obligations to those most vulnerable. Not everyone has an equal start in economic life, and hence blame for poverty does not lie exclusively with the individual. Regardless of the cause of poverty, the poor have equal dignity with all others.

CONSCIENCE AND AUTHORITY

So far in this chapter we have reviewed the Church's teachings in the areas of sexuality and social justice. Now it is time to consider the role of conscience. In the Catholic tradition both conscience and authority have important roles in helping the individual recognize what he or she ought to do in a particular situation. But both conscience and authority can easily be misunderstood.

Conscience

Catholicism values conscience as the person's ultimate guide. The Second Vatican Council described conscience as "the most secret core and sanctuary" of an individual, where he or she is alone with God (GS 16). The council here was echoing Aquinas, who taught that conscience in its most general meaning was a habit *(synderesis),* an intuitive sense deep within each person to do good and avoid evil. Aquinas understood conscience in the strict sense as the process of searching out what this sense of our obligation to do good and avoid evil means in some particular situation.[44] Since this involves a process of discernment in which the particular good may not be immediately clear, it might involve using natural reason or appealing to the revelation entrusted to the Church.

[44] *Summa theologiae* I.79.12-13.

Today many Catholic moral theologians follow Timothy O'Connell's analysis of the tradition: Conscience refers to our human moral consciousness, which includes (1) our basic grasp of the moral imperative, to do good and avoid evil; (2) the process or "moral science" of discovering the particular good to be done or evil to be avoided; and (3) the specific judgment made in a particular case.[45]

Since conscience must ultimately terminate in a practical judgment reached after a careful consideration of a situation, it is important not to reduce it to a subjective inner feeling or voice. Nor should it be identified with what Freud called the "superego," a superimposed censor that represents the "oughts" of various authority figures in our lives and relies on guilt to bring about compliance. Conscience involves the whole person: intellect, intuition, moral sensitivity, and practical judgment.

Though a person must always follow his or her conscience, that conscience can be in error, either because he or she has not developed the maturity to move beyond self-interest and social conformity in making moral judgments, or through ignorance, or because the person has not made the effort to discover the truth. Thus each person has an obligation to form a correct conscience.

Authority

The Church, which Catholics recognize as both mother and teacher, assists in this process. This is where authority comes in. As the community of the disciples of Jesus, the Church's authority is expressed in its Scripture, its tradition, and in its magisterium, or official teaching office.

Sacred Scripture relates for us the story of God and God's holy people. It gives us the Decalogue, the Ten Commandments (Exod 20:2-17), which spell out the parameters of living in covenant relationship with God. That covenant relationship is violated if we worship other gods or dishonor our parents, if we commit murder or adultery, steal, ruin the reputation of our neighbors or covet what belongs to them. From the prophets we are reminded of God's love for justice and constant command to remember the poor and the powerless—"the resident alien, the orphan, and the widow" (Jer 7:6; cf. Deut 24:21). Through the Gospels we come to know Jesus; as Pope John Paul II said in *Veritatis splendor,* following Jesus is the essential and primordial foundation of Christian morality (no. 19). The Gospels enable us to become familiar with Jesus' words and teachings, offer us the wisdom contained in his parables, and challenge us to model our lives on his example of faithful service.

---

[45] *Principles for a Catholic Morality* (San Francisco: Harper & Row, 1990) 109ff.

The tradition bears the Church's accumulated wisdom, the wisdom that comes from the Christian community's proclamation, celebration, and transmission of its faith through countless generations. The tradition is exemplified in the lives of the martyrs and saints. It includes the Church's conviction that God has infused into each human heart the "natural law" to do good and avoid evil, as well as the Church's understanding of what the human good is in particular circumstances, based on the biblical revelation and its own reflection on the moral order revealed in creation and in the dignity of the human person.

The magisterium teaches in the name of the Church and so in the name of Christ; through it the authority entrusted by Christ to the apostles and their successors, the bishops, comes to expression. Thus the magisterium not only reminds Catholics of what the Church has taught officially in the past, it also functions as a living teaching office, proclaiming moral principles and applying those principles both to our personal lives and to the social order.

Catholicism has a deep sense that every aspect of human life—personal, sexual, economic, and social—is to be transformed in light of the promise of God's reign in Jesus. Much of the Church's official teaching in the area of sexuality and marriage stands in sharp contrast to the values of popular modern culture. Catholics take this teaching mission of the Church seriously and respect it; perhaps this is why some people think that Catholics are always talking about morality and sexuality. The Church continues to insist on the sanctity of life, the indissolubility of marriage, and the inseparable relationship between matrimonial fidelity and sexual expression. At the same time, in this area of applying principles of Christian morality to everyday life, conscience and authority may occasionally come into conflict.

An Informed Conscience

How are these conflicts between conscience and authority to be resolved? The principle remains that in the final analysis one must follow one's conscience. But conscience is not autonomous. Since one's conscience can be erroneous, the primacy of conscience can never be used to avoid the responsibility of forming a correct conscience, which includes for Catholics a serious and prayerful effort to incorporate the moral vision emerging from the Catholic tradition, understood in its full sense of Scripture, the tradition of the Church, the sense of the faithful, and the teaching magisterium exercised by the pope and the bishops.

In this process of forming conscience, the magisterium has a special role to play. For example, Catholics who say that "the Church has no right to tell me what I do in my bedroom" or who argue that the Church's social teachings are an unwarranted intrusion into the realm of the political may be acting more out of self-interest or class consciousness than from a genuine desire to discover the truth. In a narcissistic and secularized society like our own we need a moral vision we can live by. It is important that the magisterium continue to perform this prophetic function of assisting Christian people in the formation of their consciences. Yet in the final analysis it remains true that authority can never be a substitute for responsible decisions made in accordance with a well-formed conscience.[46]

CONCLUSION

These issues of sexuality and justice that we have been considering are important because they attempt to express the implications of discipleship and the Christian vision of the kingdom for our personal and social lives. If they are controversial, it is because they touch each of us so personally.

Catholic teaching on sexuality is of long standing. That it has changed so little with the times is not necessarily an argument against it. Christian life should be informed by the gospel, not by the values of a particular culture. However, an ethical vision should never blind one to compassion and a recognition of the uniqueness of the individual. If the Church is uncompromising in its role as teacher, it generally is compassionate in its pastoral practice. There are also other voices in the Church that deserve a hearing.

The social doctrine of the Church is of more recent articulation, but it also has roots deep within the tradition. The Acts of the Apostles presents the Christian community as one in which "no one claimed that any of his possessions was his own, but they had everything in common" (Acts 4:32). That may represent a vision of the ideal, but perhaps our age needs such a vision.

We live in a world of an ever-increasing gulf between the rich and the poor, not just within nations but globally. At the present time some countries are simply dissolving into anarchy; their economies are no longer functioning, and their cultural, religious, and civil systems of restraint are beginning to collapse. The ensuing chaos in countries where even teenagers have automatic weapons threatens the security of even the most powerful nations. Beyond these economic divisions our natural environment itself is in crisis. The exhaustion of nonrenewable resources, the elimination of the tropical rain forests, the resulting loss of topsoil, the poisoning of the rivers, lakes, and air, the depletion of the ozone layer, the amassing of tons of toxic waste—all this has brought into jeopardy the very ability of the planet to sustain human life.

In a world so much under threat, a communitarian tradition that speaks of the common good, distributive justice, the right of all to participate in the goods of society, and a limited right to private property may be a rich

---

[46]See the helpful little book by Philip S. Kaufman, *Why You Can Disagree and Remain a Faithful Catholic* (Bloomington, Ind.: Meyer-Stone Books, 1989).

resource. But it is a threatening one because it calls those in prosperous First World countries to reexamine and perhaps to change their way of life.

For Catholics it is a given that God speaks through the Church, though not *only* through the Church. If there are times or situations when a person cannot in conscience accept what the Church teaches, then after sufficient prayer and study that person must follow his or her conscience.

But it is equally necessary today to affirm the right of the Church to teach, and the obligation Catholics have to acknowledge that teaching (cf. LG 25). If magisterial teaching must be received by the faithful in order to be effective in the life of the Church, it is also true that the bishops of the Church who constitute its magisterium have an important prophetic role to play in bringing the light of the gospel to bear on issues faced by the Church in the contemporary world.

9. Prayer and Spirituality

Thomas Merton tells a wonderful story about the first time he attended Mass in a Catholic church, shortly before his conversion. As he slipped into a pew, not at all sure of what was expected of him, he noticed near him a young girl about sixteen years old kneeling quietly in prayer. He wrote later in his famous autobiography, "I was very much impressed to see that someone who was young and beautiful could with such simplicity make prayer the real and serious and principle reason for going to church."[1] In this young woman's recollection Merton saw at once that God was near, not far away, and that we could open ourselves to God's presence.

Christianity is not a message or revelation about a God who remains distant. In Augustine's words, God is more intimate to me than I am to myself. God's self-revelation in the person of Jesus means that God is both the giver and the gift itself. In Jesus, who made us his brothers and sisters and poured out upon us his Spirit, we have been given a share in God's inner life as a Trinity of persons. Christian prayer is always Trinitarian; we pray to the Father in the Son through the Spirit. A great part of the mystery of the Trinity is precisely the mystery of our own share in the divine life. "Whoever loves me will keep my word, and my Father will love him, and we will come to him and make our dwelling with him" (John 14:23).

But we do not always recognize this divine indwelling. It is not God's distance but God's very nearness that makes it so hard for us to be aware of God's presence. God surrounds us, more closely than the air we breathe. And we often are no more aware of God's sustaining presence than the fish is aware of the sustaining waters of the sea. Prayer puts us in touch with that divine life. It nourishes our life in God just as the gentle rain falling on the earth softens it and makes it fertile.

There are many forms of prayer, but basically all prayer is an opening of ourselves to God; it is raising our minds and hearts to God. Or, in that

[1] *The Seven Storey Mountain* (New York: Harcourt, Brace, 1948) 204.

wonderful image of Henri Nouwen, to pray is to relax, to let go, to open one's hand and spread out one's palm in a gesture of receiving.[2] We pray in expectation because God is near and wants to fill us. We pray of necessity because without God we are rootless and alone, and our lives lack depth. We pray in awe because God is the Creator and we are creatures, the work of God's hands.

Prayer is inseparable from the life of God's people in the Bible. One cannot read the psalms without a vivid sense of how real God's presence was to the Jewish people; they sing of the reality of God, in praise and thanksgiving when God's presence was experienced: "The promises of the Lord I will sing forever" (Ps 89:2); "My soul rests in God alone, from whom comes my salvation" (Ps 62:2). Or in tears and lamentations when God seemed distant or absent: "I cry aloud to God, cry to God to hear me" (Ps 77:2); "My God, my God, why have you abandoned me?" (Ps 22:2). What is most remarkable is that the psalms convey this profound sense of what it meant to live in covenant relationship with Yahweh God without any idea of a life beyond the grave, for it was only very late in the Old Testament tradition, two hundred years or less before the time of Jesus, that the hope that the God of the living might also give life to the dead began to surface in Jewish religious writing.

The Gospels present Jesus as a man of prayer. He followed the religious traditions of his people, participating regularly in their official Sabbath worship "according to his custom" (Luke 4:16) and most probably reciting three times daily the *Shema,* the credal prayer that begins "Hear, O Israel! the Lord is our God, the Lord alone" (cf. Deut 6:4-5). Luke especially stresses Jesus at prayer; his experience at the Jordan after his baptism takes place while he was praying (3:21). Luke shows Jesus praying before other important moments in his own life (5:16; 6:12; 9:18, 28; 11:1; 22:42; 23:46) and counseling others to pray (11:5-13; 18:1, 9-14; 21:36; 22:40). One beautiful saying of Jesus encourages the disciples to persevere in prayer; it is a lesson for us as well: "Ask and you will receive; seek and you will find; knock and the door will be opened to you" (Luke 11:9).

Perhaps what is most suggestive of Jesus' relationship with God is the familiar term that he used in his own prayer, addressing God as "Abba," a family word that means not just the more formal "father," but something like "loving father," the kind of word a son or daughter would use within the intimacy of the family. No Jew at that time would have dared address God in such familiar terms; indeed, devout Jews would not even pronounce God's holy name; they would always use some circumlocution such as "the Blessed One" (Mark 14:61) rather than pronounce the sacred name. But the fact that Jesus regularly spoke to God in such familiar fashion suggests to us a great deal not just about his own experience of God but about the nature of prayer

---

[2] *With Open Hands* (Notre Dame: Ave Maria, 1972) 17.

as well. Prayer is simply speaking in a very personal way with the God who loves and cares for each of us.

At the end of his life, with his ministry apparently a failure, Jesus faced his death alone, abandoned by his friends. Even his God seemed absent. Yet he did not despair, did not cease trusting in the one he called "Abba," hoping against hope that Abba would vindicate him. And God did not abandon him; God raised him up to everlasting life.

TYPES OF PRAYER

Christian prayer is always a turning ourselves toward God through Christ in the Spirit. The language descriptive of prayer is rich, varied, and somewhat artificial. Prayer can be public liturgical prayer or private prayer. The Catholic tradition has also included a rich tradition of devotional prayer such as devotion to the Sacred Heart of Jesus, various Marian devotions, remembering the saints and asking their intercession, praying before the Blessed Sacrament, lighting candles to symbolize the ongoing nature of one's prayer, making pilgrimages or novenas (saying certain prayers for nine consecutive days), and so on. These devotions are exercises of piety meant to encourage and deepen a life of prayer.

Spiritual writers speak of different kinds of private prayer: vocal and mental prayer, affective and discursive prayer, formal and spontaneous prayer, meditation, contemplation, and mystical prayer. But neat distinctions often break down as one type of prayer shades over into another. The vocal praying of the Rosary can easily lead to a contemplative centering of the person or to an imaginative meditation on the mysteries of the life of Jesus. A discursive meditation can simplify into contemplation, including the deep contemplation verging on what the tradition has called "infused" or "mystical" prayer. For the sake of clarity we will follow the traditional distinctions of vocal *(oratio),* mental *(meditatio),* and contemplative prayer *(contemplatio),* recognizing the limitations of the categories themselves. We will also say a word about liturgical prayer.

Vocal Prayer

Vocal prayer is a way of addressing God using either formal prayers such as the Our Father, the Hail Mary, the Glory to the Father, or simply sharing with God the thoughts and concerns of our hearts in our own words. We should never think of such formal or conversational prayer as a kind of second-class prayer. Formal prayers can be a great help in those times when we want to pray but find ourselves without the words to express our feelings, particularly the emptiness we sometimes experience. Those who have been exhausted by a long illness often find it very difficult to gather their thoughts and concentrate; they welcome the presence of someone who can help them pray by repeating with them such simple prayers.

Praying to God conversationally can be a profound experience when we feel great interior joy or sorrow or struggle. We should be able to express ourselves freely to God when we are so moved. Both kinds of vocal prayer should be a part of our daily lives, just as sometimes we need to wait for the Lord in silence and expectation. What is important is that we pray honestly from the heart rather than trying to force something that doesn't truly express our inner feelings.

Some kinds of vocal prayer call not just on our minds and feelings but on our bodies and imaginations. It always strikes me as slightly ironic that so many Catholics today have to run off to some therapeutic or New Age center to learn how to pray with their bodies when the Catholic tradition has many such ways of praying. The Rosary is an ancient method of prayer that combines simple prayers hallowed by the tradition with brief meditations on events in the life of Jesus and Our Lady. It is a kind of mantra prayer, quieting the mind and the imagination by fingering the beads and repeating over and over the simple words of the Hail Mary while focusing on the mystery—the annunciation, the birth of Jesus, his crucifixion, the descent of the Holy Spirit, and so forth. The Stations of the Cross is another prayer that combines vocal prayer and meditation on the mysteries of Christ's passion with bodily movement, sometimes standing, sometimes kneeling, walking with Jesus from one scene to the next.

Another form of vocal prayer, "glossolalia," or the gift of tongues, comes out of the experience of the charismatic renewal. Mentioned in Paul's First Letter to the Corinthians (chs. 12, 14), tongues is a prayer of praise welling up from within a person to the extent that feeling overflows the constraints of language and results in a speaking or singing in unintelligible syllables. Paul acknowledged it as a genuine gift of the Spirit, but clearly as a lesser gift that needs to be regulated (1 Cor 14). Though rarely seen outside of charismatic circles, the gift of tongues should not be considered as unusual or miraculous.

Mental Prayer

When we pray discursively, using our minds and imaginations to unite ourselves with God or to consider some divine mystery, we are doing mental prayer. Meditation is the most common form of mental prayer.

The Bible is a particularly rich source for meditation. We can ponder a passage of Scripture, reading it over, savoring its language and imagery, letting the Lord speak to us through the text. We can meditate on a scene from the life of Jesus, imagining the cure of the blind man for example, placing ourselves in the scene, taking the part of one of the characters in the story, seeing ourselves as the blind man, calling out to Jesus (or perhaps finding ourselves reluctant to approach him), feeling his touch, opening our eyes as for the first time. When we meditate on the life of Jesus in the Gospels we allow its imagery and language gradually to become our own. More importantly, in making a kind of imaginative contact with the person of Jesus presented to us in the gospel mysteries, we discover the correspondence between his humanity and our own; Jesus becomes more real to us, and so we grow in love and appreciation of the Lord we cannot see.

One very fruitful way of growing in prayer is to take each day a brief passage from a particular Gospel, not a whole chapter but one simple story–a miracle story, a teaching or saying–and using it for our prayer. Some people find it helpful to use the readings for the liturgy of the day, listed in any missalette, for their daily prayer. This has the advantage of uniting them in their prayer with the liturgy or of preparing them for the liturgy if they are able to participate in the Mass on a daily basis. Others find helpful using a book of brief meditations such as the classic *Imitation of Christ* by Thomas à Kempis.

Other forms of mental or discursive prayer might include a meditative reading of Scripture, a spiritual reading, doing an examination of conscience or "consciousness examen"–which means looking for God's presence in the events of our daily lives–or keeping a personal journal in which we reflect on our prayer experience and our personal spiritual journey. Those who pray regularly often find that they are led gradually from discursive prayer to a simpler, more contemplative way of praying.

Contemplation

Contemplative prayer is a prayer of loving attentiveness to God's mysterious presence, even though that presence is not directly experienced but known only in faith. The prayer the young Samuel learns from the priest Eli provides a model: "Speak, LORD, for your servant is listening" (1 Sam 3:9). While mental prayer involves the active use of our faculties of imagination and intellect, contemplative prayer is more quiet, receptive, and affective. It is a prayer of the heart, an focus, a quiet awareness of God's presence sensed deep within us or suggested by the silence and solitude of a natural vista–a grassy meadow under an infinite blue sky or the heavens at night filled with stars. Sometimes that presence moves us to pray affectively, praising, loving, asking pardon. Thus contemplation involves not so much the imagination or discursive reason as it does the heart.

Thomas Merton, the Trappist monk who perhaps more than anyone else brought contemplation to the attention of contemporary men and women, describes it as a deepening of faith to the point where the union with God already given in our very nature is realized and experienced. It is not the result of some psychological trick but a genuine grace, something that comes as a gift and not as the result of our own use of special techniques. In his poetic language Merton describes contemplation as a door opening in the center of our being through which we seem to fall into an immense depth of silence and presence while our ordinary powers of thinking and imagination are stilled.[3] It is at this point, when our natural faculties are quiet and in darkness and prayer becomes a simple awareness, that contemplation begins to shade into what spiritual writers describe as "infused" contemplation, the first stages of mystical prayer. The latter should not be associated with extraordinary phenomena such as voices, visions, and levitations. It is better understood as a heightening of contemplative prayer, in which a person enters into a more profound awareness of God's mysterious presence.

The Church has been enriched enormously by its spiritual teachers and its mystics, men and women like Bernard of Clairvaux, Catherine of Siena, Francis of Assisi, Julian of Norwich, Jean Gerson, Teresa of Avila, Ignatius of Loyola, Francis de Sales, Dorothy Day, and Thomas Merton. Mysticism is very much part of the Catholic tradition. But contemplative prayer is not something limited to mystics or those living the monastic or religious life; it can be practiced by all Christians.

Today many people find what is known as "centering" prayer a helpful preparation for contemplative prayer.[4] Centering prayer can quiet the mind and imagination and focus one's awareness. The approach is simple; one sits quietly with the eyes closed and turns in faith toward God, ignoring the thoughts and images that continue to flow from the imagination. Many find it helpful to use a "sacred word" such as "Abba" or "Lord Jesus" to focus their attention. When the mind wanders off, one simply returns to the sacred word. Centering prayer is related to the ancient Eastern tradition variously known as Hesychasm (from the Greek *hesychia,* meaning "quiet" or "stillness") or the Jesus Prayer, a way of centering oneself by repeating over and over again "Lord Jesus Christ, Son of God, have mercy on me."

Liturgical Prayer

Liturgical prayer is the prayer of the Church gathered in worship and praise of God. In first place is the Eucharist itself, the "fount and apex of the whole Christian life" (LG 11). The Liturgy of the Hours, or Divine Office, is a liturgical prayer of praise based on the biblical prayer of the Jewish synagogues. In the early Church the Offices, or "hours," were celebrated both in

---

[3] *New Seeds of Contemplation* (New York: New Directions, 1962) 227.

[4] See M. Basil Pennington, *Centering Prayer: Renewing an Ancient Christian Prayer Form* (Garden City, N.Y.: Doubleday, 1980); Thomas Keating, *Open Mind, Open Heart: The Contemplative Dimension of the Gospel* (Rockport, Mass.: Element, 1992).

the major churches and in the monasteries. The basic structure of an hour of the early cathedral Office would have included several psalms and canticles, the *Gloria in excelsis,* some intercessions, and a closing blessing and dismissal.

Vatican II sought to restore the original rhythm of the Office so that it might become again a prayer not just for priests and religious but for the entire Church (SC 100). It singled out Morning and Evening Prayer as "the two hinges on which the daily Office turns; hence they are to be considered the chief hours and are to be celebrated as such" (SC 89). Today the Liturgy of the Hours is prayed by an increasing number of lay Christians. Many religious communities pray the Office in the morning, at noon, and in evening, establishing a rhythm of prayer to the day.

SPIRITUALITY

Christian life is life in Christ. Like Christian prayer it is a movement toward God through Christ in the Spirit. The word "spirituality" derives from Paul's use of *pneumatikos,* "spiritual," in the sense of whatever is characterized by spirit or influenced by God's Spirit. In the past spirituality was too often seen as pertaining to the spiritual life of monks and nuns, often described as the "interior life." Today the term is understood much more comprehensively; it is used to describe many different ways in which people experience the transcendent and is often used popularly of a multitude of self-improvement programs that draw upon a person's inner resources. In the Christian tradition spirituality has been used to describe particular ways of experiencing and fostering life in Christ. It "refers to the unfolding, day by day, of that fundamental decision to become or to remain a Christian which we make at baptism, repeat at confirmation, and renew each time we receive the Eucharist."[5]

Since there are many visions of what life in Christ means concretely, there are many different spiritualities.[6] Some are identified by a particular movement or way of life in the Church such as monasticism, apostolic religious life, and various lay movements such as Marriage Encounter, Cursillo, and the charismatic renewal. Others are known by their association with a person in Christian history such as Francis of Assisi, Ignatius of Loyola, or Dorothy Day.

Monastic spirituality, concerned always with the search for God alone, is contemplative. Monks and contemplative nuns seek to center their lives on God through their celibacy, their silence, and for many, a vow of stability. The centrality of the *opus Dei,* or liturgical prayer, gives a strong liturgical

---

[5]William Reiser, *Looking for a God to Pray To: Christian Spirituality in Transition* (New York: Paulist, 1994) 2.

[6]See Michael Downey, ed., *The New Dictionary of Catholic Spirituality* (Collegeville: The Liturgical Press, 1993).

dimension to monastic spirituality, while the emphasis on *lectio divina,* a contemplative reading of Scripture, makes it strongly biblical. Benedictine spirituality in particular places a large value on hospitality; according to the *Rule of St. Benedict* the guest is to be welcomed as Christ himself.

Franciscans are devoted to the poor and suffering Jesus of the Gospels and seek to serve him in the poor. Thus Franciscan spirituality is distinguished by a love for evangelical poverty and by a solidarity with the disadvantaged. Other aspects include the attempt to find a rule of life in the gospel, a strong sense of brotherhood and sisterhood, and a reverence for creation, which includes a deep sympathy for animals.

Ignatian spirituality, growing out of Ignatius' mystical experience, is Trinitarian. Its strongly apostolic character reflects his background as a soldier. Several aspects of Ignatian spirituality can be seen in the *Spiritual Exercises;* the meditations on Christ the King and the Two Standards emphasize following Christ in his ministry and personal identification with him in his humiliation and rejection. From the vision of God present and active in all creation at the end of the *Exercises,* known as the "Contemplation for Obtaining Love," comes the Ignatian ideal of finding God in all things. The rules for discernment of spirits exemplify Ignatius' sense that we can come to know God's will through the motions of our affectivity; Ignatian spirituality emphasizes discernment.

In all its expressions Christian spirituality is concerned with leading others to a deeper life in Christ and to growth in the Spirit. Therefore the life of charity must be at the heart of any spirituality if it is to be authentically Christian. Without it, a spirituality can easily turn inward, becoming either a kind of spiritual narcissism obsessed with the self and its needs or a world-denying asceticism that isolates one from others and deadens the spirit.

Life in Christ means a life of discipleship, a discipleship summed up in John's Gospel by Jesus' commandment "Love one another as I love you" (John 15:12). In Matthew's great eschatological sermon Jesus makes it clear that we will be judged one day on the basis of how we have cared for the poor and the needy, specifically those who are hungry, thirsty, a stranger, naked, sick, or in prison (Matt 25:31-46). This sermon supplied what in the catechetical tradition were called the "works of mercy," both *corporal* works of charity such as feeding the hungry, giving drink to the thirsty, clothing the naked, sheltering the homeless, visiting the sick, ransoming the captive, and burying the dead, and *spiritual* works such as instructing the ignorant, counseling the doubtful, admonishing the sinner, bearing wrongs patiently, forgiving offenses, comforting the afflicted, and praying for the living and the dead. These works of mercy were commended to all Christians.

In order to promote growth in faith, hope, and especially charity, most spiritualities stress prayer. Prayer is essential. Without prayer there is no inner life, no experience of God's transforming presence. In addition to prayer most Christian spiritualities teach some kind of spiritual discipline.

Spiritual Disciplines

We recognize that a certain amount of discipline is necessary for our physical health; we need physical exercise, a careful diet, moderation in the use of alcohol and stimulants, and the right amount of sleep. Similarly, we need a certain discipline in our spiritual lives. The traditional term for this is "asceticism," a word that causes a certain amount of nervousness today, though it came into Christian usage from the Greek love of athletics (the Greek *askesis* meant "athletic exercise" or "practice"). Paul himself compared his efforts to master his bodily nature for the sake of his apostolic labors to the athletic training necessary to participate in the games (1 Cor 9:25-27).

"Asceticism" means the practice of a spiritual discipline for the sake of ordering the natural appetites, centering the person, and opening the spirit to God's presence. There are a number of traditional ascetical practices that still can be very helpful.

Most religious traditions have recognized a spiritual value in fasting. In the Old Testament fasting was a sign of penance. In the history of Christianity fasting has been practiced as a way of uniting oneself with the suffering Jesus and as a preparation for prayer (cf. Acts 13:2-3). According to the second-century *Didache,* both the one to be baptized and the one that performs the baptism are to fast before the sacrament (*Didache* 7). In the patristic literature fasting was frequently linked with almsgiving. From at least the third century Christians fasted in preparation for Easter, a practice that evolved into the liturgical season of Lent.

The rules for fasting, which for centuries had been part of Catholic practice, were mitigated considerably around the time of the Second Vatican Council. In 1964 Pope Paul VI reduced the traditional fast before Holy Communion to one hour before receiving the sacrament. After the council the obligatory Lenten fast was mitigated considerably, though Catholics are still required to observe a moderate fast on Ash Wednesday and Good Friday (the norm is that what is taken at the two minor meals together should not be more than what is taken at the main meal). Today many Christians are rediscovering fasting both as a discipline for prayer and as a way of entering into solidarity with the hungry and the poor.

Abstinence, the refraining from eating meat, is another ascetical practice that has a long history in the Church. Many monastic communities abstained entirely from meat both as a discipline and as a sign of penance, a practice still maintained by the Trappists and other contemplative communities. Catholics in the United States are no longer obliged to observe the Friday abstinence except during Lent. If younger Catholics no longer remember the obligation of not eating meat on Fridays, an increasing number of Christians are voluntarily abstaining entirely from meat today, some for reasons of health, others out of concern for animals' rights, and a considerable number in protest of the disproportionate amount of grain used to feed the cattle consumed by the wealthy nations and as a way of being in solidarity with those who are hungry. Many young women today, influenced by eco-feminism, are abstaining from meat.

Finding a time and place to be alone before God, for solitude, is another important spiritual discipline. In the history of spirituality the desert has functioned as a symbol of the solitude that nourishes prayer and leads to the encounter with God. A number of modern contemplative communities make provisions for a "desert" day once a week, a day to be spent in solitude and quiet contemplation, freed from the normal community routine. In our modern urban environment, where we are surrounded by an artificial world of concrete, glass, asphalt, and steel and constantly bombarded with noise and distractions, we need to find places of solitude. We need to be able occasionally to smell the earth and the trees, to feel the grass under our feet and the breeze on our face. Solitude helps us open ourselves to the God who speaks to us in silence and in the beauty of creation. We should also be able to find places of quiet and solitude in our everyday lives, an enclosed place to walk in reflection or a corner in a room where we can light a candle before an icon or crucifix and sit in prayer and solitude. A retreat is an extended period of solitude, a time to enter more intensely into prayer and meditation. There are retreat houses in most dioceses that offer weekend retreat experiences, usually with others. Some are available for more extended retreats of five or eight days or even the traditional thirty days for making the *Spiritual Exercises*.

Spiritual direction can be a great help in our efforts to live a more conscious spiritual life. A spiritual director is more like a trusted friend than someone who "directs" or tells us what to do; it is one with whom we can share our own inner journey, reflecting out loud about our prayer and trying to discern where we stand before God and the directions in which we might be moving. The discipline of meeting regularly with a spiritual director, like writing in a journal, helps us objectify our experience and can protect us against self-deception. A good director is one who can listen well and who is himself or herself experienced in prayer. Today an increasing number of lay men and women are serving as spiritual directors.

Nonviolence

Though it is not generally included in traditional writings on spirituality, nonviolence is also an exacting spiritual discipline. No one has made this point better than Thomas Merton. In an essay entitled "Blessed Are the Meek," he set forth its principles.[7]

---

[7] Thomas Merton, *Faith and Violence: Christian Teaching and Christian Practice* (Notre Dame: Univ. of Notre Dame Press, 1968) 14–29.

Christian nonviolence is founded theologically on the Beatitudes. Those who would practice it must be willing to reject all unjust and abusive uses of power. Merton was convinced that those who resist force by using force would be contaminated by the very evil they were struggling against and, if successful, would become just as ruthless and unjust themselves. But nonviolence is not passivity; it means being for others, especially the poor and the underprivileged. The practitioners of nonviolence must avoid the self-righteousness that can so easily infect those involved in a moral struggle; they must be willing to give up the fetishism of seeking immediate results, the way of the power structure against which they are struggling.

Most of all, there must be an absolute refusal of evil, including all dishonesty, and they must be willing to recognize and admit the truth of their opponents' positions. Merton argued that nonviolence could not be conceived as a tactic to be used to obtain peace as a political end, no matter how laudatory. Nonviolence would succeed only if it was the pursuit of truth. He had learned this lesson from Gandhi and cited his words as a summation of the whole doctrine of nonviolence: "The way of peace is the way of truth. . . . Truthfulness is even more important than peacefulness."[8] Merton insisted that the nonviolent resister was not fighting for "his" truth or "her" conscience, but for *the* truth, the truth common to both the resister and the adversary, and so the resister was actually fighting for everybody.

Merton's nonviolence flowed out of his contemplation and the sense of the connectedness of all things that was its fruit. Nonviolence must give up all particular truths, no matter how much cherished, for Truth itself, the Truth which is God.

CONTEMPORARY SPIRITUALITIES

Lay Spiritualities

The religious life of vows in the Church has frequently been referred to as the "state of perfection," and all too often the Catholic tradition has tended to speak as though spirituality pertained only to the kind of lives led by religious. Philip Sheldrake has written, "The identity of lay Christians was effectively obscured for centuries because religious life became a kind of normative framework for Christian life."[9] We tend to forget that many rich spiritual traditions in the Church were created by lay men and women. The early Fathers and Mothers of the desert were lay people, not clerics or religious. The Beguines and Beghards of the twelfth and thirteenth centuries belonged to lay movements, as was initially that of St. Francis of Assisi.

[8] *Conjectures of a Guilty Bystander* (Garden City, N.Y.: Doubleday, 1968) 84.
[9] *Spirituality and History* (New York: Crossroad, 1992) 107.

All Christians, lay men and women as well as religious, are called to a spiritual life, so it is important to broaden the concept of spirituality to reflect the different circumstances and needs of lay people, whether single or married. St. Francis de Sales (d. 1622) understood the diversity of spirituality; in *The Introduction to the Devout Life* he stressed that the practice of devotion should be adapted to each person according to his or her duties and occupation:

> I ask you, Philothea, is it fit that a bishop should lead the solitary life of a Carthusian? Or that married people should lay up no greater store of goods than the Capuchin? If a tradesman were to remain the whole day in church, like a member of a religious order, or were a religious continually exposed to encounter difficulties in the service of his neighbor, as a bishop is, would not such devotion be ridiculous, unorganized, and unsupportable?[10]

The Second Vatican Council, with its emphasis on the universal call to holiness (LG 42), provided the theological basis for a number of lay spiritualities. The foundation of all spirituality is baptism, which incorporates a person into Christ and the Church and gives each, whether lay, religious, or ordained, a share in Christ's priestly, prophetic, and kingly functions (LG 31).

A lay spirituality fosters this baptismal vocation in both the Church and the world. As a vocation in the Church it is nourished by the Word of God and by the sacraments. As a vocation in the world it must be incarnational; it should be able to find God's presence in the midst of the ordinary and the everyday, and it recognizes that work can be an expression of one's Christian commitment. It can be lived out in marriage or in the single life.

Married couples are called to a spirituality that is essentially relational; their primary vocation is their marriage and family. They are called to live a shared life that both respects and overcomes differences. Their sexual love is an expression of their spirituality; it is an important sign of God's tender and life-giving love. Indeed, as Andrew Greeley has often emphasized, sexual pleasure bonds husbands and wives to each other and heals the frictions and conflicts a shared life so often brings.[11] In a real sense husbands and wives image God for each other and for their children; their home and family becomes a place where others can experience the joy and security of God's love.

Both marriage and the single life can bring people closer to God. The Marriage Encounter movement has done much to promote a spirituality of marriage; it has helped married couples to discover what it means to live Christian marriage as a sacrament. Some lay men and women choose the single life as a way of fostering intimacy with God and in order to give them-

---

[10] *The Introduction to the Devout Life,* trans. and ed. John K. Ryan (New York: Harper & Brothers, 1950) 6.

[11] *Sex: The Catholic Experience* (Chicago: Thomas More, 1994).

selves more completely to a particular ministry in the Church; their single lives can be an expression of celibacy for the sake of the kingdom (cf. Matt 19:12).

The charismatic renewal has helped many lay people to experience a more intense life in the Spirit. The Cursillo movement, based on a weekend spiritual renewal, promotes a spirituality that finds God's presence in everyday life, at home, at work, and in particular in the community of the local Church. The recovery of the idea of lay ministry calls for a spirituality of service.

Justice and Solidarity with the Poor

One of the most powerful currents affecting spirituality in the twentieth century has been the combination of a contemplative spirituality with a commitment to the struggle for social justice and solidarity with the poor. The spirituality of liberation, developing out of the theology of liberation in Latin America, is an expression of this current. The idea of solidarity with the poor is not a new one in the history of the Church. Though the rhetoric was different, the call to follow the poor Jesus, heard by Francis of Assisi and his Little Brothers, and their practice of an itinerant poverty certainly represented an expression of what today would be called "the preferential option for the poor."

Charles de Foucauld, in his efforts to preach the gospel by modeling in his own life among the tribesmen in the Sahara the hidden life of Jesus at Nazareth, is a modern exemplar of this tradition; he has had an enormous influence on certain contemporary religious communities. And there are a number of communities founded by lay men and women such as Dorothy Day's Catholic Workers and Jean Vanier's l'Arche communities, whose members seek to combine in their lives contemplation, simplicity of life, and direct service of the poor.

The spirituality of the Catholic Worker movement is rooted in the gospel. In an engraving done by Quaker artist Fritz Eichenberg, which has become a quasi-official icon of the movement, Jesus stands cold and unrecognized in a line of patiently waiting poor men and women. Catholic Workers see an obvious connection between their Eucharistic practice and the meals they serve the hungry in their kitchens. They continue to repeat the words of Dorothy Day: "We know Christ in the breaking of the bread. And we know each other in the breaking of the bread."

Those drawn to l'Arche sense in the developmentally disabled a vulnerability that makes them open to God in a special way. Their spirituality is based on a basic truth of the gospel: Jesus identifies himself with the poor and the suffering, and when we open ourselves to the poor, we come to know his peace and presence. They could not sustain their daily life of taking care of the handicapped if they were not convinced of this truth. The Beatitudes (Matt 5:3-12; Luke 6:20-26) stand at the center of their spirituality. Those called blessed by Jesus are the poor, the suffering, and the merciful, not the comfortable and the powerful. The Beatitudes stand as a constant challenge to us, for they turn our conventional values upside down and open up a whole new vision of the world.

In North America and other parts of the world the AIDS crisis has challenged Christians to respond to those living and dying with this terrible disease. There are presently approximately 13 million people infected with HIV. It is estimated that the number will rise to 110 million by the year 2000.[12] Many have to face in addition to the terrible suffering brought on by the disease stigmatization by society, abandonment by their families, the loss of loved ones. Many of those ministering to persons with AIDS as well as those with the disease discover a spirituality of compassion, prayer, and hope in seeking to come to terms with AIDS as a fact in their lives.

The efforts of Christians and Churches in Latin America to live the option for the poor in the midst of their often violent and repressive societies have led to a spirituality of discipleship and even martyrdom. The costs have been very high. The number of priests, sisters, brothers, and Protestant pastors killed in Central and Latin America since the end of the Second Vatican Council is in the hundreds. In the 1980s more than twelve priests and at least three Protestant ministers were murdered or disappeared in Guatemala. During the same period in El Salvador, Archbishop Romero, the four Church women mentioned earlier, and at least seventeen priests were murdered. In 1989 six Jesuit priests along with their cook and her daughter were murdered when Salvadoran troops entered their residence and shot them in cold blood. If lay leaders are included throughout Central and Latin America, the number climbs to the thousands.

Jon Sobrino, one of the Salvadoran Jesuits not at home the night that the members of his community were murdered, has done much to develop what he calls a spirituality of liberation, a spirituality of justice and solidarity with the poor.[13] He tells a story about that tragic night, which symbolizes more powerfully than any of his writings God's solidarity with the poor and powerless.[14] In his room among his books was a book by German theologian Jürgen Moltmann entitled *The Crucified God*. After the murders the soldiers dragged the body of one of the dead Jesuits into Sobrino's room, knocking Moltmann's book off the shelf in the process. It fell next to the dead Jesuit, where it was found the next day, soaked in his blood. Far better than any

[12]See Kenneth R. Overberg, *Aids, Ethics, and Religion* (Maryknoll, N.Y.: Orbis, 1994) 3.
[13]*Spirituality of Liberation: Toward Political Holiness* (Maryknoll, N.Y.: Orbis, 1988).
[14]*A Question of Conscience: The Murder of the Jesuit Priests in El Salvador,* dir. Ilan Ziv, First Run Features, 1990, videocassette.

theological treatise, that blood-soaked book with its powerful title spoke of God's own passion, God's solidarity through the crucified Jesus with victims of violence and injustice throughout human history.

What are some of the characteristics of a spirituality of justice and solidarity with the poor? First, it must be rooted in prayer and contemplation, which, as Henri Nouwen has observed, is always a struggle to get *at* reality, to see things as they really are. Reading the Bible so that one's daily life might be understood in its light plays a vital role here.

Second, simplicity of life. It is difficult if not impossible to be in solidarity with the poor while maintaining an affluent lifestyle. Indeed, the culture of affluence, which can so deaden the spirit, is a product of the economic networks and social structures that allow the few to prosper at the expense of the many. An "immersion experience," in which one takes a period of time to live and work with the poor, can be a great help here. So can some kind of regular contact with a community engaged in direct ministry to the disadvantaged. Sustained social analysis can also deepen a commitment to simplicity of life and solidarity with the poor.

Third, a sense for an inclusive human community that transcends all boundaries and barriers. The Church itself is to be a sign of the union of all humankind in the coming of the kingdom of God. Divisions between the baptized whether based on race, sex, wealth, or social status fracture the unity of the body of Christ; they are, as Paul says, an offense against the Body and Blood of the Lord (1 Cor 11:17-31).

Finally, a commitment to action on behalf of justice. Authentic prayer leads to a concern for justice. To be actively involved in the struggle for justice is part of the responsibility of all Christians; it is an expression of their participation in the mission of the Church. The 1971 Synod of Bishops makes this clear in the introduction to its document *Justice in the World:* "Action on behalf of justice and participation in the transformation of the world fully appear to us as a constitutive dimension of preaching the Gospel, or, in other words, of the Church's mission for the redemption of the human race and its liberation from every oppressive situation." A spirituality of justice and solidarity with the poor must always be concerned with moving from *proclaiming* the truth to *doing* the truth.

Many young adults today learn the values of a spirituality of social justice from giving a year or more of their lives to the service of the poor through service groups such as the Jesuit Volunteer Corps, the Claretian Volunteers, or the Glenmary Associates. They generally join these programs after graduating from college; with only a small amount of monthly spending money, they live in small communities and work in various placements: shelters for the homeless or for abused women, inner-city schools and parishes, advocacy programs for migrants or the elderly. The Maryknoll Lay Missioners is another popular and effective program for lay missionaries.

Feminist Spirituality

Feminist spirituality is a relatively new field that has grown out of the struggle of women for equality in both society and Church. It is a particular expression of liberation theology. Like feminist theology (for it is often difficult to separate theology and spirituality), feminist spirituality covers a broad spectrum of positions and persons in the contemporary Catholic Church. Some feminist theologians have moved explicitly beyond the Christian tradition; their theological interests focus on the pre-Christian European worship of the Goddess, a nature religion also known as Wicca. Mary Daly is among those feminists who identify themselves as post-Christian. Others, like Rosemary Radford Ruether and Elisabeth Schüssler Fiorenza, have challenged the tradition in a radical way from within. What is common to most feminist theologians is a concern to bring the often neglected experience of women into the theological enterprise.

Feminist spirituality seeks to articulate a vision of the spiritual life that can embrace the experience of women, particularly their experience of oppression; it seeks to address their particular needs and help them reappropriate their own spiritual power. Consciousness raising is a first step toward a genuine feminist spiritual vision. Women who have so often been defined in terms of their sexual and reproductive functions insist that their value and personal possibilities cannot be determined by biology. Thus feminist spirituality offers women an alternative vision that includes a critique of those forces and movements that have oppressed women and alienated them from themselves. Patriarchy, the structuring of society and culture in terms of male interests and power, and hierarchy, organizing society and Church in terms of higher and lower status, are both rejected. Feminist spirituality emphasizes equality, inclusivity, and mutuality. It prefers the discussion to the lecture, the circle to the square.

Feminist spirituality differs from much of traditional spirituality in its nondualistic approach to all of reality; it seeks to overcome the split between body and spirit, between spirituality and sexuality, transcendence and immanence, reason and feeling, the sacred and the secular, between this world and the next. It seeks to read the Gospel in such a way that women will be empowered; thus it is uncomfortable with the emphasis in classical theology on losing the self by putting others first, seeing here a reinforcement of the passivity and submission to which so many women have been conditioned by a patriarchal culture and Church. Displacing one's own ego is fine if one's temptation is to pride, but for many women the real task of a genuine conversion is to be more assertive, to affirm their own value, and come to a genuine love of self.[15]

[15]See, for example, Rosemary Chinnici, *Can Women Re-Image The Church?* (New York: Paulist, 1992) 11–36.

Sandra M. Schneiders lists the following as major characteristics of feminist spirituality: First, it must be rooted in women's experience. Thus there is generally an emphasis on a personal sharing of stories as a way of recovering what has been repressed and of raising consciousness. Second, it celebrates those aspects of bodiliness, particularly those feminine experiences such as childbirth and menstruation, that religion has been silent about. They are life giving, not shameful. Third, it is concerned with nonhuman nature, with its sense of our organic relationship with the universe; its vision is ecologically sensitive. Fourth, it emphasizes rituals that are inclusive rather than hierarchical, joyful and participative rather than unemotional and dominative. Feminist spirituality is concerned for the renewal of Church ministry, liturgy, organization, and community. Finally, feminist spirituality sees an intrinsic relationship between personal growth and social justice. From the perspective of feminist spirituality, the personal is always political.[16]

MARIOLOGY

Devotion to Mary the mother of Jesus has been an important part of Catholic spirituality since the early centuries. It is difficult to imagine a Catholic church without a statue or image of Mary prominently displayed. The development of the Church's Mariological doctrine is a complicated question, but there is no question about the place that Mary holds in the hearts of Catholics. Mary has long appealed to Christians as a symbol both of the human person's openness to the divine and of the Spirit's transforming power in human life. Because of this, Mary is often seen as a type of the Church.

Mary in Scripture

Symbolism is perhaps the best approach to Mary in the Scriptures. Using the topological (as opposed to literal) interpretation so popular in the early Church, the Christian tradition has seen Mary foreshadowed in passages such as Genesis 3:15, proclaiming enmity between the offspring of the woman, Eve, and the serpent, and Isaiah 7:14, where the Hebrew *almah,* "young woman," was translated as "virgin" by Jerome in the Vulgate: "The virgin shall conceive, and bear a son, and his name shall be Emmanuel" (cf. Matt 3:23).

There is little about Mary in the earliest New Testament documents; Mark seems to include Mary among the members of Jesus' family, who consider

---

[16]See Sandra M. Schneiders, "Feminist Spirituality," *The New Dictionary of Catholic Spirituality,* ed. Michael Downey (Collegeville: The Liturgical Press, 1993) 400.

him to be out of his mind (Mark 3:21). But she plays a greater role in later books, in the infancy narratives of Matthew and Luke with their report of the virginal conception of Jesus, and in the Gospel of John. Much of this material sees Mary as a symbol: as the true disciple (Luke 8:21), as an intercessor (John 3:2), as mother of the disciple (John 19:26-27).

Mary in Tradition

The Fathers of the Church continued to develop the rich symbolism suggested by the image of the mother of Jesus. All of them taught the virginity of Mary. Justin Martyr (d. 165), Irenaeus of Lyons (d. 202), and Tertullian (d. ca. 221), building on Paul's notion of Jesus as the new Adam, developed the idea of Mary as the new Eve. Irenaeus, stressing Mary's active role in the work of redemption through her obedience, associated her with the Church, as did Tertullian, Hippolytus, Ambrose, and Augustine. Ambrose's description of Mary as a type of the Church was affirmed by Vatican II.

One of the most important titles of Mary is *Theotokos,* "Mother of God" (literally, "God-bearer"), so venerated in the Eastern Church. It was apparently used as early as 220 by Hippolytus of Rome and later became popular in the struggle against the Arians in the fourth century because of its obvious Christological significance. Though the title was rejected by the Nestorians, it was accepted by the universal Church after the definitions of Ephesus (431) and Chalcedon (451).

Parallel to this developing theology of Mary was the important place she held in the piety and devotion of the early Christians. One indication of this is the frequency with which she appears in the apocryphal writings. Though this material represents mostly pious imagination trying to fill in the gaps in the gospel stories of Jesus and Mary, it is evidence of the interest that Mary evoked.

Much more significant is the fact that Christians were praying to Mary as an intercessor as early as the third century. A manuscript from that time preserves this prayer: "We fly to thy protection *(sub tuum praesidium),* holy Mother of God *(Theotokos);* do not despise our prayers in our needs, but deliver us from all dangers, glorious and blessed Virgin." Another form of the prayer appears today in the still-popular *Memorare,* a prayer that dates from the Middle Ages: "Remember O most gracious Virgin Mary, that never was it known that anyone who fled to your protection . . ." From the fifth century on, churches began to be named in honor of Mary. For Catholics Mary is foremost in the communion of saints.

Mary was also celebrated in the liturgy. The first independent Marian feast originated outside Jerusalem in 430; it was celebrated on August 15 in honor of Mary, Mother of God, but was changed within a few decades to a commemoration of Mary's "dormition," or falling asleep. Her name was mentioned in the Roman Eucharistic Prayer as early as the fifth century. By the seventh century the feasts of the Annunciation (March 25), Dormition or Assumption (August 15), Nativity (September 8), and Purification (February 2, now called the Presentation of the Lord) were being observed in both the Eastern and Western Churches.

The Church has generally encouraged popular Marian devotion, but it has also been careful to distinguish carefully between what is popular piety and its public professions of faith, as in the Marian dogmas. Even apparitions and visions such as those at Tepeyac, Lourdes, and Fatima, though they might be approved by the Church, remain essentially private devotions; they are not part of the Church's official faith.

Some of these apparitions have played an important role in the development of popular Catholicism. The story of the appearance of Our Lady of Guadalupe in 1531 to the Aztec peasant Juan Diego at Tepeyac, near Mexico City, was enormously influential in enabling the Indian peoples of Mexico to recognize themselves in the religion of their conquerors. In the famous image, still venerated by Mexican and Mexican American people, Mary appears as a *mestiza,* a woman of Spanish and Indian blood, and she seems to be pregnant. The appearances to Bernadette Soubirous, a young French girl, in 1858 at Lourdes led to a church and a place of pilgrimage that has become a place of grace and healing for millions.

The Marian Doctrines

Catholic Marian devotion emerges out of the interplay between interest and imagination, prayer and liturgical celebration, popular piety and theological reflection. The long process illustrates the principle that the Church's prayer and liturgy helps shape its faith *(lex orandi, lex credendi)*. The Church has taught the perpetual virginity of Mary since the fourth century. The Council of Trent affirmed the sinlessness of Mary (DS 91). The two most recent teachings are the dogma of the immaculate conception, solemnly defined by Pope Pius IX in 1854, and Pius XII's solemn definition of the assumption in 1951. Though neither dogma can be "proved" from Scripture, each has a long history in the tradition, and each was proclaimed only after a process of consulting the faith of the Church through a polling of the bishops.

In proclaiming that Mary was conceived "immune from all stain of original sin," Pius IX's decree *Ineffabilis Deus* cited texts such as Gabriel's greeting Mary as "full of grace" (Luke 1:28) and Elizabeth's exclamation "Blessed are you among women" (Luke 1:42). The doctrine seems to have originated in the liturgical tradition of the Eastern Christianity, which began celebrating Mary's conception around the end of the seventh century. The feast came to Europe in the ninth and tenth centuries, occasioning considerable controversy over the doctrine. It is interesting to note that theologians such as Anselm, Bernard, Albert, Aquinas, and Bonaventure—all of them saints of the Church—opposed the doctrine, not being able to reconcile it with the idea that all human beings are saved through Christ.

The dilemma was resolved by Duns Scotus, who proposed that Christ can save human beings by preserving them from sin as well as taking it away from those touched by it. The dogma of the immaculate conception does not deny that Mary was saved by Christ; what it affirms is that because she was destined to be the mother of the Redeemer she was united to God in a most intimate way from the beginning of her life.

The tradition of the assumption of Mary is considerably older; it has been celebrated by the Church since at least the end of the sixth century. The dogma affirms that from the moment of her death Mary shares fully in the resurrection of Jesus—that is, that she has entered into heaven in her full humanity, "body and soul." It is an important affirmation of our own share in the resurrection of Jesus, even if the Church has not definitively answered the question of how and when the resurrection takes place for the rest of us. Some theologians today argue that what the Church has affirmed about Mary's entry into glory takes place in a similar way for all the just at the moment of their deaths.[17]

Some had hoped that the Second Vatican Council would issue a separate document on Mary, declaring her to be Mediatrix of all graces. Others argued that it was unnecessary and would do great damage ecumenically. After considerable debate, the fathers voted to have the council's teaching on Mary included as a separate chapter in the Dogmatic Constitution on the Church. Though it touches briefly on her relation to the mystery of Christ, it places more emphasis on Mary as a model of the Church, stressing her faith, charity, and union with Christ (LG 63).

Mary and Ecumenism

Although Orthodox Christianity has a deep devotion to the Mother of God, Catholic Marian devotion has frequently been misunderstood by Protestant Christians. They have sometimes accused Catholics of worshiping Mary. Mary holds a place of honor in the Catholic tradition, both in its devotional life and in its doctrinal heritage. But the tradition has always been careful to distinguish between the worship *(latria),* given only to God, and veneration *(dulia* for the saints, *hyperdulia* for Mary). It also keeps a careful distinction between what is popular piety and its public professions of faith, as we saw above. Catholics value their veneration of Mary highly, but they do not seek to impose it on Protestants. At the same time, Protestant

[17]For example, Karl Rahner, *Foundations of Christian Faith: An Introduction to the Idea of Christianity* (New York: Seabury, 1978) 388.

Christians should not see Catholic veneration of Mary as something contrary to the gospel or as an obstacle to Christian unity. The Marian dogmas should be understood as a legitimate example of doctrinal development within the Catholic tradition.

Today both Protestants and Catholics are coming to a new appreciation of the power of Mary as a symbol. Robert McAfee Brown has observed that twenty years ago Catholic devotion to Mary was a major obstacle for Protestants who are today discovering the Mary of the *Magnificat*.[18] Elizabeth Johnson, though warning that the image of Mary may be interpreted in a way that stereotypes women in subordinate roles, argues that the Marian tradition (as indeed women in general) can be a rich source of divine imagery.[19]

CONCLUSION

The temptation to reduce Christianity to a system of ethics or simply to the practice of the Golden Rule is a great impoverishment. Jesus says that he came so that we might have life and have it more abundantly (John 10:10). The life he offers us is not just eternal life in the kingdom but a share in God's life now. "Now this is eternal life, that they should know you, the only true God, and the one whom you sent, Jesus Christ" (John 17:3).

Prayer, whether vocal, mental, or contemplative, unites us to God so that we might experience something of that abundance of life that Jesus offers us. Liturgical prayer is the official prayer of the Church. Spiritual disciplines help to prepare the soil of our hearts, to weed and water it, so that the divine life in Christ might take deep root in us. Spirituality fosters that life and gives it expression in our own lives. An authentic spirituality is one that promotes psychological and spiritual maturity and opens one to others. The Church has been enriched by a host of mystics and spiritual teachers.

The rich diversity of spiritualities in the Catholic tradition—monastic, apostolic, social justice, charismatic, matrimonial, lay, feminist—shows a truly catholic comprehensiveness. At the same time, as Catholics see life in Christ lived out within the community of the Church, there is generally an ecclesial aspect to Catholic spirituality. A Catholic spirituality is communal and liturgical; it includes the ancient tradition of honoring the Mother of God. As a symbol, Mary shows both God's power and human possibility.

---

[18]"Protestants and the Marian Year," *Christian Century* 104 (June 3, 1987) 520–21.
[19]"Mary and the Female Face of God," *Theological Studies* 50 (1989) 525–26.

10. The Fullness of Christian Hope

Our human destiny is everlasting life, the fullness of life with God, which is both revealed and promised in Jesus' victory over sin and death. This is the ultimate meaning of our salvation in Christ Jesus. In the words of Pope John Paul II, "To save means to *liberate from radical evil.*"[1]

The Christian tradition uses a number of symbols, images, and concepts to express the fullness of Christian hope, which in the final analysis is beyond our ability to imagine. The resurrection of the body, the second coming of Christ, the particular judgment at the moment of death, a general judgment on the last day, the immortality of the soul, heaven, the beatific vision, eternal life—all these "eschatological" (from the Greek *eschatos*, "last," or "end") concepts represent efforts to express the theological truth of our eternal destiny, a destiny rooted in the resurrection of Jesus. These are salvific terms speaking about the future God has in store for us. But salvation was not always an eschatological concept.

SALVATION AND ESCHATOLOGY

Salvation in the Hebrew Scriptures

The Hebrew word "salvation" and its derivatives comes from the root *YS*, which connotes open space, security, and freedom from constriction. In the tradition of ancient Israel the notion of salvation is concerned with God's interventions on behalf of the people of Israel. Though God "saves" the people in many ways, the paradigm of salvation for ancient Israel is always the great event of the Exodus, God's deliverance of the people from bondage in Egypt (Exod 15:2; Ps 78:22; Isa 63:9).

---

[1] *Crossing the Threshold of Hope,* ed. Vittorio Messori (New York: Random House, 1994) 67.

For most of the period of time reflected in the Bible there was no belief in life beyond the grave, nor does the resurrection of the dead play a very large role in the Hebrew Scriptures. We can learn a great deal about how powerful the Jewish experience of God was by reading the psalms; they are alive with the joy of living in covenant relationship with God, of sensing God's presence, of praising God's name in the assembly of the people–and all this without any idea of life after death. This may seem difficult for many of us to understand, but then we are the product of almost two thousand years of Christian history; because of the resurrection of Jesus we take the resurrection of the dead for granted.

Our way of thinking has also been greatly influenced by the dualistic anthropology inherited from Greek philosophy. The Greeks thought of the human person as a composite of soul and body or, as the Platonists taught, a soul "imprisoned" in a body. In the Jewish tradition the person was not conceived dualistically. A human being was always a living body. Once a person died, the "spirit" or principle of life and activity *(ruah)* departed and the self *(nepes)* went down to Sheol, the underworld or abode of the dead. But Sheol was not the place for another kind of life; it was a place of darkness, worms, dust, a pit (Job 17:13-16). Sometimes the word "sheol" was used simply as a synonym for death or the grave.

The state of the dead in Sheol is the opposite of everything meant by life. It is a state of utter passivity; there is no work, no reason, no knowledge, no wisdom in Sheol (Eccl 9:10). Worst of all, there is no longer any relationship with Yahweh, for the dead cannot remember or praise Yahweh (Pss 6:6; 88:12). It was only in the intertestamental literature, written close to the time of Jesus, that Sheol appears as a place reserved for the wicked.

The Resurrection of the Dead

During and after the sixth-century Exile in Babylon Judaism began to wrestle seriously with the questions of Yahweh's faithfulness and salvation in the context of shattered hopes, evil, and death. Ezekiel's vision in 37:1-14 shows Yahweh reanimating the dry bones of the nation and bringing it new life. The story of Job, the just man who suffer., raises the question of the mystery of evil.

The first clear evidence of a Jewish hope for a resurrection of the dead appears in the Book of Daniel, written during the persecution of Antiochus IV Epiphanes (167–164 B.C.), a little more than 150 years before the time of Jesus. Antiochus had forbidden the Jews the practice of their religion; those who disobeyed were put to death. Their fidelity to the Law did not save them from torture and death (cf. 2 Macc 6–7); thus their martyrdom raised the question of their relationship with Yahweh in a new way. Where was their God? The author of the Book of Daniel assured the people that God's intervention was at hand. For those who had died for their faith, he expressed the hope that the coming apocalyptic judgment would see the dead raised to everlasting life (Dan 12:1-3). In 2 Maccabees (2:7; 14:46), another book from the same period, belief in the resurrection of the dead is clearly present. The same idea is present in the noncanonical apocalyptic books (Enoch 51; Bar 50; 4 Ezra 7.29). What this means is that in some expressions of the Jewish tradition in the century before Jesus salvation had become an eschatological concept. At the time of Jesus the Pharisees believed in the resurrection of the dead, while the Sadducees did not (Luke 20:27-38).

Thus the idea of the resurrection of the dead was a late development in the Jewish tradition. But the Jewish concept of the resurrection was an apocalyptic notion; it involved the resurrection of *all* the dead, which was to take place at the end of time. Because of this many of the early Christians, influenced by Jewish apocalyptic thought, believed that the resurrection of Jesus meant that the end of the world was at hand (1 Cor 7:29).

The Resurrection of Jesus

The death of Jesus was a shattering experience for his disciples; it left them disoriented, confused, and terrified for their own safety. Something of their experience is captured by Luke in his story of the two disciples on the way to Emmaus. As the disciples make their way along the road, they tell a stranger who joins them about their distress over Jesus' death: "We were hoping that he would be the one to redeem Israel" (Luke 24:21). The disciples are slow to recognize the stranger as the risen Jesus, a theme that a close reading of the texts finds in the other Easter appearance stories as well. Yet these two disciples, as well as Peter, Mary of Magdala, and other men and women who had followed Jesus, are convinced by their Easter experience beyond any shadow of doubt that God had delivered Jesus from the realm of the dead and given him new life.

The disciples' Easter experience of the Crucified One's presence among them in a new way challenged their powers of expression. Jesus' new life is a mystery not easily captured in language. It is something completely different from the raising of Lazarus. The risen Jesus now lives on the other side of time and space, in God's presence. In Paul's words, "As to his death, he died to sin once and for all; as to his life, he lives for God" (Rom 6:10).

The language of resurrection predominates in the New Testament, though it has other ways of expressing what remains the mystery of Jesus' new life with God. An early tradition speaks of God "releasing him from the throes of death, because it was impossible for him to be held by it" (Acts 2:24). Some traditions use the language of exaltation rather than resurrection (Phil 2:9; Luke 24:26; Eph 4:8; Acts 5:6). In contrast to the much later stories of his conversion that appear in Acts, Paul himself does not give many details of his Easter experience. He says simply in Galatians that God "was pleased to reveal his Son to me" (Gal 1:16). And there are other ways of expressing the belief that Jesus has been vindicated and lives with God. But it is not surprising that the language of resurrection predominates, for the idea of a general resurrection of the dead at the end of time was already a part of Jewish eschatological hope.

CHRISTIAN ESCHATOLOGY

The Resurrection of the Body

The resurrection of the body rather than the immortality of the soul is the foundational concept of Christian eschatology. Paul presumes the resurrection of the dead in his First Letter to the Corinthians; in fact, he twice goes so far as to argue from the resurrection of the dead to the resurrection of Jesus (1 Cor 15:13, 16) to assure the Corinthians of their own hope of sharing in the resurrection. In other words, our resurrection and his are inseparably linked. Paul describes the risen Jesus as "the firstfruits of those who have fallen asleep" (1 Cor 15:20) and as the "last Adam" (15:45).

But when it comes to trying to explain to them what a risen body is, Paul's language begins to break down. He speaks of that which is raised up as "incorruptible" (15:42), of a "spiritual body" *(soma pneumatikon)* as opposed to a natural one (15:44), of a body clothed "with immortality" (15:53). But what is a spiritual body? The expression itself sounds like a contradiction in terms. What Paul is affirming is essentially a personal existence, for the resurrection of the body means that we enter into life with God in the fullness of our individual humanity, which to the nondualistic Jewish way of thinking is inseparable from our bodily existence. Thus it means a kind of existence that is beyond the limitations of space and time but at the same time is much more than the survival of our soul. Paul says that the Lord Jesus "will change our lowly body to conform with his glorified body" (Phil 3:21). Indeed, for Paul "creation itself" is destined to share in Christ's redemptive work; it will be "set free from slavery to corruption and share in the glorious freedom of the children of God" (Rom 8:21). God's transforming grace is at work not just in human beings but in the cosmos itself.

Some contemporary theologians speculate that the resurrection of the just takes place at the moment of death.[2] This opinion has the advantage of resolving one of the unanswered questions of a more traditional understanding of Christian eschatology that saw the soul "entering heaven" after the particular judgment but having to wait until the resurrection of the dead

[2]See Karl Rahner, *Foundations of Christian Faith* (New York: Seabury, 1978) 270–74.

at the end of time in order to be reunited with its body. Such a literal understanding of biblical texts such as John 6:54 and Revelation 20:12-13 represents a temporal way of conceiving the eschaton, which, by definition, is beyond space and time. Furthermore, it leaves unexplained how personal identity and consciousness can be maintained in a soul separated from the body through which it knows and is self-aware. As Rahner says, "Eternity is not an incalculably long-lasting mode of pure time, but a mode of spirit and freedom which has been actualized in time, and therefore it can be grasped only from a correct understanding of spirit and freedom."[3]

The resurrection of the body remains the most basic theological statement of Christian hope; it is a formula of faith professed in the Apostles', Nicene-Constantinopolitan, and Athanasian creeds. It is a powerful symbol. But there are other symbols expressive of Christian eschatological hope, some of which have been interpreted in an overly literal manner.

Heaven

The symbol of heaven represents the most popular expression of Christian eschatology. In the Old Testament, heaven, or "the heavens," as it frequently appears, means both the area above the earth and the place where God dwells. In the New Testament heaven becomes both the dwelling place and the reward of Christians (Matt 5:12; 1 Thess 4:16-17). Of course, heaven is not a place; to be in heaven means to be fully in God's presence. Or as Kasper says so well, heaven does not simply exist but comes into being "when the first created being is eschatologically and finally taken up by God. Heaven takes shape in the Resurrection and Exaltation of Christ."[4]

Other biblical ways of expressing the destiny of the just include the term "eternal life" (Rom 2:7; 6:23; 1 Tim 1:16; John 3:15, 36; 6:68; 12:50; 20:31); Paul's expression "inheriting the kingdom of God" (1 Cor 6:9; 15:50; Gal 5:21; Eph 5:5); and his beautiful idea that we already see the glory of God reflected on the face of Christ (2 Cor 4:6) and will one day see the face of God directly (1 Cor 13:12). The later Church expressed this idea of seeing God face to face by the term "beatific vision."

The Second Coming

The second coming of Christ, sometimes referred to as the *parousia* (from the Greek "presence," or "arrival"), is another concept that has often been interpreted in a too-literal way. The concept has a long history and represents the fusing of several different biblical images. Its roots are in the

---

[3]Ibid., 271.
[4]Walter Kasper, *Jesus the Christ* (New York: Paulist, 1976) 152.

image of the Son of Man in Daniel 7:13, described as "coming on the clouds of heaven." In this passage the Son of Man functions as a symbol for the people of Israel. But in the later apocalyptic literature the Son of Man appears as the agent of God's judgment, coming on the clouds of heaven at the end of the world. Jesus frequently spoke of the Son of Man in this context of the final judgment (Matt 24:30; 25:31; Mark 8:38; Luke 12:8).

But it was the early Christian community that began proclaiming the imminent coming of the risen Jesus in judgment, from which the image of the second coming developed. In a very early Christological development, two associations were made. First, the resurrection of Jesus was interpreted against the background of the apocalyptic expectation of a general resurrection of the dead at the end of the world, then popular in Palestinian Jewish communities. If Jesus has been raised from the dead, then the end of the world must be at hand. This led to the apocalyptic expectation so evident in the earliest stages of the tradition (cf. Luke 12:8), including Paul (1 Cor 1:8; 7:29). Paul describes Jesus as the Lord coming down from heaven at the sound of the archangel's voice and God's trumpet (1 Thess 4:16). Second, the risen Jesus was identified with the heavenly Son of Man, the agent of God's judgment and bringer of God's salvation. The Synoptic evangelists frequently represent Jesus as referring to himself as the Son of Man.

Fundamentalist Christians have used texts such 1 Thessalonians 4:17 and Revelation 3:10 to teach a very literal coming of Jesus in judgment in the manner of Michelangelo's famous painting of the Last Judgment in the Sistine Chapel. Some talk about the "rapture," when those faithful Christians still living on earth will be taken up to meet the Lord with all the saints, though there is disagreement as to whether this happens before or after the "great tribulation," which will bring God's judgment upon the wicked. But these are not the only possible interpretations. Catholic faith does not obligate us to believe that the Lord will come literally some morning or afternoon on the clouds of heaven; there are many ways to imagine the end of the world, some of them, unfortunately, entirely of our own doing. What is clear is that each of us must one day face God's judgment, but how or when or under what circumstances we do not know. At least we can say that for the dead the parousia has already happened.

Final Judgment

What becomes of the wicked? The idea that they must one day face God's judgment and pay the price of their sins can be found in both Hebrew and Christian Scriptures. Popular Christian eschatology uses the image of hell (from the German *Hel,* "place of the dead") to portray in highly imaginative terms the destiny of the wicked. Behind this image can be found the biblical notion of judgment and the image of Gehenna.

The Old Testament notion of God's judgment *(mispat)* was probably derived from the earthly judgments exercised by tribal elders and kings. God's judgment was either awaited eagerly or feared, depending on one's moral state. For the righteous it meant vindication (Deut 10:18; Pss 7:7; 9:5; 76:10; Isa 11:4), but for the wicked God's judgment brought condemnation and punishment (Ezek 5:7; 7:3).

The idea of a day of judgment, the Day of Yahweh, first appears in the prophet Amos, but it must come from an earlier period, since Amos does not explain it. The pessimistic Amos associates the Day of Yahweh with God's judgment on Israel; it will be a day of darkness and gloom (Amos 5:18-20; 8:9). In the subsequent prophets the Day of Yahweh stands for the future day when God would manifest the divine righteousness, often with cosmic displays of power. Isaiah broadens the concept to include the other nations without excluding Israel; it will be a day when Yahweh brings down the proud and arrogant (Isa 2:12), a day of wrath and anger when the sun and the stars are darkened, the moon does not shine, the land will be wasted, and sinners destroyed (Isa 13:9-11). In some of the later prophets the Day of Yahweh is conceived more eschatologically. Joel (4:12-14) sees it as a day that brings God's judgment to all the nations. Zephaniah (1:15) describes it in the language of anguish and distress, of destruction and desolation, which would be echoed in the medieval Christian hymn *Dies Irae.*

In the New Testament the day of judgment became the Day of the Son of Man, when Jesus would return to judge the living and the dead (Mark 13:26; Luke 17:24; Matt 25:31), as we have seen.

The image of hell comes from the Aramaic word *Gehenna,* a shortened form of "valley of the son of Hinnon." Located on the outskirts of Jerusalem, the place had a bad reputation as having once been a shrine where human sacrifice was offered (2 Kgs 23:10). Jeremiah cursed it (Jer 7:31-33). Though Isaiah does not name it, he refers to it as a place where those who rebelled against Yahweh will end up, and he supplies the images of fire and torment: "Their worm shall not die, nor their fire be extinguished" (Isa 66:24). In the extrabiblical Jewish writings this imagery is used again to depict Gehenna as the place where the wicked are punished after death. It appears in the New Testament as a place of fire (Matt 5:22; 18:9), which is unquenchable (Mark 9:43), as a pit into which the wicked are cast (Matt 5:29; Mark 9:45), "where 'their worm does not die, and the fire is not quenched'" (Mark 9:48). From this comes our popular image of hell.

What about the devil? Though belief in evil spirits was widespread in the ancient world and entered the Hebrew tradition by way of Mesopotamia, it does not play an important role in the early Hebrew Scriptures. The figure of Satan, whose name means "accuser," functions as an adversary or one who tests the virtue of human beings in the earlier literature (cf. Job 1:6; 2:1). In the Septuagint translation of the Hebrew Scriptures, "Satan" was translated as *diabolos* (whence "devil"), which also means "accuser." It is only much later, in the intertestamental literature, that demonology becomes much more important and Satan is seen as a ruling evil spirit dedicated to the destruction of humankind. In the apocryphal Jewish writings the demons are described as fallen angels and Satan gives as the reason for his expulsion from heaven his refusal to honor man as the image of God.

The New Testament takes for granted Satan's power and hostility to the reign of God (Matt 13:19; Luke 22:3; John 13:2). Jesus' exorcisms are described as a "casting out" *(ekballein)* of evil spirits (Matt 8:16; Luke 11:14) or a "healing" *(therapeuein)* others of them (Mark 1:34; Luke 6:18; 8:2). The existence of the devil and evil spirits is presupposed in traditional Catholic belief, but it is not clear that their existence has been formally defined. Where the devil has been mentioned by the magisterium, it has been in the context of the theology of creation, affirming that the devil and other spirits were created good but became evil by themselves (DS 800).

Not all New Testament writers describe the destiny of the wicked in terms of a hell with fires and demons, but the idea that they must one day face God's judgment is everywhere. Paul teaches that sinners will not enter the kingdom of God (1 Cor 6:10; Gal 5:19-21) and will be punished with eternal destruction (Phil 3:19). For John sinners have already come under judgment in Jesus (3:18; 5:22-24; 12:31) and will be excluded from eternal life (5:29; 8:24; 10:28).

Does God inflict eternal punishment on sinners? Certainly the New Testament speaks of eternal damnation as the destiny of the wicked (Matt 25:41; Luke 16:23; Rev 20:10). Some Christians today argue that the presence of so much evil in the world demands the existence of hell for those who have chosen to live without God, or in more biblical terms, those who sought to be their own gods (Gen 3:5). Others express the hope that in the end all will be saved.

It is important to reflect further on this question of eternal punishment. It does not make much sense theologically to think of God as a God who condemns the evil to eternal torment. God does not punish, either in this life or in the next. The suffering and alienation that our sins bring into the world are their own punishment. God is at once the author of life and our final destiny, calling us to communion in the divine life. But God always respects our human freedom; our response must be freely given. If we refuse to respond, the choice is ours; God cannot force love and communion upon us any more than we can force love and communion on one another. Love that is not freely given is not love. To exclude God from our lives is sin; to die in that state is to have refused God's offer of communion in the divine life. That is the real meaning of hell, apart from any sulfurous imagery; it is the final alienation, which comes from sin. It is to be forever without the God for whom we were created and for whom our hearts are yearning. Or in that powerful image from Jean-Paul Sartre's play, *No Exit,* hell is to be forever what we have made ourselves to be.

Edward Schillebeeckx offers a very suggestive interpretation of hell. He finds the view that all will be saved too superficial, one that trivializes the real struggle between good and evil so obvious in our human history. But he holds that heaven and hell cannot be considered on the same level; they are asymmetrical affirmations of faith. Nor does it make sense to imagine the just living in glory, while others "next to them"—so to speak—are suffering the pains of hell. Here is where the asymmetry comes in. Schillebeeckx is convinced that God indeed offers an eternal communion or life to those who have been in communion with the divine mystery and in solidarity with others during their earthly existence; this is the bond that cannot be destroyed by death. But rather than seeing a God who condemns the wicked to eternal punishment, Schillebeeckx suggests that those who have rejected solidarity with their fellow human beings and thus communion with God will not survive their own deaths. "So there is no future for evil and oppression, while goodness still knows a future beyond the boundary of death, thanks to the outstretched hand of God which receives us. God does not take vengeance; he leaves evil to its own, limited logic."[5]

Schillebeeckx's approach is attractive precisely because it takes both God's justice and human freedom seriously; it respects both without in the process turning the God of mercy and life into a vindictive judge who sustains the wicked in torment for eternity.

Purgatory

The doctrine of purgatory grounds the Catholic practice of praying for the dead (cf. 2 Macc 12:43-46); it refers to the purification to be undergone for the "temporal punishment" due to sins already forgiven, in other words, for the damaging effects of sin. The basic idea is one of purification before coming into God's presence. There is considerable evidence that Christians have been praying for the faithful departed since the early centuries. In the Middle Ages the Western idea of purgatory became much more juridical, stressing the need for expiation. The Eastern Church continued to stress purification and spiritual growth. The notion of purgatory as a place seems to date from the twelfth century. The doctrine of purgatory was affirmed by the Second Council of Lyons (1274) and by the Council of Florence (1439). It was reaffirmed by Trent against the Reformers.

As an eschatological concept, purgatory should not be imagined temporally or spatially. Contemporary theology tends to understand it in relation to the encounter with God at the moment of death or perhaps even

---

[5] *Church: The Human Story of God* (New York: Crossroad, 1990) 138.

earlier, an encounter that burns away our resistance to the brilliance of the divine presence and purifies us of whatever self-centeredness remains as an obstacle to union. Catholics commend a departed member of the community to God by a celebration of the Mass of Christian Burial; they remember those in purgatory on All Souls Day, November 2.

Limbo

What about limbo? Many Catholics grew up believing that infants who died without baptism, thus in original sin, went to limbo, a state of natural happiness, since they had not committed any actual sin, but without the joy of the beatific vision. But the magisterium has not taken an official position on the question of limbo.

Belief in limbo developed in the Church to counter the teaching of Augustine on the fate of unbaptized children. In response to the Pelagian teaching that such children were granted access to a place of beatitude, Augustine taught that they were consigned to eternal punishment, though of the mildest kind (*Enchiridion* 93). His position was mitigated by Peter Abelard and other medieval theologians in the twelfth century who held that unbaptized infants were not subject to punishment but could not receive the beatific vision. This intermediate state was known as limbo (from the Latin *limbus*, "border"). Though belief in limbo became part of popular Catholicism and was widely held, the Church has no formal doctrine regarding the fate of unbaptized children. Thus limbo remains a theological opinion.

Today Catholic theology assumes that infants who die without baptism enter eternal life, since they have had no chance to reject the salvation merited for all humanity through the death and resurrection of Jesus. Jesus himself held up little Jewish children as examples of openness to God's kingdom (Mark 10:14). The *Catechism of the Catholic Church* does not mention limbo and expresses the hope that there is a way of salvation for children who have died without baptism (1261).

The fact that an infant has not been baptized does not exclude the child from God's grace; indeed the practice of indiscriminately baptizing children whose parents are not practicing their faith needs at least to be questioned, as it risks reducing baptism to a cultural rite of passage rather than a sacramental celebration of faith. Nevertheless, the Church continues its tradition of baptizing infants in immediate danger of death that they might be incorporated into the dying and rising to new life of Jesus and become members of his body, the Church.

THE COMMUNION OF SAINTS

One of the distinguishing characteristics of Catholicism is its awareness of a relationship between the living and the dead. This relationship is expressed in the doctrine of the communion of saints, the belief that those in the Church on earth enjoy some kind of fellowship with all those who have died in the Lord, the "saints," canonized or not, the holy ones of the Old Testament, and the souls in purgatory.

The original term *communio sanctorum* is ambiguous; it can mean a communion of holy things as well as a communion of holy persons, or "saints." The term originated in the Eastern Church, where it was used in the sense of "holy things" *(ta hagia),* probably in connection with Eucharistic communion. In the West *communio sanctorum* appears in a creed, probably from southern Gaul, in the fifth century. J.N.D. Kelly argues that in its original Western usage it stood for "that ultimate fellowship with the holy persons of all ages, as well as with the whole company of heaven."[6] Though the phrase has also been used in the West in reference to the sacraments, since at least the sixth century it has been understood in the sense of a communion of persons living and dead. We are related to the Church triumphant and the Church suffering through our communion with the risen Jesus and in his Spirit.

The Second Vatican Council "accepts with great devotion the venerable faith of our ancestors regarding this vital fellowship with our brethren who are in heavenly glory or who are still being purified after death" (LG 51). Contemporary theological reflection suggests that the communion of saints is not limited to those living or dead who are members of the Church but embraces all those who have been the beneficiaries of God's salvific work in Christ; therefore, it is coterminous with the kingdom of God rather than with the Church.

Invocation of the Saints

The saints are those men and women in whom God's grace and presence has been abundantly evident—in their heroic witness to their faith in martyrdom (the word "martyr" in Greek means "a witness"), in love and compassion for others, in their work for the Church, or in their faithful living out of their vocations. Church historians have identified some ten thousand saints whose cults have been celebrated by the faithful, most of whom were never officially "canonized."[7] A "saint" was someone who was remembered, venerated, and invoked by the faithful. The process of canonization did not really develop until after the year 1000 and was not reserved to the

---

[6] *Early Christian Creeds* (London: Longman, 1972) 391.
[7] Kenneth L. Woodward, *Making Saints* (New York: Simon & Schuster, 1990) 17.

papacy until 1234 when Pope Gregory IX in his *Decretals* claimed absolute papal jurisdiction over all causes of saints.[8] But even today some are unofficially acclaimed as saints by the people—men and women like Archbishop Romero of El Salvador, Mother Teresa of Calcutta, and Pope John XXIII—because of the closeness to God evident in their lives.

Conscious of their fellowship or communion with the saints, Christians have invoked their intercession from perhaps as early as the middle of the second century. In the early third century Origin wrote that intercessory prayers addressed to the saints are both valid and powerful (*On Prayer* 11.2). Augustine extolled the power of the saints and encouraged their invocation (*City of God* 22.8ff.)

Invoking the saints is very much a part of Catholic piety and the Catholic liturgical tradition. The Litany of the Saints, prayed on solemn occasions such as an ordination or the baptizing of candidates at the Easter Vigil, can be a powerful expression of the Church's communion with the holy men and women of the past. The feast days of many of the saints are remembered in the liturgical calendar. The feast of All Saints, celebrated on November 1, honors all those who have died in communion with Christ, even if they have not been officially recognized as saints by the Church.

Protestant Christians have difficulties with invoking the intercession of the saints as well as with praying for the dead; they find neither practice warranted by the Bible. Furthermore, they fear that invoking the saints might compromise the one mediatorship of Christ. But both practices have their origin in the faith experience of Christian peoples over the centuries and have been approved by the Church. The invocation of the saints remains today, particularly in certain cultures, very much a part of popular religion, which the Church has been willing to accept as part of the inculturation of the faith. At the same time it has tried to guard, not always successfully, against the aberrations into which popular religion can descend.

The Lutheran-Catholic Dialogue in the United States has suggested one way beyond the impasse raised between Catholics and Protestants by the Catholic practice of invoking the saints. In 1992, after seven years of dialogue on the question of "The One Mediator, the Saints, and Mary," the Dialogue published its report. What it proposed to its respective Churches was that Lutherans acknowledge that the "Catholic teaching about the saints and Mary as set forth in the documents of Vatican Council II does not promote idolatrous belief or practice and is not opposed to the gospel" and that the Catholic Church acknowledge that Lutherans "would not be obliged to invoke the saints or to affirm the two Marian dogmas."[9] Essentially that makes

[8]Ibid., 66–67.
[9]H. George Anderson, J. Francis Stafford, and Joseph A. Burgess, eds., *The One Mediator, the Saints, and Mary* (Minneapolis: Augsburg, 1992) 62.

the traditional invocation of the saints a matter of piety and the Mariological dogmas a legitimate example of doctrinal development within the Roman Catholic Church, neither of which should be imposed on other Churches (just as the practice of invoking the saints is not imposed on Catholics).

Indulgences

The notion of indulgences is related to the doctrine of the communion of saints; it presents a complicated and at times unfortunate chapter in the history of the Church. Indulgences are concerned not with taking away sins themselves, which are forgiven through God's grace, but with removing entirely (plenary indulgence) or mitigating the "temporal punishment" attached to sins committed after baptism.

In the early days of Christian history a person who had committed a serious sin would be enrolled in the order of penitents to complete a period of public penance. Later, as private confession was introduced, a penitent would often be given a "commutation," or reduction, of the canonical penance but would still do some good work in its place. This was similar to the "penance" we receive today in confession.

The first indulgences appeared in the eleventh century when bishops and confessors would assure their penitents that the Church would pray for the remission of the temporal punishment due their sins and at the same time would grant a remission of part or all of their canonical penance. But gradually the two elements of prayer and reduction of penance coalesced into one act of remitting the temporal punishment due to sin. Hugh of St. Cher (1230) justified this on the basis of the "treasury of the Church," the merit or, better, superabundant grace of Christ and the saints applied by the Church, increasingly through the authority of the pope, on behalf of the sinner. The idea of doing some good work, the remnant of the older commutation of the canonical penance, was still required, but no longer made sense, once the Church began granting a simple juridical remission of temporal punishment, now outside the forum of confession.

From the fifteenth century on, indulgences began to be applied to the dead. The practice of granting them, accompanied by a donation, which originally had been a good work of almsgiving, was obviously open to abuse. John Tetzel's "selling" of indulgences in Germany in the sixteenth century triggered Luther's protest at Wittenburg; it was the straw that broke the camel's back. By the time Trent condemned the abuses connected with indulgences, the damage was done.

Pope Paul VI specifically linked the doctrine of indulgences with that of the communion of saints in his 1967 apostolic constitution, *Indulgentiarum doctrina*. In this context it makes sense, for the practice of praying for the dead with whom we are in communion through Christ is an ancient one.

The communion of saints is a real communion. However, as Richard McBrien observes, "a calculating, egocentric approach to Christian destiny, where an individual is concerned primarily with the accumulation of spiritual 'credits,' is so antithetical to sound theological and doctrinal principles that the disappearance of that sort of interest in indulgences can only be welcomed."[10] Pope Paul further reformed the discipline connected with indulgences by dropping the specific times attached (thirty days, seven years, etc.) and limited their availability.

SALVATION OUTSIDE THE CHURCH?

The Church's traditional emphasis on the necessity of baptism for salvation has led to other theological anomalies besides the old belief in limbo. Also problematic is the axiom "no salvation outside the Church" *(extra ecclesiam nulla salus)*. It suggests not only an overbearing pride and intolerance on the part of Catholics and other Christians but, what is worse, a very narrow and impoverished concept of God.

The Traditional Doctrine

The axiom has a long history in the tradition.[11] Most of the Church Fathers prior to Augustine applied it to Christians who had separated themselves from the Church through either heresy or schism. In other words, it was used in reference to errant Christians. But toward the end of the fourth century, when most of the Roman Empire had become Christian, the axiom began to be used as a warning to pagans and Jews; John Chrysostom, for example, used it particularly against the Jews, regrettably referring to them with "some of the most offensive language about Jews to be found in Christian literature."[12]

Augustine's emphasis on the necessity of baptism and the Church intensified the position; he specifically rejected the possibility of salvation for Jews or for pagans, whether they had heard of the gospel or not. Even unbaptized children were damned, as we saw above. His influence was to so shape the subsequent tradition that it is not difficult to find popes and councils throughout Christian history repeating what had become a traditional teaching. As late as 1863 Pope Pius IX could proclaim: "It is a well-known Catholic dogma that no one can be saved outside the Catholic Church" (DS

---

[10] *Catholicism* (San Francisco: Harper, 1994) 1171.

[11] See Francis A. Sullivan, *Salvation Outside the Church? Tracing the History of the Catholic Response* (New York: Paulist, 1992).

[12] Ibid., 26.

2867). The pope's concern was religious indifferentism, but at the same time, he was apparently unable to recognize any truth or good in non-Christian religions.[13]

There is, however, another tradition that recognizes the possibility of salvation for those who through no fault of their own remain outside the Church. Its roots can be traced back as far as Thomas Aquinas in the thirteenth century. Though Thomas believed that no one could be saved without explicit faith in Christ, he also believed firmly in the universality of God's salvific will and seems to have recognized the possibility of an ignorance of Christ that was not culpable. He also spoke of an implicit desire for baptism. After the discovery of the New World, with its huge continents and millions of peoples who had never heard of Christ, theologians began to raise the question of salvation outside the Church in a new way. The Dominicans at Salamanca in Spain, building on some of Thomas' ideas, explored the concept of invincible or inculpable ignorance as well as the possibility that the Indians of the New World were unable to accept the faith because of the scandalous conduct of their Christian colonizers. They as well as the Jesuits in Rome came to the conclusion that "salvation must be possible, even in the Christian era, through faith in God without explicit faith in Christ."[14]

A New Direction

It was only in the middle of the nineteenth century that Pius IX acknowledged that some people who remained outside the Church because of invincible ignorance might be saved if they cooperated with divine grace. As Sullivan says, this is the first time in the history of the Church that "we have papal authority for explaining that this axiom means: "No salvation for those who are *culpably* outside the church."[15] Prior to Vatican II Catholics formed on the *Baltimore Catechism* recognized the possibility of salvation for those outside the Church who at least implicitly desired the grace of Christ. According to the catechism, an unbaptized person who "loves God above all things and desires to do all that is necessary for his salvation" could receive "baptism of desire."[16]

The Second Vatican Council officially changed the attitude of the Catholic Church toward other religions. The Dogmatic Constitution on the Church recognizes the Jewish people as "most dear to God, for God does not repent of the gifts He makes nor of the calls He issues." God's plan of

[13]J. Robert Dionne, *The Papacy and the Church: A Study of Praxis and Reception in Ecumenical Perspective* (New York: Philosophical Library, 1987) 92.
[14]Sullivan, *Salvation Outside the Church?* 98.
[15]Ibid., 114.
[16]*A Catechism of Christian Doctrine,* rev. ed., Baltimore Catechism (Paterson, N.J.: St. Anthony Guild, 1948) no. 323, p. 263.

salvation also includes the Moslems, who "along with us adore the one and merciful God." The council clearly acknowledges that others can be saved:

> Those also can attain to everlasting salvation who through no fault of their own do not know the gospel of Christ or His Church, yet sincerely seek God and, moved by grace, strive by their deeds to do His will as it is known to them through the dictates of conscience. Nor does divine Providence deny the help necessary for salvation to those who, without blame on their part, have not yet arrived at an explicit knowledge of God, but who strive to live a good life, thanks to His grace (LG 16).

Most Catholics today recognize that salvation is available outside the Church for those who are unaware of God's revelation in Jesus. God's grace is not confined by the structures of the Church; the Spirit moves where it will. As the Pastoral Constitution on the Church in the Modern World points out, the Holy Spirit offers to all people "in a manner known only to God" the possibility of being associated with the paschal mystery (GS 22).

Yet at the same time Christians will insist that the Church contains the fullness of truth. The Church is the universal sacrament of salvation (LG 48). Through the Church is revealed the triune nature of God, the salvation of all people in Jesus, and life in the Spirit. Those who are members of the Church consciously live, proclaim, and celebrate this mystery of faith. The Church must continue to proclaim it to all nations. But it must do so in a way that is profoundly respectful of those who follow other religions, for the Spirit of God is not absent from their lives.

CONCLUSION

In the past an overemphasis on the future dimension of Christian eschatology led to a neglect of the gospel's salvific and liberating meaning for our life in the world. A faith that looks only to the future can easily become an ideology, teaching the poor and the oppressed to accept their condition without complaint and legitimating oppressive social structures. Karl Marx's dismissive remark about Christianity being an "opium for the people" was a reaction to such a one-sided interpretation of the gospel.

It is equally an ideologizing of the gospel to reduce it to a message of social transformation without any reference to our ultimate destiny of eternal life with God. Christianity begins with the resurrection of Jesus; it is the mystery that is at the heart of the preaching of the first disciples. That mystery is interpreted by a wealth of symbols and images comprising Christian eschatology that cannot always be interpreted literally. But the resurrection of Jesus is not just a symbol; it is an eschatological event, God's future breaking into human history, revealing Jesus' victory over sin and death and the promise of our own resurrection.

The doctrine of the communion of saints, in gathering into the Church not just the baptized on earth but the faithful departed as well, is an expression of the eschatological nature of the Church. Christians have a fellowship with the saints in heaven and the souls in purgatory, which will be fully realized in the eschaton when all things will be restored in Christ (Eph 1:10; Col 1:20). They have been invoking the saints and praying for the dead since the early centuries; both practices are rooted in popular piety and have been approved by the Church.

Catholics believe that grace and salvation are offered to all humanity through the death and resurrection of Jesus; thus they see the community of the Church as the most complete symbol of the means of salvation. But grace is never confined by the limits of the Church or its sacraments. Though Catholics have taught and believed for some time that those who cooperate with God's grace can be saved even though they have not heard the gospel, the Second Vatican Council made that explicit. Thus in effect it reinterpreted the axiom "no salvation outside the Church" to more adequately take account of the universality of the salvation that is available through Christ Jesus.

11. The Unfinished Agenda

Did the publication of the documents of the Second Vatican Council signify the completion of the renewal of the Church that the council represented, or did those documents mark only the beginning of a process that has not yet been completed? This question is still being debated.

Some Catholics feel that the Church has gone too far too fast, accommodating itself to the spirit of the times rather than challenging the times with its timeless truth. Some join associations of conservative Catholics—Catholics United for the Faith (CUF), Opus Dei, or the Fellowship of Catholic Scholars. Some write letters to sympathetic officials in Rome denouncing the laxity of "waffling" bishops and the errors of "modernist" theologians. Such Catholics are often identified as "integralists," a term used to describe those who see all Catholic doctrines as equally important and so closely interconnected that to challenge one is to undermine the whole divinely revealed structure.[1] Integralism represents a type of Catholic fundamentalism. Other Catholics are even more discontent; some travel miles to take part in Latin liturgies; others, having rejected the Second Vatican Council, have joined schismatic Tridentine communities such as Archbishop Marcel Lefebvre's Society of St. Pius X, thus separating themselves from the Church.[2]

Other Catholics today are equally unhappy, but for the opposite reason. They feel that the Church has not moved fast enough, that it has failed to carry out the reforms that were indicated by the council documents, that a reaction has set in that seeks to restore the closed and centralized Catholicism of an earlier era. Many work for change through the institution, working in chanceries, ministering in parishes, teaching in catechetical programs, schools,

---

[1]See Gabriel Daly, *Transcendence and Immanence: A Study in Catholic Modernism and Integralism* (Oxford: Clarendon, 1980) 187.

[2]For a survey of conservative Catholic groups see Michael J. Walsh, "The Conservative Reaction," *Modern Catholicism: Vatican II and After,* ed. Adrian Hastings (New York: Oxford Univ. Press, 1991) 283–88.

and universities. Some join associations advocating change such as the Call for Action, the Women's Ordination Conference, or CORPUS, an organization of laicized priests and their wives working for a broader expression of priestly ministry. Some seek a more congenial Church by joining small communities where they hold their own liturgies with sympathetic priests or sometimes without an ordained presider. Some have simply given up completely and left the Church.

If there is dissatisfaction on the two wings of the Church, there is also considerable anxiety in Rome. Both Catholics and Protestants are concerned about what they see as an effort on the part of Rome in the latter years of Pope John Paul II's pontificate to bring about a retrenchment, or "restoration," a term used by Cardinal Joseph Ratzinger, prefect of the Congregation for the Doctrine of the Faith, in an interview given to an Italian magazine shortly before the 1985 Extraordinary Synod of Bishops. To many John Paul II seems to be concerned primarily with holding his fractious flock together and restoring discipline. While progressive on social questions, he is conservative on doctrinal and moral issues, and he has appointed bishops—now over half the total number of bishops in the Church—who reflect his views.[3]

But for the vast majority of Catholics throughout the world, Vatican II belongs now to history, and the changes it introduced into Catholic life are taken for granted. Those under thirty have known no other Church. In more technical language, the council has been received by the Church. The conciliar documents established the parameters for renewal, and they remain a normative expression of the self-understanding of the Catholic Church as it approaches the third millennium.

But the currents of renewal that preceded the council as well as new ones the council unleashed continue their reshaping of contemporary Catholicism. In a real sense the issues raised by these currents constitute the council's unfinished agenda; we mentioned a number of them at the end of chapter 4. In this final chapter we need to consider some of those issues, among them liturgical renewal, the question of authority, women in the Church, the ecumenical movement, and interreligious dialogue. These are issues that will continue to transform the way Catholics experience themselves and their Church well into the next century.

LITURGICAL RENEWAL

One of the primary goals of the liturgical movement from the beginning has been the encouragement of a "full, conscious, and active participation in

---

[3]See Heinrich Fries, *Suffering from the Church: Renewal or Restoration?* (Collegeville: The Liturgical Press, 1995).

liturgical celebrations" by the faithful (SC 14). The Second Vatican Council moved a considerable way toward this goal by making possible the use of vernacular language in the liturgy and by opening to lay men and women a number of liturgical roles previously reserved to clerics.

Liturgical Change

In the years following the council Catholics experienced a succession of changes designed to reduce the physical and psychic distance between priest and people and to refocus attention away from an overemphasis on the consecration and back to the celebration of the gathered community. Beginning in 1966 the altars in many churches were moved forward so that the priest could preside facing the congregation rather than standing at a distance with his back to them. Communion rails began to disappear, removing the physical barrier that had once separated the people from the sanctuary, communicating implicitly the mistaken notion that only the ordained could enter the holy place. With congregational participation the Mass became a dialogue between priest and people rather than a whispered conversation between the priest and the altar boys, who for centuries had responded in place of the people. As congregations began to experiment with different types of music, guitars were introduced and "folk Masses" became popular. The kiss of peace, which had become a relic ritually exchanged only by the three clerical ministers at a solemn High Mass, was restored to the congregation. Three new canons, or Eucharistic Prayers, were added to the Sacramentary in 1968, and a new Mass order was approved in 1969. Additional Eucharistic Prayers were approved subsequently, so that the Sacramentary for the Church in the United States currently has nine options. A newly revised Sacramentary should appear in 1996.

Most of the changes in a liturgy that had remained essentially the same since the sixteenth century were accepted with a combination of stoicism and good humor. Often the needed explanations of the changes were given poorly if at all. Some people were confused about why they should "interrupt their prayers" to exchange a greeting of peace with those around them or were uncomfortable receiving Communion from an "extraordinary minister" rather than from a priest. When receiving Communion in the hand was approved, some felt that the Blessed Sacrament was not receiving its proper reverence, while others argued that the hand of a Christian baptized and anointed in the Spirit was as worthy a receptacle as any vessel of gold blessed by a priest.

The Liturgical Assembly

Beyond these relatively minor changes, liturgical scholarship has effected a shift in the way that liturgy is understood. Especially significant has been the emphasis in recent liturgical theology on the liturgical assembly as the real celebrant of the liturgy. The liturgical language of the first millennium indicates that it is the entire assembly that celebrates the Eucharist. The General Instruction for the revised Roman Missal (1970) has returned to this view, which one finds as well in the new *Catechism of the Catholic Church* (no. 1140). From this perspective the priest is more appropriately referred to as presider rather than celebrant. But putting theology into practice is not always easy. The challenge still remains to find appropriate ways to move from "priest-centered liturgies with congregations" to "assembly-centered liturgies with presiders," so that the assembly's role in the celebration might be more clearly expressed.[4]

The arrangement of liturgical space should reflect the importance of the assembly. In the primitive Church the place of God's presence was not a building but the assembly itself. Paul told the Corinthians, "Do you not know that you are the temple of God, and that the Spirit of God dwells in you?" (1 Cor 3:16; cf. Eph 2:19 22). The early communities assembled for Eucharist in private homes. As the Church grew, larger buildings became necessary, but a church should not look like a theater in which the focus is on a distant "celebrant" and all one sees of the other members of the assembly is the backs of their heads.

The church should be built around the assembly; the people of God should be able to see one another and to gather around the Eucharistic table. The whole place is holy, not just the "sanctuary." Thus modern church architecture tends to move the altar forward, into the assembly. There is a "stational" dimension to liturgy; the focus of the liturgical action moves to the president's chair for the introductory rite, to the ambo or lectern for the Liturgy of the Word, to the altar for the Liturgy of the Eucharist, and finally back to the chair, from which the priest dismisses the assembly with a blessing and commission to bring to others the mystery of God's love that they have celebrated.

The recovery of the concept of the liturgical assembly has also meant a declericalization of the liturgy. This has created not just new liturgical roles for lay men and women but new expectations as well. Catholics today, especially young Catholics, expect to be able to take an active part in the liturgy. They are eager to serve—as lectors and Eucharistic ministers, as planners, music ministers, and in some cases preachers at non-Eucharistic liturgies and presiders at Communion services in the absence of a priest.

Today these lay men and women resent being told by the official Church that they are only "extraordinary" ministers of the Eucharist and

---

[4]Cf. Bob Hurd, "Liturgy and Empowerment: The Restoration of the Liturgical Assembly," *That They Might Live: Power, Empowerment, and Leadership in the Church*, ed. Michael Downey (New York: Crossroad, 1991) 132.

hence that they cannot minister the bread or the cup at large liturgies when there are a sufficient number of concelebrating priests. They do not understand why unordained men can be installed into the ministries of acolyte and lector but women cannot. Some ask why qualified lay men and women could not on occasion give the homily at the Eucharist, a role canon law (can 767.1) reserves for the ordained. While preaching cannot be separated from the ordained minister's role of presiding over the local community, some would argue that the priest's pastoral responsibility could be legitimately exercised by occasionally recognizing other members of the assembly who have a charism for effective preaching. Certainly as more lay men and women take on full-time ministerial roles within the Church or gain reputations as theologians and spiritual directors, there will continue to be tensions over restricting the roles lay ministers can fulfill at the Eucharist.

Renewed Theology of Priesthood

There is also an increasing need to rethink the question of *who* can be ordained. Although the council made significant steps in developing the theology of the episcopal office and that of the laity, it said little about the priesthood except to describe priests as "prudent cooperators with the episcopal order" (LG 28). Without a renewed theology of the priesthood and with new expectations of priests on the part of the laity, what had been the clear vision of the priest's vocation seemed to disappear after the council.[5] Since then, fifty thousand priests have resigned from their ministry. And with fewer candidates for ordination the Church is experiencing today a severe shortage of priests. It has been estimated that about 50 percent of the parishes and mission stations in the Third World lack a resident priest, and even in the United States an increasing number of Catholic communities are unable to celebrate the Sunday Eucharist because they lack an ordained celebrant. According to sociologist Richard Schoenherr the number of active diocesan priests stood at 35 thousand in 1966 but will fall to about 21 thousand by the year 2005. Meanwhile, the Catholic population of the country will increase in this same period from 45 million to at least 74 million.[6] Unfortunately, the Church's leadership has been reluctant to address honestly the problems raised by the growing shortage of priests.

The Church has been able to welcome married episcopal priests into an active ministry (though they must be reordained), but it has been unwilling

[5]See Thomas P. Rausch, *Priesthood Today: An Appraisal* (New York: Paulist, 1992).
[6]"Numbers Don't Lie: A Priesthood in Irreversible Decline," *Commonweal* 122 (April 7, 1995) 11–12; see also Richard A. Schoenherr and Lawrence A. Young, *Full Pews and Empty Altars: Demographics of the Priest Shortage in United States Catholic Dioceses* (Madison: Univ. of Wisconsin Press, 1993).

to reconsider the rule of celibacy for its own candidates for ordination. Edward Schillebeeckx has suggested that the right of a Christian community to the Eucharist should take precedence over the Church's disciplinary law of celibacy.[7] Contemporary theology of the priesthood stresses that ordination is not to a specifically cultic function but to leadership in the Christian community, and there is a much clearer sense that one who leads a Christian community should be able in a real sense to represent it. Thus the argument is frequently put forward that pastoral leaders in local communities such as the Basic Christian Communities in many Third World countries should be ordained to function as priests in the context of their communities.[8] Whatever forms the Church's priesthood takes in the not-so-distant future, the ministerial demographics we have been considering will have much to do with bringing about a change.

Rethinking the Diaconate

Another issue is the permanent diaconate, restored by the council. There are at present more than 9,500 permanent deacons in the United States. But there is still some confusion as to the deacon's proper role. Though deacons functioned in the early Church as ministers in charge of the community's outreach to the poor, today their ministry is too often conceived almost exclusively in liturgical terms. While their liturgical role is important, it would make sense today, as the Church continues to rediscover that ministry to the disadvantaged is an essential dimension of its mission, to recover the caritative meaning of the deacon's ministry.

THE QUESTION OF AUTHORITY

A number of developments in recent history have played an enormous role in changing the way in which Catholics understand Church authority. First, Catholic theology since the end of the council has gone through a virtual revolution in methodology. Second, that same period has seen an increasing laicization of theology. Finally, the explosion in lay ministries in recent years represents a third development.

Methodologically, Catholic theology prior to the council was largely speculative and deductive; it saw its role as that of analyzing and clarifying the divine truth taught by the magisterium. But the Church's eventual acceptance of modern biblical criticism and the shift from an abstract, dog-

---

[7] *The Church with a Human Face* (New York: Crossroad, 1985) 48.

[8] See Leonardo Boff, *Ecclesiogenesis: The Base Communities Reinvent the Church* (Maryknoll, N.Y.: Orbis, 1983) 63.

matic, "classicist" way of understanding to one based on historical consciousness effected a major change in approach. As the old Scholastic framework was largely abandoned, theology became a far more critical discipline–probing foundations, investigating historical developments, reinterpreting traditional formulas, and turning increasingly toward experience.

In terms of its practioners, most Catholic theology up to the time of the council was done in seminaries by priests. No theological school in the United States would accept women as students until 1943, when Sr. Madeleva Wolff, C.S.C., established a School of Sacred Theology for women at St. Mary's College, Notre Dame, Indiana. In September 1963 Marquette University began the first doctoral program in theology (called at that time religious studies) in a Catholic university open to lay men and women. Other institutions followed Marquette's lead. As the council came to an end, lay men and increasingly lay women began enrolling in doctoral programs in theology. In recognition of this the Catholic Theological Society of America, previously an association largely of seminary professors, began admitting lay members in 1964. As these men and women received their degrees and began moving into faculty positions, the locus of theological reflection began to shift from the seminaries to the universities and graduate schools, and it was increasingly being done not by clerics but by lay men and women.

These developments and shifts in Catholic theology have resulted in a number of significant changes. First, Catholic theology is far more independent than in the days when it was done almost exclusively by priests and religious. This new independence lies behind the efforts of the Vatican in the late 1980s and 1990s to bring Catholic theologians under the juridical control of the local bishop, particularly through the insistence that each should receive a canonical mandate to teach (cf. can. 812).

Second, many Catholics today are theologically much better educated than in the past, when for the most part, only priests and religious had the benefit of a theological education. They are aware of the diverse nature of the biblical sources and the different historical contexts out of which Catholic doctrine has developed and are far more ready to recognize development and change. This in turn has changed the ways they understand Church doctrine and Church authority.

Thus they recognize that revelation is not given in formulated doctrines or timeless propositions but is mediated by symbols emerging out of the experience of the religious community; only later is that religious experience formulated in doctrinal statements that remain limited and historically conditioned. They have a new appreciation of the historical Jesus, much closer to the Jesus of the Synoptic Gospels than the Jesus of John's Gospel, who speaks so openly and consciously of his divinity. They understand the Church not as an institution established in all its details by the historical Jesus but as a community of disciples, which under the guidance of the Holy Spirit develops out of the communities of primitive Christianity into a worldwide communion of Churches. They appreciate the importance of a strong teaching magisterium, but at the same time they are aware that the magisterium is an office within the Church, not an independent authority placed above it.

A third development is that in the years since the council the number of lay men and women preparing for ministry has increased dramatically, while the number of priests and religious has continued to decline. According to a 1992–1993 study funded by the Lilly Foundation there are significantly more men and especially women in graduate programs in theology and ministry in Catholic institutions than there are candidates for the priesthood today. This "virtual revolution in how ministry functions in the Catholic Church in the United States" means that the institutional culture of the Catholic Church will be quite different in the future.[9]

The Exercise of Authority

The developments we have been considering have all brought into sharper focus the question of how authority is exercised in the Church. This question will continue to be a matter of controversy into the next century. There are many issues—among them, the shortage of priests, the place of women in the Church, and the Church's sexual morality—that the Church needs to face honestly today. These issues have to be discussed openly. Unfortunately, it is too often the case that episcopal efforts to raise these issues are discouraged. One such effort, the U.S. bishops' pastoral letter on women, after several Roman interventions was revised in its fourth draft into insignificance. At least two bishops described the final draft as sexist, and on November 18, 1992, the bishops voted to abandon the project.

Lay Catholics have even fewer opportunities to shape Church policy or to influence its decision-making processes. A recent survey of lay Catholics reported a growing disagreement between Church leaders and the laity on questions such as birth control, divorce and remarriage, abortion (to a lesser extent), and the ordination of women.[10] The survey found that the majority of lay Catholics are consistently in favor of democratic decision making in their parishes, in their dioceses, and in Rome. Yet lay people have little opportunity to have their voices heard at the levels where decisions are made or to have any say in choosing those who make such decisions.

---

[9]Association of Graduate Programs in Ministry, "A Same and Different Future: A Study of Graduate Ministry Education in Catholic Institutions of Higher Learning in the United States" (Executive Summary) 1.

[10]William D'Antonio and others, *American Catholic Laity in a Changing Church* (Kansas City: Sheed & Ward, 1989).

To many people today the institutional Church still seems a monolithic and monarchical structure whose organs of teaching and government are beyond the influence or reach of those for whom it speaks. To whom are Church authorities accountable? As Jesuit sociologist John Coleman has pointed out, there is something anomalous about the Church as an institution in which the same people and bodies fill the legislative, judicial, and executive functions without any system of checks and balances.[11] This disenfranchises the laity, leaving them little say in the Church's decision-making process, in the formulation of the Church's teaching, and in the selection of their pastors.

The Church, however, is far more flexible than it often appears. If it is not a democracy, neither is it an absolute monarchy. It is not simply an institutional structure but a living organism, a genuine community of lay and ordained members. How can the Church better express the shared responsibility for its life that its interdependent nature indicates? There are a number of steps that could be taken, giving recognition to the dialectical relation that ought to exist between office and charism, without changing the fundamental structure of the Church.

Shared Decision Making

Representatives of the clergy and laity could participate in Church decision-making structures without taking anything away from the leadership role of the pope or the episcopal college. As Coleman observes, participation in the shaping of one's community is a matter of justice. Vatican II insists that individuals are codeterminants of their social structures and "conscious that they themselves are the artisans and the authors of the culture of their community" (GS 55). This means even the community of the Church.[12]

The fact that university doctors of theology and representatives of the religious orders took part in Church councils of the late Middle Ages is precedent for a broadening of the way the Church's teaching magisterium might be exercised in the Church of tomorrow. The presence of theological experts and lay auditors at the 1987 Synod of Bishops on the laity, able to participate in the small-group discussions but not to vote, is one model for a more participatory style of decision making. And there are others.

The Selection of Bishops

How bishops are selected is another crucial question today. For the first thousand years of the Church's history the right of local Churches to select

[11]"Not Democracy but Democratization," *A Democratic Catholic Church,* ed. Eugene C. Bianchi and Rosemary Radford Ruether (New York: Crossroad, 1992) 235. Coleman's article is a nuanced treatment of the renewal of authority structures.
[12]Ibid., 233.

their own bishops was clearly recognized. Pope Celestine I declared: "Let a bishop not be imposed upon the people whom they do not want."[13] Pope Leo I stated: "He who has to preside over all must be elected by all."[14] In the Middle Ages bishops were usually appointed by kings. In 1305 Pope Clement V tried to reserve the right of appointing bishops to himself for the purpose of raising revenue, but bishops continued to be chosen by local authorities, sometimes kings, sometimes cathedral clergy. Now, however, the new bishop had to be recognized by the pope and pay for his approval. This increased papal funds, but it also served to express and maintain the communion between the local Church and the bishop of Rome. In the late seventeenth and eighteenth centuries bishops were frequently nominated by the rulers of the increasingly secular states of Europe.

It was only in 1884 that the papacy claimed the right to name bishops throughout the world. According to historian James Hennesey, when John Carroll was elected by his fellow priests as the first bishop of the new Church in the United States, he failed to set up a system for choosing bishops on the local level. What resulted was the practice of the selection of bishops by Rome, a practice that by the end of the nineteenth century became the pattern for the entire Western Church.[15]

Still, even in more recent times secular governments have had considerable say in the process of naming bishops. In Spain candidates for the episcopacy were subject to veto by the dictator, Francisco Franco. The governments of France, Austria, Germany, Ecuador, Portugal, the Dominican Republic, Poland, Venezuela, Argentina, El Salvador, and Colombia are recognized as having the *droit de regard,* or "right to consultation," enabling the government to make known any objections it might have to a candidate for the episcopal office.

If there is a long history of bishops being selected on the local level and if even in more recent times the Church has been willing to make accommodations with governments, even repressive ones, there is no reason it could not grant local Churches the right to name their own bishops or at least to present a *terna* (list of three candidates) to Rome. The new Code of Canon Law recognizes this possibility. It states that the pope "freely appoints bishops or confirms those lawfully elected" (can. 375). What remains necessary is that a bishop selected locally would have to be recognized by the Apostolic See in Rome in order to be in communion with the universal Church.

Thus the alternative to the present practice of Roman appointment is not necessarily local elections with candidates running for bishop, which

[13]J. Migne, *PL* 50, 434.

[14]Ibid., 54, 634.

[15]"Rome and the Origins of the United States Hierarchy," *The Papacy and the Church in the United States,* ed. Bernard Cooke (New York: Paulist, 1989) 90–92.

could politicize the episcopal office. But there is both historical precedent and canonical provision for the laity and clergy of local Churches to have considerable more say in the process of selecting their bishops. It would also recognize more effectively in the Church's life the principle of subsidiarity so important in its social teachings.

WOMEN IN THE CHURCH

Perhaps the most radical challenge to the status quo in the Church comes from the questions being asked today by so many women. In spite of the advances women have made in recent years in secular society, many Catholic women feel like second-class citizens in a Church that maintains it is not able to admit them to its ordained ministry and thus to the ranks of its official leaders and decision makers. Ecclesiastical pronouncements notwithstanding, such women feel that their baptism is not taken seriously, that the overcoming of divisions on the basis of race, social status, and gender that baptism is said to bring about (Gal 3:28) has not yet been recognized by the official Church. And so an increasing number of women are being alienated from the Church.

If the women's movement in the Church grew out of the broader contemporary feminist movement, its roots are to be found much earlier in women who challenged what was then considered the biblical view of women's place in Church and society. Sarah Grimke (1792–1873) was among the first of many women to suggest that the problem lay not in the biblical text but in the way that Scripture was interpreted. Elizabeth Cady Stanton (1815–1902) went much further, rejecting the Bible itself as hopelessly oppressive and publishing her own *Woman's Bible*. In a real sense, their different approaches to the problem of biblical interpretation suggest the spectrum of the feminist movement today, which ranges from those who want to reappropriate the Christian tradition in a more inclusive way to those who dismiss Jesus and his redemptive work with the argument that women cannot be saved by a male God.

But the women's movement in the Church today is also part of the liberation movements unleashed by the Church's turn to the world, the poor, and the oppressed after the Second Vatican Council. Pope John XXIII called attention to women's growing consciousness of their dignity in his 1963 encyclical *Pacem in terris* (no. 41). There are obvious similarities between Latin American liberation theology and feminist theology. Within the context of the Church feminism represents a whole new consciousness on the part of women who are demanding their full equality in both Church and society. What is the women's movement asking of the Church today? That it take women's experience seriously, that it acknowledge that its sacred texts are conditioned by an androcentric or patriarchal culture, that it speak more inclusively, and that it provide for a more inclusive ministry.

Taking Women's Experience Seriously

Woman today are insisting that truth comes from experience and not necessarily from authority, and they want their experience to be taken seriously. Rosemary Chinnici argues that both feminist theology and psychological theory presume "1) that personal experience lies at the heart of truth; 2) that women's experiences are valid; and, 3) that women have had the power to name their experiences stolen from them."[16] Taking women's experience seriously means recognizing at least two things.

First, *what* women experience is very often different from what men experience. *What* they experience is oppression and exclusion. They are very much aware that many women throughout the world are denied their full rights, that they work two-thirds of the world's working hours, represent two-thirds of the world's illiterate people, and are often physically abused or sexually exploited. Some of these things they have experienced themselves in a very personal way. They know there are things they cannot do, not because they are limited by talent or biology but because of social roles that are determined solely on the basis of gender.

This kind of exclusion on the basis of gender often leads to a diminished sense of self-worth. When some particular experience makes a woman suddenly realize this for the first time, she often experiences a deep hurt and anger. But even in these cases there are rules that tell her how she should react. If she expresses anger for being stereotyped or excluded, she is made to feel guilty, told that it is inappropriate, or that she should think of others instead of herself. It is little wonder that many women consider both society and Church as hopelessly patriarchal and oppressive. Neither allows them to be what they might be.

Second, as feminist theology argues, *how* women experience themselves and the world is different from the way men do the same. These differences are rooted in the different ways boys and girls develop their sense of identity from their earliest years.[17] Girls experience early on that they are "like" their mothers. As this sense of attachment and connectedness is transferred to others, there develops a sense of self-in-relation. Conversely, boys experience that they are "unlike" their mothers and so come to experience the self-as-separate. For adults, then, men tend to experience themselves as separate or distinct from other persons and things in the world, while women tend

---

[16] *Can Women Re-Image the Church?* (New York: Paulist, 1992) 11.

[17] See, for example, Carol Gilligan, *In a Different Voice: Psychological Theory and Women's Development* (Cambridge, Mass.: Harvard Univ. Press, 1982).

to experience themselves and the world in terms of relationships. This means that both men and women have different developmental tasks. According to Chinnici,

> maturity for both women and men lies in their ability to be both related and separate at the same time. . . . Women view themselves as people-in-relation and, therefore, in order to achieve a healthy self they must be encouraged to develop their independence and self-assertiveness. Men view themselves as people/as/separate and must learn to develop the side of their personality which encourages relationships. . . . This difference in development is crucial to our understanding, for, if men's experiences are taken as normative, the societal communication that women hear will be the message needed by males, one that will encourage the development of relationship but which will prove detrimental to women's development.[18]

Marga Bührig, a former president of the World Council of Churches, gives a marvelous example of the different ways men and women perceive things. She tells of a sermon she heard in which the preacher, a male, used as an example the Golden Gate Bridge, comparing the two great commandments to the two great towers from which the bridge was suspended. He saw the bridge in terms of its structure. But she saw it very differently. She saw its beauty, that it is to be crossed, that it links two shores separated from each other.[19] She saw it in terms of relationships.

At least one implication of the different ways men and women experience the world is that the Church should find some more adequate way to include both, particularly in the way it arrives at decisions and formulates its teachings.

Feminist Hermeneutics

Perhaps the most radical challenge to contemporary Christianity comes from feminist theologians using a feminist hermeneutics (or theory of interpretation) to deconstruct the New Testament and reinterpret the message of Jesus in terms of feminist concerns. Not all of their efforts will be acceptable to the majority of Christians. Some move beyond the limits of orthodoxy or so radically reinterpret the Scripture that its reconstructed meaning is accessible only to the specialist. But the extremes of the movement should not blind us to the genuine insights of feminist scholarship.

Feminist biblical scholars are asking that we approach the biblical text with an awareness that it is conditioned not just historically but also by the androcentric or patriarchal culture out of which it comes.[20] That is to say, the bib-

---

[18] *Can Women Re-Image the Church?* 14.

[19] *Woman Invisible* (Valley Forge, Pa.: Trinity Press International, 1993) 56–57.

[20] See Elisabeth Schüssler Fiorenza, *In Memory of Her: A Feminist Reconstruction of Christian Origins* (New York: Crossroad, 1983).

lical texts tend to reflect male interests, for they were written by men, translated by men, and in the subsequent tradition interpreted and commented upon by men. For example, there are a number of early Christian leaders whose names in some early texts are given as feminine, though in later texts the names appear as masculine (Junia/Junias in Rom 16:7; Nympha/Nymphas in Col 4:15). Even today we assume that the two disciples on the road to Emmaus (Luke 24) were men, though only one of them is identified as a man, or that Mary of Magdala was a prostitute, even if Scripture never describes her as such.

Feminist critics therefore ask that we approach the Bible with a "hermeneutic of suspicion," a critical approach to the text that recognizes its patriarchal bias and seeks to recover the often-suppressed stories of women in primitive Christian history. Why, for example, should the word *diakonos* when predicated of Phoebe in Romans 16:1 be so often translated as "deaconess," when scholars are aware that there were neither deacons nor deaconesses in the Churches of the 50s, that *diakonos* here is masculine, not feminine, and the same word when predicated of Paul is always translated as "minister." A more accurate translation would be "Phoebe our sister who is the minister of the Church at Cenchreae."

Or should not the "household codes" that appear in later New Testament writings (Col 3:18–4:1; Eph 5:22–6:9; 1 Pet 2:13–3:7; Titus 2:5-9) be recognized for what they were, rules of domestic order originating from the patriarchal Greco-Roman society in which the early Church was struggling for acceptance rather than an eternally valid statement of divine revelation? These rules, insisting that wives be submissive to their husbands, children obedient to their parents, and slaves obedient to their masters, were cultural imports; the New Testament writers borrowed them from their milieu while giving them a new rationale in terms of Christian faith. The author of Ephesians sees Christ's love for the Church as the model of how husbands should love their wives (Eph 5:25) and argues that the relationships between masters and slaves should be different for those who are Christians (Eph 6:5-9). It was only centuries later that the Church would challenge slavery as an institution. The incorporation of these pagan household codes into Christian writings is a good example of an early effort at inculturation, even if their effect was to subordinate women, diminishing the equality of the sexes that was more typical of the primitive Christian community.

One must be careful not to force the New Testament evidence one way or the other. On the one hand, it does not name women as apostles or show them presiding at the Eucharist. The New Testament does not give much information about who presided at the Eucharist. On the other hand, one cannot assert dogmatically that women did not exercise leadership roles in the primitive Christian communities. The fact that some women are identified as ministers (Rom 16:1), as hosts for the local ecclesial assembly (Col 4:15), as wandering husband and wife co-workers or evangelists (Rom 16:3-5, 7; 1 Cor 16:19), as exercising prophetic roles in the assembly (1 Cor 11:5), or as "prominent among the apostles" (Rom 16:7) should make one very cautious. Nor can it be denied that as the Christian communities became more structured and inculturated toward the end of the New Testament period, they also became more restrictive in terms of what women could do. The introduction of the household codes mentioned above, the restriction of the term "charism" to Church leaders, and the injunctions against women teaching (1 Tim 2:12) all witness to a loss of the openness to the ministry of women that can be glimpsed in the earliest communities.

Inclusive Language

The question of gender-inclusive language is a difficult one. How do we speak of ourselves as a community when we pray, how do we name God? Many Christians today, both men and women, are sensitive to the fact that the way we use our language does not seem to specifically include women. Our language uses the generic noun "man" to refer to both men and women. God is described in masculine terms and addressed as father, even though we understand that God is neither masculine nor feminine. When our liturgical language continues to speak as though God were male or does not make the effort to include women, many object that it is sexist or noninclusive.

Noninclusive language is not just offensive to many, it is also damaging, for it perpetuates the idea that the female sex is secondary and derivative. This sense of gender inferiority, combined with the fact that when we habitually speak of God as masculine we begin to experience God as such, results in a limitation of both our experience of God and our perception of women.

How can we make our language more inclusive?[21] There is much that can be done, without going so far as to substitute "Goddess" for God or changing the sign of the cross into gender-free terms. A first step is to make the effort to be inclusive, to say "brothers and sisters" or "men and women." We can make the effort to avoid referring to God as "he." Second, we need to recognize that all our God-language is metaphorical and analogical. The metaphor of God as father is appropriate; it is deeply rooted in the Christian tradition, stemming as it does from Jesus' use of the term "Abba" in his prayer. But it is not the only one. There are also feminine metaphors for God in the biblical tradition. God is said to have given birth to Israel (Deut 32:28), and God's love for Israel is compared to a mother's love for her child (Isa 49:15), suggesting that maternity can image the divine just as paternity has done. In the New Testament Jesus compares God working mysteriously

---

[21]A helpful book is Thomas H. Groome's *Language for a "catholic" Church* (Kansas City: Sheed & Ward, 1995).

in the world to a woman kneading yeast into the bread dough so the bread would rise (Matt 13:33).

The Church will continue to struggle with this issue of how we speak about God; the issue is not insignificant. The fact that the English translation of the *Catechism of the Catholic Church,* first prepared in an inclusive-language version, was finally published after a two-year delay in traditional noninclusive language was deeply offensive to many Catholics, both women and men. It suggests that the official Church is not willing to take even this small step toward accommodating the concerns of so many women. It is important to find ways to make our language, particularly our liturgical language, more inclusive and to recover and include the feminine images of God, which are also part of the tradition. At the same time, we need to remind ourselves that while we must use language to speak of God, our language will always be metaphorical and God remains beyond our images and our concepts. Some women theologians are seeking to build a bridge between classical and feminist theology, as is Elizabeth A. Johnson in her book on God-language, *She Who Is,* or Sandra M. Schneiders with her studies on how language impacts on and in turn shapes the religious imagination.[22]

Women and Ministry

Women today exercise many roles and ministries in the Church that in the past were closed to them. They run catechetical programs in parishes, teach theology in universities, graduate schools, and seminaries, and do spiritual direction. According to one survey, in the nineteen thousand Catholic parishes in the United States about twenty thousand lay men and women are employed half-time or more in ministerial positions. Of these, 85 percent are women.[23] In the liturgical assembly women serve as lectors and Eucharistic ministers. In 1994, after years of controversy, the Vatican Congregation for Divine Worship finally decided that women (including girls) could assist at Mass as altar servers.[24] More to the point, many women today are serving as administrators in parishes unable to secure a resident priest; their roles are as much pastoral as administrative.

The exclusion of women from ordination remains a difficult and painful issue. The official Church does not see how it can admit women to the ordained ministry, arguing that the constant tradition of the Church is opposed, that Jesus did not call women to be among the Twelve, and that the

[22]Elizabeth A. Johnson, *She Who Is* (New York: Crossroad, 1992); Sandra M. Schneiders, *Women and the Word* (New York: Paulist, 1986).

[23]Philip Murnion, with David DeLambo, Rosemary Dilli, and Harry Fagan, *New Parish Ministers* (New York: National Pastoral Life Center, 1992) 9.

[24]See "Use of Female Altar Servers," *Origins* 23 (1994) 779.

priest, to act sacramentally *in persona Christi,* should be male, as Jesus was.[25] But the argument against the ordination of women has not been convincing to many Catholics, including many Catholic theologians. At the same time, the tide of popular opinion shows an increasing readiness to accept the ministry of ordained women. Pope John Paul II sought to bring closure to this issue in his 1994 declaration, *Ordinatio sacerdotalis,* declaring that "the Church has no authority to confer priestly ordination on women and that this judgment is to be definitively held by all the church's faithful" (no. 4).[26]

Will there be new developments on this question? If the future is difficult to predict, it is also difficult to say with certainty what the Church might eventually do on any given question. Those who have tried to do so in the past have often been proved wrong. Many Christian Churches today take the ordination of women for granted. If the Catholic Church hopes one day to live in communion with those Churches, it may eventually have to rethink its inability to find a place for women in the Church's ordained ministry.

The alienation from the Church that many Catholic women experience today is very real; it is very painful not just for them but for many men as well. Those who love the Church and are aware of its possibilities and its needs anguish when they see talented and dedicated women give up their efforts to minister within the Church or join other Churches; they feel the pain of these women and they grieve because the Church and its witness are diminished by the alienation, the anger, the hurt, and the loss. It is important to respond to the genuine concerns of these women and men today. One thing is certain; the women's movement has already changed the Church and will continue to do so in the years ahead.

ECUMENISM

If the Catholic Church was late in joining the ecumenical movement, it more than made up for it in the years following the Second Vatican Council. Under the direction of the Secretariat for Promoting Christian Unity, now renamed the Pontifical Council for Promoting Christian Unity, the Catholic Church entered into official bilateral dialogues with most of the world's Churches. Those dialogues include the Anglican-Roman Catholic International Commission (ARCIC), the International Roman Catholic-Lutheran Joint Commission, as well as dialogues with the Orthodox Churches, the World Methodist Council, the World Alliance of Reformed Churches, the Baptist World Alliance, the Pentecostal Churches, the Disciples of Christ,

---

[25]See Congregation for the Doctrine of the Faith, *Declaration on the Question of the Admission of Women to the Ministerial Priesthood* (Washington: USCC, 1977).
[26]*Origins* 24 (1994) 49–52.

and a dialogue with the Evangelical Churches still in its initial stages. A Joint Working Group was set up between the World Council of Churches (WCC), headquartered in Geneva, and Rome; and Catholic theologians became members of the WCC Faith and Order Commission. The thirty years since the end of the council have seen an incredible proliferation of agreed statements.

So where does the ecumenical movement stand as Christianity approaches its third millennium? The first millennium was that of the undivided Church, the catholic and universal Church that understood itself and functioned as a communion of Churches. The second millennium saw the unity of that communion broken, first in the division between East and West, traditionally dated from 1054 when Michael Cerularius, patriarch of Constantinople, and the legates of Pope Leo IX excommunicated each other, then in the sixteenth century when Luther's protest in Germany led to the Protestant Reformation and to new divisions of the Church's unity in the West. Will the third millennium see a restoration of communion between those divided Churches?

At the present time the signs are not good. There is a clear sense today that the ecumenical movement has lost its momentum. A number of commentators have observed that the excitement generated by Vatican II has given way to a sense of discouragement because of so many unrealized expectations. Pope John Paul II has made some dramatic gestures, visiting the Archbishop of Canterbury in his cathedral, the WCC headquarters in Geneva, and a Jewish synagogue in Rome, the first ever such visit by a pope. But those gestures remain mostly symbolic, and there is a general sense that John Paul is more interested in reasserting discipline and doctrinal integrity within the Roman Catholic Church. So where have all those years of activity and dialogue led?

Past Differences

One of the most significant accomplishments of the ecumenical movement has been the broad consensus reached on issues that have divided the Churches since the sixteenth century: the doctrine of justification, the nature of the Eucharist, the theology and structure of the ordained ministry, the exercise of authority, episcopacy, even the question of papal primacy.[27] Or more accurately put, a great deal of progress has been made over the years in the agreements worked out between Church representatives and theolo-

---

[27]George Lindbeck, a Lutheran observer at the council and long-time member of the Lutheran-Roman Catholic Dialogue, states that after the dialogues "it ought to be possible on both sides to say that none of these disagreements need necessarily be considered ecclesially divisive." In George Weigel, "Re-viewing Vatican II: An Interview with George A. Lindbeck," *First Things* 48 (December 1994) 48.

gians, but these agreements have not yet been officially received by the sponsoring Churches themselves.

After sixteen years of work, the Anglican-Roman Catholic International Commission (ARCIC I) found "substantial agreement" on Eucharist and ministry and a convergence on the question of authority. The members of ARCIC have stated that in any future union of the whole Christian community a universal primacy serving the communion of the Churches should be exercised by the See of Rome, the only see that has exercised and still exercises such a ministry.[28]

The Lutheran-Roman Catholic Dialogue in the United States has published a series of agreed statements on the creed, the Eucharist as sacrifice, ministry, the Petrine ministry, infallibility, justification, as well as Mary and the saints. Lutherans have spoken of a "Petrine function," a ministry of unity on behalf of the Church as a whole. The Lutheran-Roman Catholic Dialogue in the United States has expressed an interest in a papal primacy renewed in the light of the gospel for tomorrow's Church.[29] On the difficult subject of justification by faith, the Dialogue found a "fundamental consensus on the gospel" (no. 163), even though it acknowledged some remaining differences in theological formulations and pastoral approaches (no. 157).[30]

Another report, published in 1988 in Germany by the Ecumenical Study Group, chaired by a Roman Catholic cardinal and a Lutheran bishop, argues that the condemnations Protestants and Roman Catholics hurled at each other in the sixteenth century were often based on misunderstandings and should no longer be considered Church-dividing.[31] On the basis of an international consultation of Catholic and Lutheran bishops and theologians that met in Florida in 1993, the two traditions are working toward a declaration that the condemnations no longer are applicable.

Perhaps the most significant ecumenical document since Vatican II's Decree on Ecumenism was the 1982 WCC text, *Baptism, Eucharist and Ministry (BEM)*, approved by the Faith and Order Commission at its meeting in Lima, Peru. This document, the product of over fifty years of work, provides a common understanding of baptism, Eucharist, and ministry that to a remarkable degree incorporates the doctrinal positions and concerns of the different Churches. It also gives evidence of a growing consensus on the issue of authority. *BEM* sees the historical episcopal succession "as a sign,

[28]"Authority in the Church I" (no. 23); text in the Anglican-Roman Catholic International Commission, *The Final Report* (Washington: USCC, 1982) 64.

[29]Paul C. Empie and T. Austin Murphy, eds., *Lutherans and Catholics in Dialogue V: Papal Primacy and the Universal Church* (Minneapolis: Augsburg, 1974) no. 32.

[30]H. George Anderson, T. Austin Murphy, and Joseph A. Burgess, eds., *Justification by Faith: Lutherans and Catholics in Dialogue VII* (Minneapolis: Augsburg, 1985).

[31]Karl Lehmann and Wolfhart Pannenberg, eds., *The Condemnations of the Reformation Era: Do They Still Divide?* (Minneapolis: Fortress, 1990).

though not a guarantee, of the continuity and unity of the Church" (M no. 38) and suggests that those Churches that lack it "may need to recover the sign of episcopal succession" (M no. 53b). What *BEM* cannot accept is any suggestion that a ministry should be considered invalid until it enters the line of the episcopal succession (M no. 38).

Another encouraging sign of progress is the new interest in ecumenism shown by the Evangelical and Pentecostal Churches, at least in the Northern Hemisphere. An international Roman Catholic-Pentecostal dialogue initiated in 1972 has led to increased understanding on both sides. As the late Pentecostal theologian Jerry Sandidge observed, "Pentecostals have been asked questions by their Roman Catholic dialogue partners which they have never faced before and it has challenged them to be more articulate in their theological expressions and biblical interpretation. And, Pentecostals in this dialogue have discovered that Roman Catholics *are* Christians."[32]

New Issues

If considerable agreement has been reached on many of the issues that have historically divided the Churches, the latter part of the twentieth century has seen new divisions appearing that make the Churches seem as far apart as ever. Foremost among these are ethical questions and the place of women in the Church.

The fact that the Churches generally have not explored their differences on ethical questions may indicate that they are at least implicitly aware of the often considerable distance between them in this area. Furthermore, they are often divided as to how specific issues should be identified. For example, is abortion to be considered a human-life issue or a women's-rights issue? There are considerable differences in regard to questions such as divorce and remarriage, abortion, birth control, sex outside of marriage, homosexual relations, new reproductive technologies, surrogate parenthood, and sterilization.

The question of the ordination of women, taken for granted in many Churches today, presents perhaps the most significant obstacle to the reconciliation of the Churches and to the sacramental sharing that should follow it. Those Churches that have ordained women are not about to reverse the decisions made after considerable theological reflection, prayer, and discernment. The Catholic Church and the Orthodox Churches remain opposed to the ordination of women on the basis of what they consider to be the ancient tradition of the Church. Even if the Churches officially accept the consensus emerging through the dialogues, the question remains, how can Churches

---

[32] "The Pentecostal Movement and Ecumenism: An Update," *Ecumenical Trends* 18 (1989) 103 (italics in original).

that cannot accept the ordination of women enter into Eucharistic fellowship with those that do? The situation is at an impasse.

These ethical and ecclesial issues can be the Achilles' heel of the ecumenical movement. There is a real danger today that the strong feelings some of these questions arouse can lead to a single-issue mentality, for example, on the ordination of women or the right to life of the unborn. Such a mentality easily can become a kind of litmus test for ecumenical engagement, which makes dialogue impossible and risks new and even deeper divisions.

At the same time, the seriousness of these issues should not blind us to the necessity of being able to live with strong differences in regard to them. Ecumenical encounter does not mean that everyone must believe, think, and do the same; its whole point is to discover what is held in common in spite of differences and to work toward reconciliation. It must also be acknowledged that there are considerable differences on these questions today, not just *among* the various traditions but often *within* a particular Church as well.

Future Directions

If there are new challenges today to the reconciliation of Churches, it is also evident that a number of directions for the future are emerging from the more than thirty years of encounter and dialogue. The ecumenical movement has shown that the principle *Ecclesia semper reformanda* (the Church always in need of reform), applies to all the Churches, Protestant as well as Catholic and Orthodox. It just may be that the apparent lack of movement today may indicate that the initial enthusiasm that followed the council has given way to a more sober and realistic recognition that the Churches need time to assess and assimilate the considerable progress that has been made as well as the positive steps toward renewal and the recovery of the tradition that each of them will be called upon to make.

The mainline Protestant Churches are being challenged by the ecumenical dialogue to a renewal of their structures of ministry and authority. The WCC *Baptism, Eucharist and Ministry* text suggests that the recovery of the sign of communion with the ancient Church through the ordination in the historical episcopal succession may be necessary. Other, later bilateral agreements such as the Catholic-Lutheran report, *Facing Unity,* and the Anglican-Lutheran *Niagara Report,* call for a joint exercise of the episcopal office, including joint ordinations, which will lead to a mutually recognized ministry.[33]

The Evangelical and Pentecostal Churches are being called to a recovery of the liturgical and sacramental tradition of the ancient Church, particularly

---

[33]Roman Catholic-Lutheran Joint Commission, *Facing Unity: Models, Forms, and Phases of Catholic-Lutheran Fellowship* (Geneva: Lutheran World Federation, 1985); Anglican-Lutheran Consultation, *Niagara Report* (London: Church Publishing House, 1988).

the centrality of the Eucharist. They also need to find some way to give institutional expression to the universality and catholicity of the Church.

The Catholic and Orthodox Churches are being called to reform the way in which authority is exercised so that decisions are made in a manner both truly collegial and in some way inclusive of the laity. They will have to acknowledge the authenticity of ordained ministry in other Churches, even if it lacks the sign of continuity with the ancient Church through ordination in the episcopal succession. They must be willing to accept a much greater diversity in theology, spirituality, and ecclesial life and to recognize that the doctrinal inheritance of one communion need not be imposed on another. And they will ultimately have to come to terms with the ordination of women, though this is an issue that must be addressed by the whole Church, not just by a particular communion.

Finally, all the Churches are being challenged to practice much more seriously ecumenism at the local level. An official ecumenism of Church leaders means nothing if it is not matched by a grass-roots ecumenism, for reconciliation cannot happen until Christians from different Churches are able to recognize one another as sharing the same faith. Interchurch covenants, agreements between local congregations or Churches of different traditions pledging mutual cooperation, common prayer, and, where possible, shared ministry, can help express their common faith and be a significant step toward reconciliation and full communion.

The Churches must also work together to find a way to reexpress the gospel message in a language that can address the deepest hopes and desires of contemporary men and women. Evangelical Christians generally use a language that is highly individualistic, speaking of personal salvation through accepting Jesus as Lord and Savior. Middle-class Catholics and mainline Protestants often understand new life in Christ therapeutically, in terms of healing from psychological wounds, addictive behaviors, and dysfunctional families or communities. Others interpret the gospel in terms of liberation from injustice and oppressive social structures or from discrimination against particular groups—women, gays and lesbians, ethnic minorities. The Church of tomorrow needs an evangelical language that recognizes both personal and social sin, that integrates personal morality and social justice, grace and human initiative, evangelization and social reconstruction.

Tomorrow's Church

How might tomorrow's Church be envisioned? The contemporary Catholic Church has returned to the concept of the Church as *koinonia*, or communion, which characterized the Church's self-understanding during the first millennium. As a communion the Church has both visible and invisible elements. Invisibly, ecclesial communion is based on sharing in a common life with God through Christ in the Holy Spirit. Visibly, the common life is mediated through sacramental and institutional structures—specifically baptism, the Eucharist, and the visible bonds of communion of the particular Churches. The Church is thus a communion of Churches.

Each local or particular Church, to be fully Church, must be part of the communion. The authentic character of the respective Churches in the first millennium was exhibited precisely through the visible signs of the *communio,* which linked them together into the *Ecclesia catholica.* Within this communal ecclesiology the pope has and will continue to have a crucial role to play. It is precisely through communion with the bishop of Rome that a particular bishop and Church are shown to be visibly in communion with the Church catholic, the communion of Churches.

Today an increasing number of Protestant Christians are coming to recognize the important role that the bishop of Rome should play in the Church of tomorrow. Anglicans and Lutherans are willing to consider a papal or Petrine ministry, renewed in the light of the gospel, as we have seen. Gordon Lathrop, a Lutheran theologian, suggests that the bishop of Rome might one day be elected by representatives of the Church of Rome (which is what cardinals originally were) as well as by "a few Waldensians, Anglicans, Baptists, Lutherans, and Orthodox who serve assemblies in Rome—in any case not church administrators who have no local assembly charge."[34]

In a perceptive article Lutheran pastor Mark Chapman observes that "only Rome has the traditional, ecclesiological, and moral authority to work the reunion of the Church." But what is so frustrating is that after so many years of dialogue and so much progress "Rome cannot figure out a way to re-open the ancient aqueducts so that the waters of unity that spring from her font might again flow to her marooned and isolated daughters."[35] Chapman may be right in suggesting that the reconciliation of Churches must wait for some action on the part of Rome. Pope John Paul II took a significant step in this direction in his 1995 encyclical on ecumenism, *Ut unum sint.*[36] Without minimizing the questions that remain, he observed that the ecumenical dialogue "has been and continues to be fruitful and full of promise" (no. 69), and he invited representatives of the other Christian Churches to join him in the search for "a way of exercising the primacy which, while in no way renouncing what is essential to its mission, is nonetheless open to a new situation" (no. 95).

[34]*Holy Things: A Liturgical Theology* (Minneapolis: Fortress, 1993) 200–01.
[35]"Rome and the Future of Ecumenism: Rome as the Future of Ecumenism," *Ecumenical Trends* 23 (1994) 8/40.
[36]*Origins* 25 (1995) 49–72.

INTERRELIGIOUS DIALOGUE

The council's shortest document, the Declaration on the Relationship of the Church to Non-Christian Religions *(Nostra aetate),* may well turn out to be one of its most significant. Its history is complicated. Pope John XXIII's wish that the council include a statement on Jewish-Catholic relations was originally to be a part of the council's Decree on Ecumenism. Later the bishops decided that a separate statement be prepared on Jewish-Christian relations. Finally the Jewish-Christian statement was enlarged to include the other world religions.[37]

For the first time the Catholic Church acknowledged the presence of truth within the great world religions, mentioning specifically Hinduism, Buddhism, and Islam: "The Catholic Church rejects nothing which is true and holy in these religions. She looks with sincere respect upon those ways of conduct and of life, those rules and teachings which, though differing in many particulars from what she holds and sets forth, nevertheless often reflect a ray of that Truth which enlightens all men" (NA 2).

The council fathers then exhorted the members of the Catholic Church to work with the followers of other religions "through dialogue and collaboration" so that they might "acknowledge, preserve, and promote the spiritual and moral goods found among [them], as well as the values in their society and culture" (NA 2).

A special section was devoted to relations with the Jewish people. Recalling the "spiritual bond" linking Christians and Jews, the declaration calls for mutual understanding, respect, and dialogue, and it "deplores the hatred, persecutions, and displays of anti-Semitism directed against the Jews at any time and from any source" (NA 4).

With the publishing of *Nostra aetate,* the Church had come a considerable way, moving from its traditional teaching that no one outside the Church could be saved to a recognition that truth is also reflected in the other great world religions and that those who cooperate with God's grace can be saved. This is an "inclusivist" position, more tolerant than the "no salvation outside the Church" approach but one that still acknowledges Christianity's claim to being the definitive revelation of God's salvation.

Are Other Religions Salvific?

The council fathers did not explicitly raise the question of the salvific value of the other great religions. But that question has been increasingly dis-

---

[37]For the fascinating history of this text see John M. Oesterreicher, "Declaration on the Relationship of the Church to Non-Christian Religions," *Commentary on the Documents to Vatican II,* ed. Herbert Vorgrimmler (New York: Herder & Herder, 1969) 1–136.

cussed since the council. Certainly it is difficult to maintain that Christianity is the only way to salvation when it is the religion of only one-third of the world's people. In 1966 Heinz R. Schlette described the great world religions as the "normal" or ordinary way of salvation for those who follow them.[38] Is not Islam the ordinary way of salvation for the devout Muslim, or Buddhism for the devout Buddhist? Is either any less close to God than the devout Christian? Francis A. Sullivan identifies the "mainstream" of Catholic theology today as holding that both non-Christian religions and secular realities (devoting oneself to transcendent values such as justice, peace, humanity) serve as mediations of salvation for non-Christians.[39]

Other theologians concerned with interreligious dialogue go even further. John Hick, one of the most radical, calls for a new "Copernican revolution," which would induce Christian theology to renounce its claims of absolute superiority by moving beyond its doctrine that salvation is through Christ alone. Hick and others like him hold that Christianity should move from a position of inclusivism to one of genuine pluralism.[40]

Yet many Christians find this reevaluation of the truth and salvific value of non-Christian religions difficult to accept. Evangelical Christians continue to insist that there is no salvation except in the name of Jesus.[41] Catholic theology still maintains that the salvation of the world has been once and for all accomplished through the death and resurrection of Jesus. Sullivan writes that he does not see "how a Catholic could espouse the kind of religious pluralism that John Hick and others are advocating."[42] The council called the Church to enter into a genuine dialogue with representatives of those religious traditions. But as Paul Knitter suggests, an interreligious dialogue in which one party continues to hold its own truth as absolute, "as the full and final expression of divine revelation," cannot be a genuine dialogue.[43] Consciously or not, one side has assumed a position of superiority. Knitter's solution is to base interreligious dialogue on a "soteriocentrism," an active concern for "promoting human welfare and bringing about liberation with and for the poor and nonpersons."[44] This means moving beyond the traditional understanding of Jesus

[38] *Towards a Theology of Religion* (New York: Herder & Herder, 1966) 102.

[39] *Salvation Outside the Church? Tracing the History of the Catholic Response* (New York: Paulist, 1992) 181.

[40] "The Non-Absoluteness of Christianity," *The Myth of Christian Uniqueness: Toward a Pluralistic Theology of Religion,* ed. John Hick and Paul F. Knitter (Maryknoll, N.Y.: Orbis, 1987) 22–23.

[41] For a nuanced presentation of the Evangelical presentation see John Sanders, *No Other Name: An Investigation into the Destiny of the Unevangelized* (Grand Rapids: Eerdmans, 1992).

[42] Sullivan, *Salvation Outside the Church?* 170.

[43] *No Other Name? A Critical Survey of Christian Attitudes Toward the World Religions* (Maryknoll, N.Y.: Orbis, 1985) 142.

[44] "Towards a Liberation Theology of Religions," *The Myth of Christian Uniqueness,* 187.

as God's final and definitive voice (Christocentrism) to a "nonabsolutist" Christology.

More recently Knitter has proposed a "relational or dialogical" understanding of Christian uniqueness; salvation in Jesus truly has meaning for all people, without excluding the probability of other saving words in the other religious traditions. The uniqueness of Jesus' message is to be found in his insistence that God cannot truly be known unless one is "actively, historically, materially engaged in loving one's neighbor and working for the betterment of the world."[45]

Dialogue and the Magisterium

Not many Christians at the present time will be comfortable with such a move. Nor does it reflect the official position of the Church. In his 1975 document on evangelization *(Evangelium nuntiandi),* Pope Paul VI spoke of the non-Christian religions as carrying within them "the echo of thousands of years of searching for God." He praised their spiritual values, speaking of them as "seeds of the word" and a "preparation for the gospel." But he also insisted on the exclusive nature of Christianity's claim to truth, stating that "our religion effectively establishes with God an authentic and living relationship which other religions do not succeed in doing, even though they have, as it were, their arms stretched out towards heaven" (no. 53). The pope was not merely concerned that a new appreciation of other religions should not in any way diminish the Church's work of evangelization; in reaffirming that Jesus came to reveal "the ordinary paths of salvation" (no. 80), he was very possibly reacting to those Catholic theologians like Schlette who were maintaining that the world religions were the ordinary ways of salvation for their believers.[46]

Pope John Paul II has gone further in his appreciation of non-Christian religions but not so far as to recognize them as salvific. He holds firmly to the absolute centrality of Christ in his 1990 encyclical on missiology, *Redemptoris missio,* stating that "Christ is the one savior of all, the only one able to reveal God and lead to God" (no. 5). Like Paul VI, he insists "that the Church is the ordinary means of salvation" (no. 55).

But John Paul also sees signs of the working of the Spirit in other religions. He has gone out of his way to meet with other religious leaders and affirms that interreligious dialogue is a part of the Church's evangelizing mission (no. 55). In his careful analysis of John Paul's teachings on evangelization, Francis Sullivan notes that although the pope has not explicitly rec-

---

[45]"Christian Salvation: Its Nature and Practice—An Interreligious Proposal," *New Theology Review* 7/4 (1994) 43.

[46]Sullivan, *Salvation Outside the Church,* 188.

ognized other religions as mediating salvation for their followers, he might be able to recognize them as "participated forms of mediation," dependent on Christ's own mediation; yet he seems to feel that this is a question that needs further study and reflection before any position can be taken by the magisterium.[47]

Interreligious dialogue will continue to challenge the Church, even if its importance is not always recognized by Christians in western Europe and in North and South America. But in Asia, India, and parts of Africa where Christians are not just a minority but often a threatened minority, interreligious dialogue is a pressing and deeply felt need. It may well be one of the most important issues on the Church's agenda in the twenty-first century.

CONCLUSION

The Catholic Church at the dawn of the third millennium is very different from what it was as the twentieth century began. It has come through these last decades of turmoil and change better than many religious communities, thanks to the wisdom of Pope John XXIII, who called the Church into a period of intensive self-examination and renewal. The Second Vatican Council was clearly a council on the Church itself. It meant that the Church was able to draw on its tradition, its scholarship, and the vitality of its members in a conscious effort at renewal rather than simply being swept along by the winds of change.

But the currents of renewal unleashed by the council have not yet run their course. Indeed, they seem to have outdistanced the ability of the Church's leaders to control or channel them. The Church today is facing challenges as great as any in its history. Some of these are challenges to the inner life of the Church, questions such as liturgical participation, the shortage of priests, the right of communities to the Eucharist, a more collegial style of Church leadership, allowing the laity some say in the Church's decision-making process and in the formulation of its teaching, reexamining the way we name God, and granting women full participation in the Church's life and ministry. As the majority of the world's Catholic population shifts from western Europe and North America to Africa, Asia, and the Southern Hemisphere, it will become increasingly important to allow these newer Churches to express their ecclesial life and faith in terms of their own cultures, to balance more adequately universality and particularity.

Other challenges concern the relation of the Catholic Church to the other Christian Churches, to other religious faiths, and to the world. The Church needs to consider the concrete steps that might be taken toward

---

[47]Ibid., 197–98.

Christian reconciliation so that other Churches might share in the fullness of the Catholic tradition without having to repudiate their own particular heritages; it needs to engage in a constructive and truly mutual dialogue with other faiths, and it will have to develop a credible language of evangelization in a broken and secularized world. Will the Church be able to bring the redemptive and liberating message of Jesus to a world in which there is so much injustice and suffering so that the millions of poor might share more equitably in the goods of the earth? Will it be able to find in its sacramental vision of creation a resource for the threatened biological life of the planet? Will it be able to bring its Catholic vision of universality, comprehensiveness, and inclusivity to the competing communities and peoples of the twenty-first century? Or will it become a sectarian movement, concerned only for its own institutional survival? The way the Church responds to questions such as these will determine its viability in the third millennium.

The Church will continue to proclaim the good news of God's salvation in Jesus Christ because its real life comes not from itself but from the presence of the risen Jesus in the midst of the community gathered in his name. What St. Paul said of the Church's ministry could also be said of the Church's life: "We hold this treasure in earthen vessels, that the surpassing power may be from God and not from us" (2 Cor 4:7). The Church itself is a fragile vessel; if it is to effectively be the sacrament of the unity of humankind (LG 1) for the third millennium that the council envisioned it as being, it must continue the renewal of its life and its structures. That is never easy; it means a dying to what has been so that new life can be born. It is part of the paschal mystery.

Certainly the reform of its structures of authority will continue to be a central issue for the Church in the twenty-first century. But Paul's words also refer to the promise of God's presence. That is the Church's strength and its hope.

Appendix I

OUTLINE OF BOOK, WITH REFERENCES TO THE
CATECHISM OF THE CATHOLIC CHURCH

Numbers in the outline refer to the corresponding sections in the Catechism

1. The Church and the Council
   Pre-Vatican II Catholicism
      Modernism
   Currents of Renewal
      The Modern Biblical Movement
      The Liturgical Movement
      The New Theology
      Pius XII
      John XXIII
   The Second Vatican Council
      The Preparatory Phase
      The Work of the Council
      The Church
      Revelation
      The Liturgy
      Ecumenism
      Religious Liberty
      Non-Christian Religions
      The Church and the Modern World

2. Faith and the Believing Community
   The Nature of Faith, 26, 142, 150–55, 176
      The Act of Faith, 150, 154–55, 166, 180
      The Revealing Spirit, 304, 683–89, 798–801, 813, 1831
      The Content of Faith, 150–52, 167, 198–1065
   The People of God, 62–64, 709–10, 761–62, 781–86
      Creation and Fall, 198, 279–421

Appendix II

BASIC REFERENCE WORKS ON CATHOLICISM

Abbott, Walter M., ed. *The Documents of Vatican II*. New York: The America Press, 1966.

Bokenkotter, Thomas. *Essential Catholicism: Dynamics of Faith and Belief.* Garden City, N.Y.: Doubleday, 1985. A contemporary presentation of Catholic doctrine from a historical perspective.

Brown, Raymond E., Joseph A. Fitzmyer, and Roland E. Murphy, eds. *The New Jerome Biblical Commentary*. Englewood Cliffs, N.J.: Prentice Hall, 1990. The best and most comprehensive Catholic biblical commentary, covering all the books of the Bible with many useful articles on biblical topics, revised and updated since the 1968 edition.

Catechism of the Catholic Church. Vatican City: Libreria Editrice Vaticana, 1994. The official compendium of Catholic faith and doctrine commissioned by Pope John Paul II.

Cunningham, Lawrence. *The Catholic Faith: An Introduction*. New York: Paulist, 1987. A popular presentation of the foundational elements of Catholicism.

Downey, Michael, ed. *The New Dictionary of Catholic Spirituality*. Collegeville: The Liturgical Press, 1993. An excellent resource on the currents and developments in Catholic spirituality, done from an ecumenical perspective.

Dulles, Avery. *The Catholicity of the Church*. Oxford: Clarendon, 1985. A study of those elements by which the Church's catholicity is expressed by one of its premier theologians.

____. *Models of the Church*. Garden City, N.Y.: Doubleday, 1974. Dulles' classic study of five different ways of understanding the Church theologically.

Dwyer, Judith A., ed. *The New Dictionary of Catholic Social Thought*. Collegeville: The Liturgical Press, 1994. A fine compendium of articles on historical issues, principles, movements, and documents that have shaped Catholic social teaching.

Eagan, Joseph F. *Restoration and Renewal? The Church in the Third Millennium*. Kansas City: Sheed & Ward, 1995. An exploration and critique of the post-Vatican II Catholic Church, building on seven key council documents.

Fink, Peter, ed. *The New Dictionary of Sacramental Worship*. Collegeville: The Liturgical Press, 1990. Articles covering the Church's liturgy and sacraments from a theological and pastoral perspective.

Flannery, Austin, ed. *Vatican Council II: The Conciliar and Post Conciliar Documents*. 2 vols. Northport, N.Y.: Costello, 1975–1982. A very useful collection with its inclusion of postconciliar documents on the liturgy, ecumenism, the religious life, ministry, current problems, education, and the synod of bishops.

Fiorenza, Francis Schüssler, and John P. Galvin, eds. *Systematic Theology: Roman Catholic Perspectives*. 2 vols. Minneapolis: Fortress, 1991. A contemporary presentation of the major themes of Catholic systematic theology.

Glazier, Michael, and Monika K. Hellwig, eds. *The Modern Catholic Encyclopedia*. Collegeville: The Liturgical Press, 1994. A handy one-volume encyclopedia for English-speaking readers, treating over 1,300 topics with particular emphasis on contemporary concerns and figures.

Hastings, Adrian, ed. *Modern Catholicism: Vatican II and After*. New York: Oxford Univ. Press, 1991. A very useful volume on the council and its aftermath.

Hennesey, James. *American Catholics*. Oxford: Oxford Univ. Press, 1981. A history of the Roman Catholic community in the United States.

Komonchak, Joseph A., Mary Collins, and Dermot A. Lane, eds. *The New Dictionary of Theology*. Collegeville: The Liturgical Press, 1991. An excellent one-volume dictionary of Catholic theology.

McBrien, Richard P. *Catholicism*. San Francisco: Harper, 1994. A revised and updated version of McBrien's compendium of Catholic teaching; provides a well-organized synthesis of the biblical foundations, historical development, and contemporary interpretations of Catholic faith.

____. *The HarperCollins Encyclopedia of Catholicism*. San Francisco: HarperSanFrancisco, 1995. More than 4,200 entries on all aspects of Catholicism.

McCarthy, Timothy G. *The Catholic Tradition: Before and After Vatican II: 1878–1993*. Chicago: Loyola Univ. Press, 1994. A fine study of the contemporary issues in the Church, done in terms of the history of the Church in the twentieth century.

McKenzie, John L. *Dictionary of the Bible*. Milwaukee: Bruce, 1965. Still the best single-volume, reasonably priced resource for information on biblical persons, places, terms, concepts, and books.

Rahner, Karl, ed. *The Teaching of the Catholic Church*. Originally prepared by Joseph Neuner and Heinrich Roos. Staten Island, N.Y.: Alba, 1967. Lists the official teachings of the magisterium topically, based on Denzinger's *Enchiridion Symbolorum*.

Rausch, Thomas P. *The Roots of the Catholic Tradition.* Wilmington: Glazier, 1986. An introduction to the Catholic tradition as it emerges out of the Bible and the period of Christian origins.

Sanks, T. Howland. *Salt, Leaven, and Light: The Community Called Church.* New York: Crossroad, 1992. A study of the contemporary Church that integrates historical, sociological, and theological perspectives.

Sullivan, Francis A. *Magisterium: Teaching Authority in the Catholic Church.* Mahwah, N.J.: Paulist, 1983. A very balanced study of the Church's teaching office.

Vorgrimler, Herbert, ed. *Commentary on the Documents of Vatican II.* 5 vols. New York: Herder & Herder, 1967–1969. The definitive commentary on the development of the documents of the council.

Wilhelm, Anthony. *Christ Among Us: A Modern Presentation of the Catholic Faith for Adults.* San Francisco: Harper, 1990. One of the most widely used introductions to Catholicism.

Index of Names

Index of Subjects

Biblical Institute, 9

Biblical Movement, criticism, 5–6, 14, 208–9

Birth control, 142, 143–44

Bishop of Rome, 53, 48–49, 225

Bishops, 45–46, 56. *See also* Synod of Bishops
selection of, 211–13

Blessed sacrament, 83

Body, 187, 189

Body of Christ, 41–42

Book of the Sentences, 81, 101

Born again experience, 21

Buddhism, 226, 227

Call to Action, 204

Calvinist theology, 53, 58, 70, 75

Camaldolese, 109

Canon, 68

Canon Law, 87, 145, 212

Capitalism, 153, 154, 155

Capuchins, 111

Carmelites, 111

Carthage, Synod of, 105, 125

Carthusian, 109

Casti connubi, 141, 143

Catechism of the Catholic Church, xi, xvi, 149, 155, 195, 206, 218, 231–35

Catechumenate, 45, 92–94

Catholic action, 2

Catholic devotions, 80, 90, 131, 167

Catholic Theological Society of America, 209

Catholic Worker, 97, 114, 177

Catholics United for the Faith, 203

Catholicism, Catholic, xii–xvi, 48, 52–61, 185, 224–25
and modernity, 3
and world religions, 16, 226, 228–29
books on, xi–xii, Appendix II
characteristics, xiii, 60, 73–77, 196
colleges and universities, xv, 3
culture of, xv, 62
popular, 183, 195
social principles, 159–60
word "catholic," xii, 56–57

Catholicity, xiii, 56–57

CELAM, 129, 157–58

Celibacy, 42, 47, 105–6, 115, 148, 149, 208

Celtic monasticism, 108

Censorship, 1

Centering prayer, 170

Centesimus annus, 155

Chalcedon, Council of, 37, 53, 182

Challenge of Peace, The, 158–59

Charism, charismatic gifts, 13, 23, 42, 45, 49, 100, 101, 116, 139

Charismatic renewal, 171, 177

Charity, 172

Chrismation, 86

Christian Brothers, 111

Christianity, 52–53, 185
and other religions, 226–28

Christmas, 80

Christology, 33–37. *See also* Jesus

Church, 12–14, 39–61
and religious liberty, 15
and state, 18
as communion, 54, 61, 224–25
as sacrament, 81
domestic church, 86
house church, 41
marks of, 51–59
membership, xiii, 56
of Rome, 48–49, 70, 225
of the poor, 11
particular and universal, 54, 225
Protestant view of, 58–60
reform of, 224–25
tensions in, 78, 229
tomorrow's Church, 78, 224–25
word "Church," 41

Cistercians, 109

Claretian volunteers, 179

Clement, first letter, 45, 48, 56, 130

Collegeville, 7

Collegiality, 13, 17, 49

Common good, 145, 151, 159, 163

Common worship, 15, 92

Communion *(koinonia),* xiii, 13, 15, 37, 46, 51, 52, 107, 212
and *koinonia,* 52